The Guinness Guide to

EQUESTRIANISM

The author's daughter, Carola, at six years old,
on her champion Leading-rein pony

The Guinness Guide to

EQUESTRIANISM

Dorian Williams

GUINNESS SUPERLATIVES LIMITED
2 CECIL COURT, LONDON ROAD, ENFIELD, MIDDLESEX

Editor: Anne Smith

Layout: David Roberts

ISBN 0 900424 94 X

Published by
Guinness Superlatives Limited
2 Cecil Court, London Road,
Enfield, Middlesex

Printed and bound in Great Britain by
Hazell Watson & Viney Ltd, Aylesbury, Bucks

Colour origination: Newsele Litho Ltd

CONTENTS

PREFACE

Ancient mounted warrior, showing early use of stirrups

Even in an age when knowledge is so profound, two mysteries still exist about the horse. The first is its origin: the second is its subservience to man. The fact that this animal can weigh up to a ton, is capable of a speed of up to 30 miles an hour, has the strength to pull ten times its own weight, is prepared to submit itself wholly to puny man is no less a mystery today than it was when man first dominated the horse and put it to his use 10 000 years ago. Nor has there ever been a wholly satisfying solution as to its origin.

Many believe that all modern breeds of horse were descended from one original wild horse which at some time became domesticated. This original wild horse is believed to have existed, probably in North America, some 50 million years ago. The domesticated version became known as *equus caballus*, known originally as *eohippus*. Others, however, are of the opinion that a number of wild horse types existed in the Stone Age which followed the Ice Age. Some suggest that there were six types; others only two. It is believed, however, that it is from these comparatively recent types that the modern horse is descended.

When man first started breeding horses for his own use he produced an animal capable of all that at that time he required: something to carry his goods and chattels: thus the packhorse evolved and it can certainly be traced back to the earliest nomadic tribes who similarly in different parts of the world bred donkeys, camels, even cattle for the same purpose. When man started riding a horse the requirements were rather different, so we find a different type of horse being bred in the north-east where we first learn of the Mongolian horse. It would seem that over the centuries there was considerable warfare, the cause of which was simply the acquiring of horses either for riding or for work. It was the wearing of some kind of body protection – armour – initially in Iran that led to the breeding of a stronger horse. This was developed through the centuries until one gets the famous Great Horse of the Middle Ages, the progenitor of many of the heavy breeds of horses known today.

The next great influence in the breeding of horses was the turnpike roads built across Europe by the Romans. These new roads, replacing the tortuous tracks, enabled horses to go faster which led to the breeding of faster horses. It also led to the use of stirrups. One never sees in a frieze or in sculpture a Roman riding with stirrups: but by the time we get to William the Conqueror the use of the stirrup is regular: this, quite simply, was because riders found it difficult to manage the trot, a pace only rarely used in the early days, without stirrups. To walk or to canter is no problem without stirrups: to trot is impossible. It was the new roads which made trotting a much more generally used pace, particularly with horses in harness, and so we get the Hackney, the Norfolk Roadster and others bred specifically for harness but descended from riding horses. Gradually, too, the packhorse, as such, became obsolete; the successor, bred specially for local use, was the Fell Pony or Dale Pony or, indeed, the Fjord Pony and the Arriegeois in southern France.

The introduction into Europe of Arab blood in the 16th century was to have enormous influence, the British Thoroughbred as we know it today being a direct result. A section of this book will deal in more detail with the different breeds. Suffice it to say that by the time one reaches the 20th century, specialisation has been carried as far as is possible, each type of horse or pony being bred for a particular purpose. From the original domesticated horse, *equus caballus*, probably about 14 hands in height, we now cover the complete equine spectrum from the immense Shire standing as much as 18 hands 2in to the minute Shetland only 10·2 hands and the even smaller Falabella.

Each has a part to play, each has a role to fill in the design of man, to whom the equine race has so mysteriously subjected itself. There can be little doubt that the fact that the horse allows man to control it is because in the earliest association between man and horse, the horse was a herd animal. In domesticating it man has taken it from its herd environment. It is therefore permanently 'lost', forever looking round for the rest of the herd. Evidence of this lies in the way a horse, when turned loose into a field, will immediately trot round not, as some people sometimes suggest, looking for water but rather looking for the rest of the herd. Further evidence is provided by the frequent disinclination of a horse or pony to leave the collecting ring at a show or gymkhana. Again it is reluctant to leave the rest of the herd. If this were more generally appreciated those responsible for building show jumping courses, especially for children, would think twice before building the first fence going straight away from the collecting ring. If the first one or two fences are taking a pony back towards the collecting ring the chance is that by the time it has to turn away from the collecting ring it will have been warmed up.

Without the herd, the horse has lost his natural confidence. There is a similar situation with a pack of hounds. Take a hound away from the rest of the pack and it becomes soft, inept and entirely dependant upon man. As part of a pack it is ruthless, effective and totally fearless. Similarly a horse is dependent upon man for its thinking. As part of a herd it acted instinctively, but without the herd it has to be guided, instructed. Flatteringly it puts its trust totally in man. How sad that man should so often abuse it: usually due to ignorance. By attempting to present the whole spectrum of the equestrian world in this book it is hoped to allay a little of the ignorance that can bring so much distress to this generous, long suffering servant and friend of man.

It has been said that the first requirement of education is that it should give a person self-confidence. Certainly it cannot be denied that the one who possesses self-confidence is extremely fortunate. It is the same with the horse, basically nervous, naturally lacking self-confidence, once it has been weaned. In growing so large from the original little herd animal running about the desert, no more than 24 in high, it has retained a very small brain. It can therefore only absorb knowledge in a limited way: it cannot reason. Once it has acquired knowledge it will never forget it, but to acquire some knowledge it has to be very clearly presented. A horse reacts to the very slightest movement: any movement is therefore a message to a horse: it is therefore utterly confusing to a horse if there is a lot of movement on the part of the rider. A rider should be as still as possible, only moving in seat, leg, or hand when wishing to communicate some message to the horse. The less the movement, the more definite the signal, the clearer will the message be.

One further point is worth making in the hope of furthering the understanding of the horse. The horse has eyes at the side of its head, in common with all animals that are or have been hunted, unlike the predators, the fox, the cat family, the human, which have eyes at the front of the head. This means that the angle of vision for a horse is totally different to that of man. It can three-quarters see round the back which can of course be confusing. Hence the wearing of blinkers with carriage horses who could be disturbed by the sight of the wheels revolving behind it: or occasionally on race horses who can be distracted by horses galloping up behind them. The purpose is to force the horse's visual concentration forward. It is for this reason that show jumps today are built big and bold and brightly coloured – in a word, staring: this forces the horse to concentrate his vision forward, looking at the fence, rather than allowing his concentration to wander. This side vision, however, of necessity tends to make a horse nervous.

Nervous, lacking in confidence, quick in its reactions, a horse needs plenty of understanding. It is surely remarkable that it has allowed itself to be used in such a wide variety of activities. Basically, however, it is still the same horse, whether it is a child's gymkhana pony, a race horse, a show jumper or a hackney. What a debt we owe it! In this book I have attempted to cover the horse's world, partly as a tribute to his generosity, his versatility and his ability to give pleasure in so many different ways: partly to remind people that if one wants to get the most out of a horse it is as well to know exactly what one is expecting of it, and to learn as much as one possibly can of the whole equestrian scene, now so sophisticated compared with over 100 years ago. Ultimately it is the horse that will benefit as much as the man who uses it.

INTRODUCTION
The Horse in the 20th century

The story of the survival of the horse in the 20th century is indeed a remarkable one. Today, in the last quarter of the 20th century, more people are riding than ever before; more horses and ponies are being bred than ever before. That this is so is very extraordinary when one realises just what has happened since the beginning of the century in the way of invention, particularly in the development of modern transport. Already at the turn of the century cars could go at more than 60 miles an hour and, indeed, aeroplanes were flying considerable distances. There were many in those halcyon days of the Edwardian age who realised that the horse as a means of transport must surely be on the way out. Indeed, the great International Horse Show, mounted at Olympia in 1907, was promoted with American money in an attempt to boost the harness horse. People buying tickets for the show were even asked to arrive at the show in horse-drawn vehicles. The show itself was a great success though probably, less than a decade before the outbreak of the First World War, it did little to enhance the future of the horse.

As is so often the way in war time there was, during the war years, great development and invention in all forms of transport; indeed, it was in 1917 that the fearsome tank, which was virtually to put an end to the traditional use of cavalry, made its first appearance. There were many people who therefore must have thought, as the war drew to a close and in the first days of peace, that the day of the horse was past forever. That it proved not to be so was due in the first place to the natural desire for people after the war to get back to what they regarded as the good old days. They looked back to the pre-war days, the halcyon Edwardian era, and longed for everything to be just as it was then. The horse was of course very much a part of those days and so people wasted little time in reintroducing the horse into their social life. It cannot be pretended that it was a necessity, for it was now becoming cheaper to run a motor car than to keep a horse and carriage, and to get from one place to another was already far faster by car than by horse. Nevertheless, many people did continue to use horse-drawn vehicles, persuading themselves, perhaps, that it was easier to buy forage for a horse than to get petrol for a car. It was, however, in sport that the horse was reintroduced with such enthusiasm. Within months of the end of the war, hunting was started again – indeed, it had never entirely ceased: but within a few years it became almost as smart and sumptuous as in the days before the war. Polo also quickly became popular again, not only with the Cavalry regiments which still retained their horses despite the invention of the tank and armoured car, but also at the great social centres at Hurlingham and Ranelagh. It was, however, the development of two organisations, between the two wars, that was to play the greatest part in insuring the survival of the horse, though it may well not have been appreciated at the time just how great an influence the forming of the British Show Jumping Association in the early twenties and the founding of the Pony Club in the late twenties was to be.

It so happens that I was personally involved in both these developments. My father, the late Col. V. D. S. Williams, on coming out of the Army in 1920 decided to take up show jumping – then a sport with no rules and little following – as he believed that he had one or two horses that were exceptionally good jumpers. He was, however, disappointed in that despite the fact they jumped well they seldom won prizes, and he therefore decided to give it up. At about this time, however, he was invited to judge at a big local show at Banbury. On reaching the show ground he was introduced to his co-judge, who turned out to be the Mayor of Banbury. As they walked onto the ground the Mayor turned to my father and said, 'We know who is going to be first as he has given all the prize money; we know who is going to be second as he has lent us this field; who do you think we ought to make third?' Somewhat surprised my father suggested they surely ought to see them jump first. 'Jump?' replied the Mayor, 'What is the point of that? I don't know one end of the horse from another; but what I do know is that we want to be able to hold this show here next year as it makes a great deal of money for charity.'

My father, fearing that it would be sometime before he had either a big enough field in which to hold the show or enough money for the prize money, decided that perhaps it was time that something was done about it. He therefore drove over to Aldershot – then, as now, the home of the British Army – because he knew that there were a number of young Cavalry officers who were beginning to feel as he did that the time had come for show jumping to be a properly organised sport. The result was the founding of the British Show Jumping Association, the immediate improvement in the standard of show jumping, and the gradual emergence of a number of famous names such as those mentioned in Chapter 4: Tommy Glencross, the Taylor and Foster brothers, the Bullows sisters.

It was in 1927 that a guest of my father's, Maj. Harry Faudel-Phillips, was responsible with my father and mother, Col. Guy Cubitt and one or two others in forming the junior branch of the Institute of the Horse that became known as the Pony Club. There is no doubt that this extremely popular and successful movement for young people was to play a very important part in the survival of the horse in the 20th century because during the Second World War when most adults were either in the services or doing wartime jobs there were still children who had to be amused and entertained and who were therefore encouraged to ride ponies. Many even had to ride ponies to school because of the shortage of petrol in the wartime years. The result of this was that at the end of the war there was a large number of young people who were used to riding, who enjoyed riding and wanted to continue to ride. They thus provided a nucleus of the riding public that was in the post-war years to increase so dramatically.

It was of course fortuitous that, as recounted in Chapter 4, the efforts by a number of prisoners of war in their prisoner of war camp to plan the revival of show jumping as soon as the war was over resulted in show jumping of all equestrian sports getting off the ground quicker than the others. This was of course very largely due to Col. Sir Michael Ansell and his remarkable enthusiasm and vision in the late forties and early fifties. Within years, thanks to various circumstances already described and the help of a number of dedicated people from all backgrounds, civilian as well as military, he was able to make show jumping a popular sport within a few years only of the end of the war; indeed, even before the end of the forties. It is doubtful, however, whether had there not been a Pony Club and many thousands of children already competent as young riders the initial success of post-war show jumping would have developed in the way it has. It has always been the strength of British show jumping that there is an enormous reservoir of very competent young riders ready to take the places of their distinguished elders. For instance, there were such as the Barnes family – in particular Gerald, Sheila and Mary who were ready to take the place of the great heroes of post-war period Lieut-Col. Llewellyn, Ruby Holland-Martin, Wilf White and Ted Williams. The fifties were to see the emergence of such young riders as Gill and Dawn Palethorpe, Peter Robeson and David Broome. So it has been with each succeeding generation until today when we see the emergence of brilliant young riders such as Jean Germany, Sally Mapleson, John Brown, the Whitakers, Nick Skelton, Malcolm Bowey, Robert Smith (son of Harvey), and not only in show jumping, for young riders have always been available both in the three-day event field and very much more recently in dressage: it is probably true to say that the earlier lack of success in British dressage was very largely due to the fact that there were not the young riders ready to take the place of my stepmother Brenda Williams, Lorna Johnstone, Mrs Robert Hall and Mrs Gold. Today, fortunately, there are outstanding riders headed by Jennie Loriston Clarke who won the bronze medal in the World Championships in 1978 and including such as Tanya Laringan, the successes of whom have undoubtedly assured the survival and indeed the future success of dressage in Britain.

Show jumping, so spectacular, so suited to television, has always been the shop window of equestrian sports, but when in 1948 the Duke of Beaufort decided to encourage the presentation of a three-day event at Badminton it heralded the development of another aspect of equestrianism that was to experience an extremely successful development over the next two or three decades. The three-day event was of course particularly suited to British riders with their tradition of foxhunting and cross-country riding. The success of the inexperienced team at Helsinki in 1952 when it could so easily have won a medal, its triumphant winning of the gold medal at Stockholm in 1956 and its later successes in the Mexico and Munich Olympics, to say nothing of its successes in World and European Championships encouraged many people to take up eventing with the result that within a decade or so of the first three-day event being held at Badminton there were almost as many people taking part in eventing as there were taking part in show jumping. Again it was the reservoir of young riders who did much to ensure not only the popularity of the sport and its success, but even more its development into a nationwide sport that found participants from all walks of life: people who, perhaps, found show jumping slightly too professional, even too artificial, for their liking, having learned most of their riding in the hunting field.

In the sixties the enthusiasm of Prince Philip, the Duke of Edinburgh, for polo was to start a revival in that sport, too. Thus the end of the sixties and the beginning of the seventies produced an extraordinary equestrian revival in Britain. Many people enjoyed jumping, eventing, and showing horses – there were, and still are, more than 2000 shows being held in the summer months in Britain alone. The new popularity of polo resulted in more people playing it in Britain than ever before. More people are hunting than at any time in the long history of the sport, and new sports such as long-distance riding and trekking are experiencing tremendous support. Even more remarkable than all this is that the old sport of driving, if it can be so described, was being taken up by hundreds of people who had never been carried in anything other than a motor-driven vehicle before. The development of all these sports is described in detail in later chapters, but the fact that the equestrian scene was so healthy at the beginning of the seventies is without any doubt due very largely to the founding of the Pony Club in the late twenties as it has ensured that there are always people not only genuinely interested in horses, but experienced in the handling of them: the on-going thousands of young Pony Club members has indeed played their part in keeping a love of horses alive.

There is one other aspect that should be considered: breeding. Since the war a large number of breed societies have been formed; indeed, every breed of pony that is indigenous to Britain has its own breeding society. Of particular importance is the Hunters Improvement and Light Horse Society which is responsible for the breeding of all part-bred horses likely to be suitable for hunting, show jumping, eventing, point-to-pointing. Then there is the most important of them all – the Thoroughbred breeding scene. The latter has had its problems due to the decline in the value of the pound and the slump in exports, and, more recently, the incidence of *equine metritis*, but it has survived and thanks to the blood of horses such as that of *Mill Reef* and *Blakeney* – both standing at the National Stud – it would seem that there is still an important part for the Thoroughbred breeding industry to play in the economy of Britain.

It is probably true to say, regrettably, that in the fifties and sixties there was too much indiscriminate breeding. For a time people jumped on the Thoroughbred bandwagon, breeding from quite cheap Thoroughbred mares which they sent to a good, but not outstanding, stallion, being quickly rewarded by exceptional prices at the Doncaster, Newmarket and other sales. The pony world soon followed suit, far too many mares being put to stallions of no particular worth, to breed ponies in the hope of producing another of the ponies that were already fetching very big prices as a result of the popularity of show ponies and the increasing value of them if they won at the better shows. Indeed, for a time there was a steady export market for well-bred ponies, but unfortunately it was not long before these small breeders discovered that nobody was prepared to give very much money for the less well-bred pony. The result was therefore that less than high-class ponies were sold off cheap, all too often finding their way to the continent as horse meat. In the hunter world, too, many people took advantage of the Hunters Improvement Scheme of subsidised stallions and bred from many mares that were never likely to produce anything more than a very ordinary animal. It is true, of course, that many horses so bred distinguish themselves, either as show jumpers or as eventers, or give pleasure as hunters, but many more are never more than very moderate animals and therefore worth very little money, breeders invariably having to sell them at considerably less than it had cost to breed them and to bring them up to three or four years old. These animals, admittedly, could serve a useful purpose in riding schools or simply as hacks, but the fact of the matter is that both in the hunter world and in the pony world, and even in the Thoroughbred world, too many animals are being bred. Ironically, not enough top-class animals are being bred which means that in the seventies we find top-class riders having to go overseas for their show jumpers and eventers while in this country there are still far too many animals for the requirements of the riding population, the surplus, alas, being sold for meat.

Gradually the situation is righting itself, partly because people can no longer afford to breed horses which are going to cost them money; partly because of the increasing strength of feeling against the export of foals and young horses and ponies for slaughter and subsequently for human consumption on the continent. People find it difficult to accept the fact that to send a mare to a reputable stallion, to look after it for the eleven months before it foals and then to keep the foal for a further three or even four years means that the lowest economic value of that animal as a four-year-old must be well in excess of £1000. People obviously hope that they will breed the one outstanding animal that pays for all their losses, but many people have to accept the fact that when eventually they sell their colt or filly as a three-year-old, or as a four-year-old, almost inevitably they will have lost money on it.

It is also true to say, regrettably, that the enormous increase in the popularity of riding, which could justifiably be described as an explosion, has meant that it is almost impossible to provide the amount of knowledge and instruction that is required. Naturally a large proportion of the new riders are children who come from a background where horses have played no part, with the result that there is inevitably a great deal of ignorance. Ignorance, unfortunately, with animals is akin to cruelty; in addition to the fact that people who take up riding so often feel that there is little need for them seriously to learn about horses there is also an indisputable shortage of good riding schools. It is probably true to say that there are 3000 and more riding schools in the British Isles; some 500 of them are reliable and sound, another 2000 are perhaps adequate, but at least 500 are entirely disreputable and cannot be considered fit either to instruct pupils or to keep horses.

An effort was made some years ago, when it was obvious which way the trend was going, to get legislation introduced whereby all riding schools had to be licensed. This is excellent as far as it goes, but understandably the local surveyor is not always the best person to know just what a riding school should be, nor is it easy for a vet to produce a report that is so detrimental to a riding establishment that the local council will deny it a licence. There are, of course, the various approval schemes referred to in Chapter 1, but with quickly changing staff the standards of a school can equally soon go down. It is not easy therefore to ensure that any school, however well it has been reported upon initially, is still a first-class school that one can confidently recommend to any rider. The schools at the top in Britain are very highly thought of; there are more run-of-the-mill schools where the standard of instruction and horsemastership is adequate, but there are also schools that are still very much sub-standard, not only providing inadequate instruction for pupils, but also quite incompetent in staff to properly look after horses and ponies. In addition to this there is a very real danger that they will exploit young people who want to work in riding schools, virtually using them as slave labour.

It has frequently been hoped that the British Horse Society could be employed as agents for the Government to carry out all inspection and licensing. In this way they would have complete authority over all schools in the country, whereas at present they have only authority over the schools which have applied to them for approval and which have either been approved or have been refused approval.

One must also remember that whereas everyone who rode in the old days was automatically associated with horses as there was no other means of transport, this is of course not so today, people only riding for pleasure, comparatively few horses being employed between the shafts. That there is a great keenness cannot possibly be denied, that many hundreds of books are written cannot be denied either, but that there is still a great deal of ignorance amongst the riding public is also a fact. It is right, therefore, that every effort should be made to improve the standards both of horsemanship and horsemastership.

However fond of horses one may be one has to accept the fact that in this day and age the horse is an anachronism; more than that it is a luxury. It gives enormous pleasure and, indeed, it can be the cause of great wealth; it can also provide many hundreds of thousands of people with a living, but the fact of the matter is that in the world today man could survive without the horse. It is equally true to say that if man wishes to employ horses for whatever purpose it may be, from racing in the Classics to trekking, then he must accept the fact that it is going to cost money, that it can be an extremely expensive pastime and that it can never be a hobby or a pursuit that can be enjoyed for a few pounds a week. This means that the horse in the latter part of the 20th century has acquired a status totally different to its status in any other century. It started as a beast of burden; in the 18th century it became almost a deity as with the great renaissance in the world of the arts, man attempted to make the riding of the horse an art in itself; the art known then, as it is today, is *haute école*. In the 19th century it became somewhat taken for granted. At the beginning of the 20th century it almost disappeared and then, in our time, perhaps as an antedote to the pressures and the pace of modern life, the horse exists for the provision of leisure pursuits. Increasingly since the Second World War it has become for many people – it is almost true to say from all classes – an essential part of society. Whether people just ride for pleasure, or whether they indulge in one of the various equestrian sports, or whether they are fortunate enough to be involved in racing at the top, it is the horse that provides them with their pleasure. The horse, therefore, has become a very precious commodity.

That the horse has increasingly given pleasure to people cannot be denied, hence the enormous growth of equestrianism, not only in the British Isles, but all over the world in the last two or three decades. In Germany there is certainly as much riding as in Britain, but perhaps less riding purely for pleasure, the Germans as a whole being very much more interested in equitation than are riders in Britain. It also has to be remembered that with no hunting in

Germany – or, indeed, in most other continental countries – it is necessary to provide a *raison d'être* for riding. This is of course largely provided by dressage, hence the very great interest in this form of equestrianism in many of the continental countries. In France there is rather more riding for pleasure, but there is still an emphasis on equitation. In all these countries there is a far greater contribution made to equestrianism by the Government than there is in Britain.

In the USA riding is as popular as it is in Britain. It would appear that the proportion of people interested respectively in competitive riding, leisure riding and in what can be most easily described as serious equitation, is roughly the same as the proportion of people riding in those different interests as in Britain. In Australia there is almost certainly a greater proportion of people who just ride for pleasure than who are interested in competitive riding, probably because the opportunities for competitive riding are far less in Australia and New Zealand than they are in Europe and America; the distances involved making even national competitions difficult while the opportunities for international competition are almost non-existent. The same applies to South Africa, where although there is a great deal of riding for pleasure in such a beautiful country, there is, nevertheless, tremendous enthusiasm for competition in all the disciplines, the standard being remarkably high.

What of the horse in the future – in the next century? It would seem probable that the interest in riding is unlikely to wane. Everything suggests that during the next quarter of a century there will continue to be a wider distribution of wealth which in all probability will result in more and more people, as they find themselves able to afford to ride or even better to own a horse or a pony, taking the opportunity of doing so. It is to be hoped, however, that there will be proper control, supervision and organisation of riding – and breeding – for if people are allowed indiscriminately to take up riding they could very easily, though quite unintentionally, bring considerable cruelty to the animals which they ride; or find themselves breeding for the abattoir. It has been said that to learn to ride a horse is as easy as learning to ride a bicycle, which in turn is as easy as falling off a log. It is in fact equally easy to fall off a horse, or a bicycle, or a log. What is important to remember, however, is that whereas a log and a bicycle are inanimate, a horse is a living creature, sensitive and nervous, demanding a very real understanding if he is to give his best. If the horse is to continue to survive then it is essential that he should be able to continue giving his best, and thus continue giving pleasure.

PART ONE
Acquiring the Art

1
Learning to Ride

Where does one learn to ride? The obvious answer, of course, is at a riding school. But in Britain and, indeed, in most countries the standard at different riding schools varies enormously. It is important, however, that anyone taking up riding should attempt to ensure that they get correct instruction. This is by no means always the case; people very often think that they can learn to ride a horse in rather the same way as they learn to ride a bicycle – they get on and gradually by experience learn to stay on. This is obviously one way of learning to ride, as long as one is not too ambitious or indulges in any form of equestrianism that is too demanding. This method, however, is not really fair on the horse, nor can it really satisfy the rider. For some reason, especially if people take up riding late in life, they think that it is either unnecessary or undignified to receive instruction; nothing, in fact, could be further from the truth. If one wants to ride even adequately, proper instruction is absolutely essential: it must always be far more undignified to make a fool of oneself, get run away with or fall off, than to be given proper lessons.

It is also regrettably true that people often think that after they have acquired the very rudiments of equestrian knowledge they are first-class horsemen. In fact, the real horseman never ceases to learn; every horse is subtly different; every type of equestrianism demands a different approach. No rider is ever too experienced or too old to learn. It is unfortunate that there is a tendency for riders to think that they know more than they really do. This is probably due to the fact that the majority of riders live in isolated communities and are the only riders in their neighbourhood, few people therefore knowing as much about it as they do. I have often said that once a rider has learnt to rise at the trot he thinks he is capable of writing a book on equitation! Basic instruction is therefore essential.

Britain, despite frequent criticism of our instructional standards, possesses between 2500 and 3000 riding establishments and is in fact richer in riding schools than any other country in the world. Each of these, thanks to the Act that was introduced into Parliament at the behest of the British Horse Society in the sixties, has to be licensed by a Local Authority: though this unfortunately does not necessarily mean that the riding school is all that might be desired. A riding school in applying for a licence simply has to show the Authority that it is satisfactorily hygienic and that the conditions of the horses and ponies in the school are adequate. This means that there are many schools that would not win the approval of anyone who really cares for animals although it would be untrue to say that the horses and ponies were in no fit condition to be ridden. Furthermore, as anyone who runs a stable yard knows, the minimum health and hygienic requirements are in fact totally inadequate. There is a story of one of the best known riding schools in the country being turned down in its application for a licence on a trivial point because the window in one of the boxes was not the required shape although in fact there was the required area of light and ventilation.

Of the 2500 to 3000 riding schools in the country, something considerably fewer than 1000 meet the requirements of the various bodies that are prepared to award the schools their signs of approval: the British Horse Society, the Association of British Riding Schools and the Ponies of Britain. Any school, or establishment, that has been approved by one of these organisations can guarantee an adequate standard both in the accommodation provided and in the standard of instruction. Naturally, as the official body, the British Horse Society is the most important of the organisations that carry out inspections. It employs some seven or eight inspectors who not only inspect schools seeking approval, but also investigate complaints and carry out re-inspections as frequently as possible since obviously the standard of a school can deteriorate very quickly on a change of proprietorship or when one instructor is replaced by another. The objects of the British Horse Society's Approved Riding Establishment scheme are firstly to provide members of the public with information where, in the opinion of the Society, good instruction can be obtained; secondly, to assist in raising the standard of instruction, horsemanship and horsemastership; thirdly, to provide an advisory service to riding school proprietors; and fourthly, to make available at special rates third party legal liability insurance cover for the protection of both client and proprietor. The latter point is of particular importance since unless a riding school is properly insured it can in the event of an accident – and even in the best establishments such accidents are possible – suffer penal damages which could completely ruin the school financially.

The British Horse Society gives its approval to schools which in its opinion offer sound instruction in riding and horsemastership at whatever level they seek to attain. One school can cater for those who are

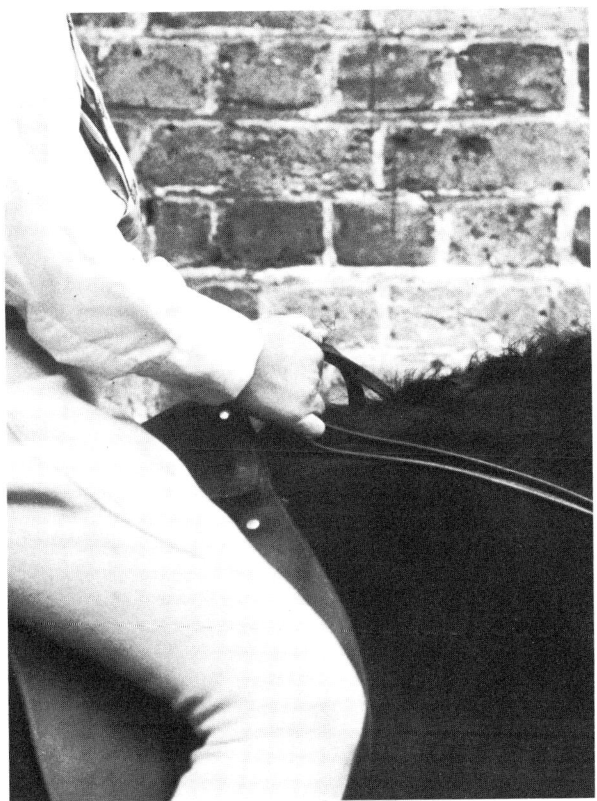

Holding the reins the right way

Holding the reins the wrong way

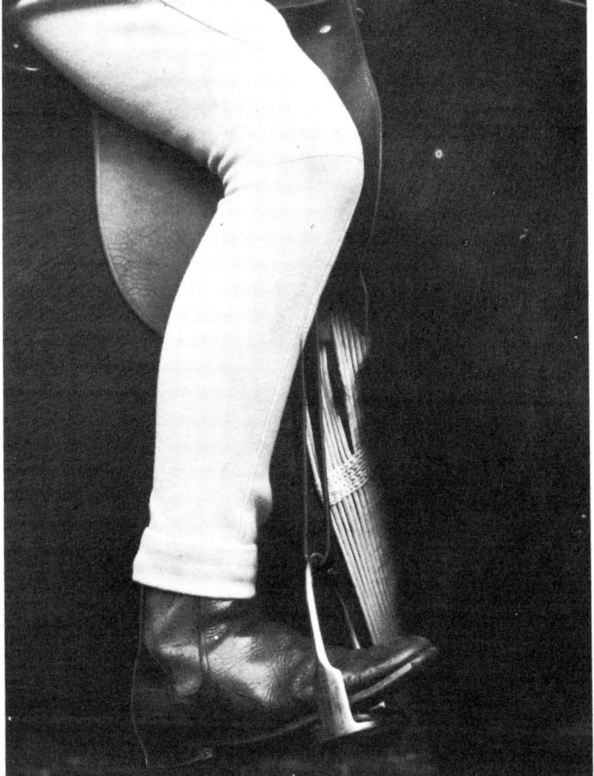

The correct leg position

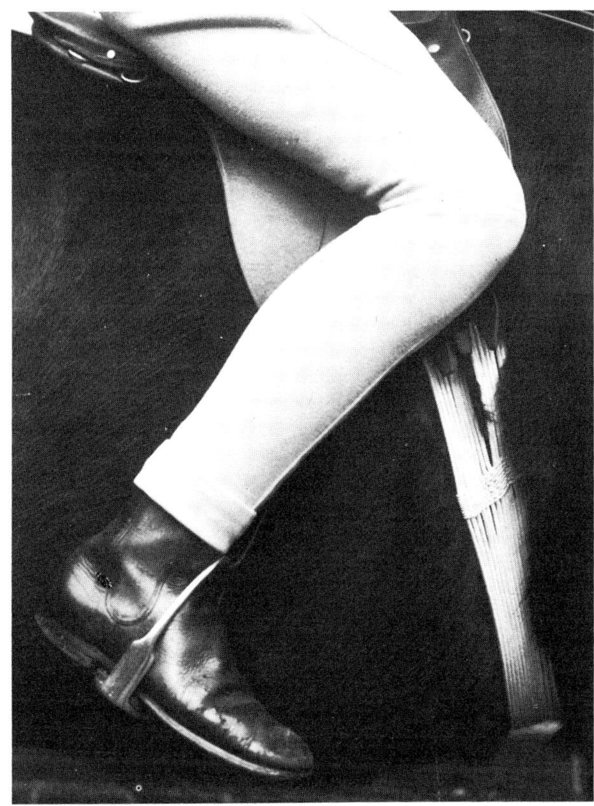

The wrong leg position

The right way to tie up hay and hold a pony

likely to represent Britain internationally, while another attempts simply to cater for complete beginners. As long as the standard is adequate for the purpose for which it is intended then that school can be approved. Indeed, often the school that is catering for beginners and the less experienced is doing as useful, if not a more useful, job than the school that is more ambitious. It could be suggested that this is because whereas most people are agreed on the requirements for basic training there are still wide regions of disagreement on the required training for the higher levels of horsemanship.

There are also schools which specialise in one particular aspect of riding; it might be jumping, dressage, riding side-saddle, or cross-country riding. If this is made properly clear, then as long as the standard is adequate for that particular purpose, the school can receive approval and recognition.

Unfortunately, there are many schools, if they can be so called, which do not practise instruction at all. They are, in fact, little more than livery yards where people can just hire a horse for an hour's riding under no supervision and with no instruction provided. It is very often these schools that are of the lowest standard, not coming under any supervision from a recognised society or from an Authority, other than acquiring the necessary licence. Naturally, it is cheaper to go to one of these schools and hire a horse than it is to go to a proper riding establishment and receive instruction, but it is an unfortunate short cut which not only does little to improve the riding of the customer, but is likely to encourage the existence of such places which provide the very minimum in the way of proper amenities or, one regrets to say, care and forage. Such establishments are often run by the bogus, quick-rich types who quickly disappear when they realise that there is likely to be a complaint about either the hygienic or welfare conditions in their yard. It has even been known for a so-called proprietor to disappear overnight leaving his animals to the mercy of anyone who cares to take pity on them. Frequently such people employ the cheapest possible labour if, indeed, it can accurately be referred to as labour; or indeed, if it can be rightly described to as employment, using the local pony-crazy girls who are willing to work for virtually no reward. It would certainly be to the great advantage of equestrianism in this country if such establishments could be rooted out altogether.

At the other end of the scale there are of course some very high class establishments. Obviously with so many good schools it is invidious to mention more than one or two by name, but certain schools in Britain have, with justification, gained an international reputation: schools such as Fulmer, presided over by Robert Hall who was for some years the trainer of our Olympic dressage riders; Porlock, founded by the late Capt. Tony Collings who was so tragically killed in an air crash, now run by John Laseter a student of the Spanish Riding School who succeeded Col. Jamie Crawford who did so much to build up the international reputation of the school; Waterstock, with its remarkable reputation in the production of successful combined training riders, thanks to the very successful techniques of Lars Sederholm; Crabbet Park, run by Brian Young who for some years was the British Horse Society's national instructor; the Talland Equitation Centre, run by Mrs Sivewright who has been particularly successful in bringing on young riders of potential. All these schools, and many others, now have an international reputation: indeed, it is probably true to say that the majority of their students today come from overseas. This is partly because with fees understandably high the likelihood is that they are patronised by people from countries rather more wealthy than Britain is at the present. This is not to suggest that these schools in any way overcharge; far from it, the cost of labour, forage and upkeep is extremely high today. It is not an exaggeration to say that it costs around £12 a week just to feed a horse; to accommodate it and to look after it is at least another £12, apart from the usual overheads, shoeing, veterinary service and transport. It is not surprising therefore, that for a student to be instructed and to have to keep

Learning over cavalleti

The first jump: a simple pole

himself and his horse could cost anything up to £50 a week. As instruction at this level is essentially extended, that is to say lasting three months rather than three weeks, it can be seen that top-class instruction is now expensive. Regrettably, not many local authorities are prepared to help as they still appear to harbour the antiquated belief that everyone who rides or who wants to improve their riding is wealthy. It is for this reason that in 1977 the British Horse Society started its Riding Foundation, a scheme whereby funds are made available to help potentially good young riders in obtaining the sort of instruction that might benefit them in reaching a standard in equestrianism which normally would have been denied them. The objects of the Foundation when it was launched in 1977 were described as follows:

There are well over a million people riding regularly today in this country, twice as many as there were twenty years ago, but this expansion has inevitably brought a lowering of standards in riding and in horse care. At international level we are now fighting to keep our place against countries we had scarcely heard of two decades ago, and in competitions in which our dominance used to be an accepted fact.

If we cannot maintain high standards at home and if we are not at the top in international competition, how long can the sport continue to thrive?

The remedy must lie in more and better instruction, better methods of instruction and better instruction facilities. We already have a solid structure of qualified instructors backed up by a corps of keen and dedicated voluntary instructors, particularly in the Pony Club and affiliated Riding Clubs, but these need support: two forms of support.

First they need financial help. It costs money to go on a course to improve yourself as an instructor, whether you are a professional or a voluntary instructor. If you are a professional and have to earn your livelihood, it takes up valuable time as well. So the refresher training of instructors, which is so important, must be subsidised.

Secondly, a centre from which inspiration, ideas and doctrine can flow is essential. Before the war there was Weedon: other countries still have national centres such as Saumur in France and Warendorf in Germany. Each of these is generously financed to the tune of hundreds of thousands of pounds by their Governments. It is from such national centres that the path to success in general standards and international achievement starts. By comparison, we, of course, have the British Equestrian Centre at Stoneleigh which has always had to pay its own way, with virtually no financial assistance. If, through an injection of support, we could turn the British Equestrian Centre into a truly national training centre, we could not only help our instructors with subsidised courses, but we could also help our rising stars with the training which is so essential in the very competitive standards in international riding today. Most valuable of all we would have a centre which would have an inspirational effect on the whole of riding in this country.

From this it will be seen that a real attempt is being made to provide the sort of instruction that is necessary if Britain is going to maintain its position at the top of the equestrian world. There is no doubt that while the famous cavalry equitation school at Weedon was in existence there was a lavish supply of first-class instruction available to riders at all levels. Unfortunately, it has never been possible to produce a civilian Weedon similar to the establishment at Saumur when the cavalry training was superseded by a civilian set-up underwritten by the Government. In Britain it has never been possible to afford an absolutely top-class instructor of world calibre to introduce a doctrine which is acceptable to all the many people who at one level or another are instructing in Britain.

While it is true to say that certain countries are fortunate enough to have schools of the highest possible calibre, such as the Spanish Riding School in Vienna, Saumur in France, Warendorf in Germany and Gladstone in the United States, most countries are in fact limited in the number of really top-class riding establishments for the simple reason that there just are not enough good instructors to go round (in the whole world let alone in any one country). That this should be so is something of a paradox considering the large increase in popularity in riding over the last few years. But, unfortunately, whereas there are proper courses which lead to diplomas and degrees in academic subjects there have seldom been similar courses for sporting activities, let alone riding. Therefore, while in a country such as the USSR where limitless money is available there is a carefully planned scheme for producing riding masters, nothing similar exists, certainly not on such a scale, in other countries, although in Germany and in a rather different way in France there are developments in this direction.

2
What to Ride on

It is vitally important that anyone taking up riding should ride the horse best suited to his or her requirements. So often people do not take sufficient trouble in choosing the type of horse that they are going to get most pleasure from riding; in particular, once they have learnt, a certain number of people tend to get a little over ambitious and are then rather inclined to buy horses that are really too much for them. It is worth, therefore, considering the different types of horses available in the British Isles and assessing their suitability for different riders.

Horses

Initially, of course, there is the Thoroughbred. It is often said that anybody who has once ridden a Thoroughbred never wants to ride anything else. This is obviously true up to a point, but it has to be accepted that a Thoroughbred requires rather more skill in riding and controlling than a less well-bred horse. This is because, in the first place, it is more highly strung, thanks to the breeding policies employed in the Thoroughbred world over the years when speed was the principal requirement. It is therefore very much faster, not only in its actual paces but also in its reactions, which can take the less experienced rider by surprise. The Thoroughbred is also that much more sensitive and reacts more quickly to the slightest movement on the part of the rider. This, again, with the less experienced rider can lead to problems; so, although there is no doubt that to ride a Thoroughbred is one of the most exciting equestrianism experiences that one can have, it must be taking a risk to start riding a Thoroughbred before one has had sufficient experience. The Thoroughbred today is mainly used for racing, but there are many Thoroughbreds that, once they have finished their careers on the racecourse and, for one reason or another, are not considered suitable for the stud, find their way into private stables as hunters or as hacks. Sometimes the temperament, as suggested, because of the experience on the racecourse, is unreliable, but very often a Thoroughbred, carefully handled when it first comes into a private stable, can prove to have as equable and generous a temperament as any other horse. If it does settle then there is no horse in the world to equal the Thoroughbred across good hunting country, especially a country such as Leicestershire where in some areas there is still plenty of grass.

Next we come to the three-quarter-bred or even half-bred. This is a horse that has perhaps a Thoroughbred stallion as its sire, but is out of a mare that is not completely clean bred. Careful breeding can in fact result in this three-quarter-bred or half-bred horse being in many ways ideal for every form of equestrianism other than racing. The English Hunter, the typical three-quarter-bred, is nowadays almost accepted as a breed, certainly as a type. It has, over the years, been assiduously developed in England and Ireland; the Irish three-quarter-bred hunter, in particular, having no peer in the world of the horse. The advantage of the three-quarter-bred or half-bred lies in the fact that by careful breeding one can eradicate those elements and qualities that can make a Thoroughbred less suited for ordinary riding. For instance, the Thoroughbred sometimes lacks stamina, being bred for speed; the Thoroughbred sometimes lacks bone, being bred for quality: a horse, therefore, with the basic qualities of the Thoroughbred, but also with substance and stamina is obviously a very valuable animal. There can be no doubt whatever that this is the ideal vehicle for the ordinary rider once he has sufficient experience and has progressed on from the learner stage.

Many people are totally devoted to the Arab. It certainly has great qualities, not least of which is its very real beauty. Those used to riding Arabs never want to ride anything else; though conversely those who have normally ridden the hunter-type seldom take to the Arab. It is certainly a totally different feel riding an Arab with its shorter stride, its apparent lack of substance and its deep saddle position; but those who are Arab-minded can see nothing wrong whatever in them and, indeed, they have a wonderful record as a riding horse. Nor should it be forgotten that the Arab is the original Thoroughbred and therefore retains many of the Thoroughbred's qualities. Not surprisingly their popularity is increasing enormously – Arab classes at all the major shows nowadays are among the best filled classes. It is true, however, that people who are not Arab-minded, despite the fact that they cannot fail to appreciate the beauty of its head and movements, tend to find something about its hind leg, tail carriage and angularity that looks totally wrong. Indeed, there are many people who have probably been brought up, for the most part in the hunting field, who still regard the Arab as something slightly inferior. It is true that Arabs do not appear to make good hunters though they have a very fine record in long-distance riding, stemming of course from their experience over the centuries in the desert. As a mount for a beginner an Arab is possibly a little sharp, but there are many people who have found the Arab with its narrowness, its great intelligence and its attractive personality to be an ideal horse for a beginner.

As is the case with every horse if fed with too much hard food, it will become stupid, while carefully planned and adjusted feeding will make any horse, or almost any horse, sensible.

Ponies

As has been suggested, the ideal vehicle for beginners, especially if they are children, is a pony. In fact, British-bred ponies are often sturdy enough to carry adults. Britain, however, is unique in the fact that it has the nine native breeds which have been such a feature of equestrian activities in the British Isles and, indeed, all over the world. The export of British-bred ponies to many other countries is now considerable. The children's riding pony in Britain is in fact something of a phenomenon. Apart from the pure individual breeds which will be discussed later, the majority of the ponies that are ridden by children and young people in Britain are crosses with a certain amount of Thoroughbred blood and a certain amount of native blood in their veins. This produces the almost ideal vehicle for everyday riding; the Thoroughbred provides the quality, speed, activity, and the temperament, and the native breed produces the sturdiness, 'toughness' and the ability to survive living out in all weathers: which, of course, in these days is a big financial saving.

Champion side-saddle pony: the author's daughter at 16

Quality Hunter

At the top end of the scale there is the unique British Show Pony which is now so beautifully bred that it is unrivalled anywhere in the world. Invariably it has Thoroughbred blood in its veins, frequently Welsh blood – whence stems the beautiful flowing movement – and very often Arab blood. A few years ago the stallion *Naseel*, a pure bred Arab, provided stock which was to become famous the world over; ponies now legendary such as *Pretty Polly*, *My Pretty Maid* and *Pollyanna*, allegedly sold to the States for £6000, being considered the almost perfect child's show pony.

Then there is the ordinary riding pony that probably has little show potential, indeed does not expect ever to see the show ring, but makes the ideal pony for ordinary children to hunt, to ride in gymkhanas, go to the Pony Club on, and generally enjoy their riding on. This, perhaps, is the most useful pony of all: after all, the number of children who can compete in high-class shows, even the lesser shows, is obviously limited. The different breeds that provide the blood which does so much to produce these eminently suitable riding ponies must now be considered.

The Connemara

The Connemara is indigenous to the western coast of Ireland. Owing to the fact that the ponies run in droves in this inaccessible part of mountainous Ireland the breed has remained virtually uncontaminated. The Connemara Stud Book was started in 1923, all Connemara stallions now having to be licensed in Ireland. There is a very considerable export trade for the Connemara as it is a pony that crosses extremely well, not only with another pony, but also with a horse – many well-known horses having Connemara blood in their veins. They can be as high as 14 hands 2 in, are very tough, sure-footed, and are also very sensible and co-operative. As a rule they make first-class hunters and jumpers, which is why so many of our leading event horses and show jumpers have Connemara blood in their veins. The most usual colour is grey, but they can also be bay, black, but are seldom chestnut (piebald and skewbald not being allowed in the Stud Book) and they frequently have an eel stripe down the back. They are short legged with a good shoulder, have seven or eight inches of bone and retain a slight degree of Arabian appearance. One of the problems of breeding Connemaras outside their natural habitat is that when fed on better land they tend to get too big and lose their true type; it has been known for a Connemara at six-years-old to grow four inches. Nevertheless, of all the native breeds they have perhaps contributed most to the general value and improvement of ponies, with the possible exception of the Welsh.

The Welsh

Welsh ponies are widely recognised as being amongst

the most beautiful in the world. In addition they possess many other desirable pony qualities; it is not surprising, therefore, that Welsh blood is to be found in so many good ponies. In fact, the Welsh Stud Book caters for four distinctive Welsh breeds; the Welsh Mountain pony (Section A) which is under 12 hands and in the opinion of many is the supreme example of all that a pony should be, namely intelligent, courageous, gentle and possessing this exquisite movement.

Active Welsh Cob

Its slightly concave face set on a graceful neck, with a deep sloping shoulder, a strong back and a tail somewhat highly set and proudly carried, makes it visually extremely attractive. Section B caters for the Welsh pony which inherits many of the characteristics of the Mountain but is bred more specifically as a child's pony with emphasis on quality, bone, substance and, of course, pony character. The Section B may be up to 13·2 hands in height. Welsh ponies of Cob-type and the Cob itself are covered in Sections C and D. The former not exceeding 13·2 hands, while the latter averages 14·2 to 15 hands. These sturdier ponies are active, strong with great substance, have quality heads, but are deep through the heart and, once again,

A selection of suitable ponies of differing native breeds

have this wonderful action. Welsh ponies have been exported all over the world and in many countries such as America, Australia, New Zealand, and South Africa they have their own Welsh Pony Societies and Stud Books.

New Forest

The New Forest pony is found in the New Forest in Hampshire. This has allegedly been the breeding ground of these ponies since the 11th century. The size varies from between 12 to 14 hands, the larger ponies having considerable sturdiness. They are ideal as an all-round family pony being intelligent, quick to learn, ideal for sporting events, but useful too in harness. All in all the New Forest pony is exceptionally reliable, being also unusually attractive in appearance. There is, as one would expect, a thriving New Forest Society. The New Forest crossed with other ponies invariably produces a genuine, reliable, child's pony: its narrowness making it a comfortable ride, while its equable temperament making it sensible.

Exmoor and Dartmoor

The Exmoor is usually thought to be the oldest native pony breed in Britain going back almost to prehistoric times. The Moors being wild and lonely, the climate harsh with little protection, these ponies have developed what is still their principal attribute – hardiness, the characteristic that has led to their considerable use as foundation stock for breeding. They are exported in large numbers, particularly to the Scandinavian countries and Canada. In the opinion of many people the Exmoor crossed with a Thoroughbred, or a pony with Thoroughbred blood in its veins, produces the almost ideal children's pony. Exmoors are quick witted, intelligent, and have great stamina. They are still bred wild on the Moor, being rounded up once a year and sold at fairs such as Bampton. Many, however, would like to see the end of this as they feel that ponies are in effect, just being bred for slaughter. Although a good ride in itself the Exmoor pony is of particular value to breed from. These ponies have a deep wide chest, powerful loins, clean legs and excellent feet. The winter coat, as can be expected, is very thick; the foals, too, are born with a thick woolly undercoat covered by a waterproof top layer of long hairs that protect them against the climate.

The neighbouring Dartmoor has to learn to withstand similar climatic conditions and therefore has many of the same characteristics as the Exmoor, but the Dartmoor is also valuable for other reasons, being an unusually versatile pony. It is a remarkable jumper for its size – it does not exceed a height of 12·2 hands, and is therefore much in demand as foundation stock in the breeding of the larger all-round ponies and, indeed, of the top-class show ponies. The value of Dartmoor blood in the veins of other ponies is proved by the fact that a part-bred Dartmoor register has now been formed. It is a good-looking pony with a small, well-bred head; it has an alert expression, carries a full mane and has particularly well-shaped feet. The Dartmoor has a good front, with a high head carriage making it a pleasant and safe ride for children. In addition to the physical advantages, the Dartmoor is intelligent, able to think for itself and has apparently a particular and genuine liking for children.

The Shetland

The Shetland is perhaps the best known of all the native breeds, and consequently people are inclined to call any small pony a Shetland. The genuine Shetland is about 40 in high at three years old and should not exceed 42 in when fully grown. The favourite colour is black, but in fact Shetlands can be any colour, including skewbald and piebald. In the summer their coats produce a lovely sheen, but in winter the coat is very protective, being a kind of double coat which is later shed. The Shetland has a broad forehead, neat little ears and plenty of hair on the mane and tail. They are extraordinarily good trotters considering their size, and astonishing speeds have been recorded. Over the years Shetlands have been exported all over the world for many different reasons, even for working at circuses and fairs. They have also worked in the mines, being ideally suited because of their size; and they have for centuries carried the Shetland islanders for farm work in a fierce climate, often on a very meagre ration of food. There is naturally a great demand for these ponies, but although in many ways they appear to be ideally suitable as first ponies for children, a Shetland pony can sometimes prove to be less ideal than might be expected. This is because being so small it has never really been broken properly and therefore tends to indulge in bad habits which are difficult to correct. They might also prove too strong for a small child and sometimes have a mind and will of their own which must not be allowed to get out of hand. On the other hand, there are many Shetland ponies which, thanks to the skill of the breeder and the breaker, have been entirely responsible for a child taking up riding. The right Shetland can give a child complete confidence, which once acquired leads on to a desire to ride a larger pony. All in all the Shetland richly deserves its reputation.

Dales and Fells

The Dales come from Northumberland and neighbouring counties and are usually dark brown and black, although occasionally one sees a grey. They are bred for power and activity and although they are very strong with particularly strong quarters and good fronts, they retain a pony-type head. They are great trotters and have proved themselves very strong and willing; they have been known to carry amazingly heavy loads of lead across the Dales to Newcastle, but they also make friendly and attractive riding ponies. Frequently they have been crossed successfully with other ponies or small horses, producing really good hunters and jumpers. The Fell ponies from next door also have a background of heavy pack work, sometimes travelling as far as 250 miles a week carrying as much as 16 stone, but they are also good ponies to ride and to hunt. They have in particular a wonderful and very comfortable walk which is long striding and rhythmic. They are sure-footed and are therefore particularly safe ponies in their own kind of country; they have very long manes and tails, good shoulders but are a little bit long in the back which is often responsible for making them a comfortable ride. The Fell pony is 13·2 to 14 hands. They are rightly considered as safe and reliable ponies for children.

The Highland

For sheer weight-carrying the Highland pony exceeds all others: carrying deer on the moors of an overall weight of 17 st is not unusual. Considering the weight being carried the Highland seems able to cover the ground at a remarkable pace. They are usually grey, though one frequently sees duns, and like the Connemara they have the eel stripe down the spine. Highland ponies are short with rather wide heads and a wide jaw bone. They have small ears and a contented expression. The Arab blood which goes far back can still be seen in their heads. The mainland Highland is a little heavier than the Highland to be found in the Western Isles; the latter making a particularly good riding pony. It is worth remembering that one of the most famous three-day event horses of all time, Sheila Willcox's *High and Mighty*, had a Thoroughbred sire but his dam was half Highland, the other half being Arab. The Highland blood showed very clearly in *High and Mighty* who had an eel stripe down his strong back. Highlands carry little hair on the heels, but are well ribbed up with broad quarters, strong thighs, plenty of bone and broad knees; everything suggesting great strength. They are not unlike the Norwegian ponies, but the Highland is probably the more attractive; certainly the more active.

To sum up, perhaps the most suitable ponies for riding are those with New Forest and Dartmoor blood in their veins. For the small child it is obviously the Shetland; for the rider, or the parent of a rider looking for quality, then it must be the Welsh. The other ponies have the advantage that they can carry not only children, but adults; indeed, the Dales and Fells and Highland ponies are frequently ridden by adults more regularly than by children. The influence

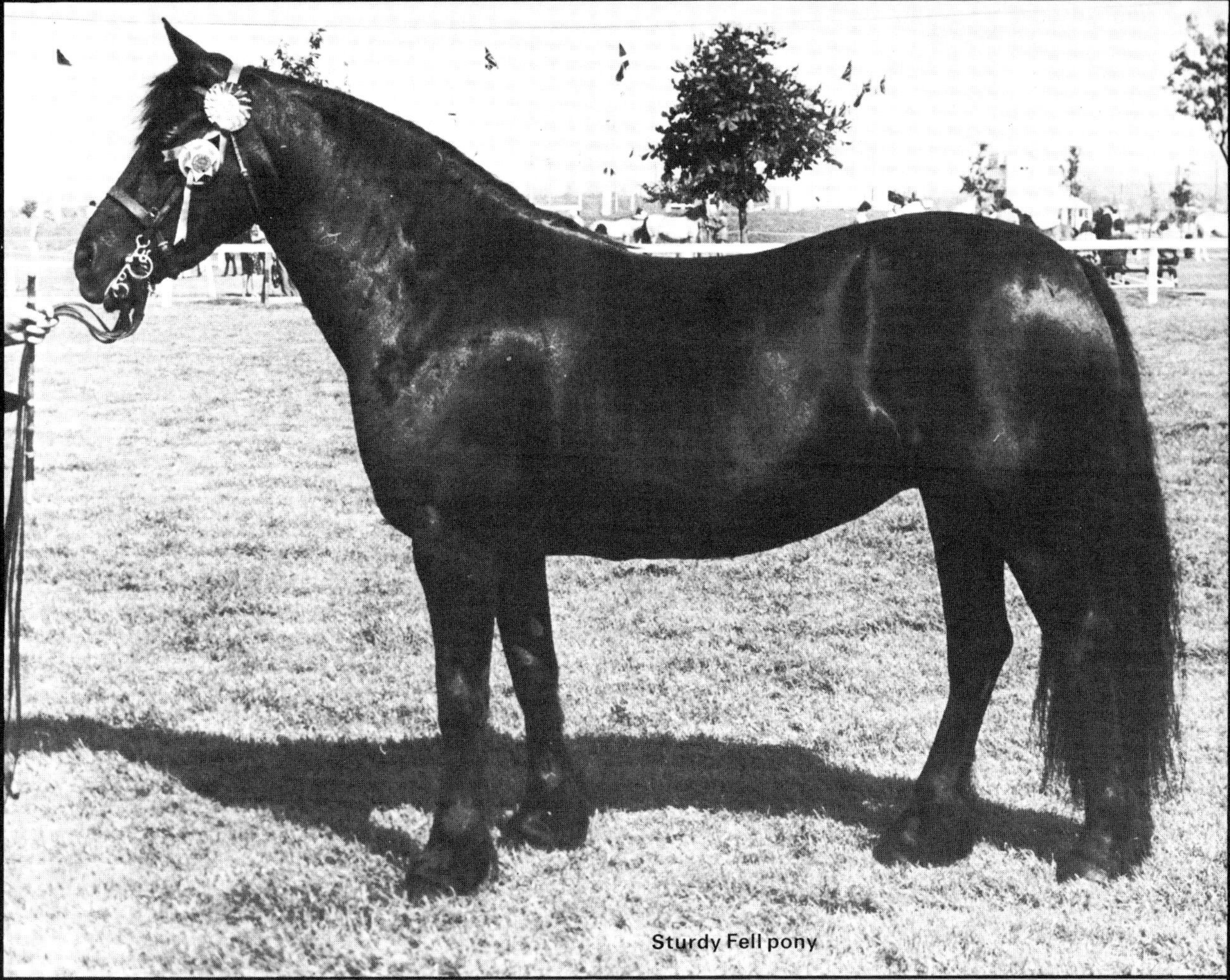

Sturdy Fell pony

Sensible Dale pony

of these ponies on riding, throughout the world, is remarkable. It has to be remembered that although today, ponies originating in Britain are used all over the world, the majority of countries do not breed ponies as such, with the result that children do not learn to ride until they are old and big enough to ride horses. This of course is a great advantage for British children and children in those countries where ponies are now available.

What to Learn on

What then is ideal for the learner? It is not, unfortunately, all that easy to find the ideal conveyance for an inexperienced rider because the safer, the more reliable a horse is the more dull it is inclined to be. A beginner, however, or the less experienced rider, is always going to find it much easier, and get much more enjoyment if the horse goes freely forward. Frequently, therefore, the horse that is so often described as the patent safety, needs a great deal of persuasion to go forward at all, not only making uninteresting hard work for the rider, but also making it difficult to learn. Perhaps the ideal animal for a beginner then is the cob-like animal; though not necessarily the true Welsh Cob, which is a splendid animal, having a very good temperament, being sturdy and solid yet also possessing great action which makes it capable of considerable speed. There are many other cob-types, however, probably with Welsh Cob blood in their veins, that can provide a very pleasant ride. It does seem to me a great pity that the Welsh Cob is not more generally used in breeding the ordinary riding horse. There are also animals with pony blood in their veins – the pony invariably providing many valuable qualities which are not as a rule found in horses. There is also, as suggested above, the half-bred, with at least some Thoroughbred blood in its veins.

Ideally, then, the less experienced rider should be able to satisfy himself or herself with a horse that is sound and reliable, capable of a certain amount of speed, but is neither a racehorse nor a show horse and is, therefore, very much cheaper.

It could be argued that in Britain we encourage our children to start to ride at too early an age; that it would be better to wait until they were sufficiently strong and were more developed mentally to know what riding was all about. I do not believe that this argument can be upheld. There can be little doubt that the possibility of learning to ride at an early age gives pleasure to countless thousands of children much earlier than if they had had to wait until they were big enough to ride a horse, even if the knowledge acquired does not necessarily appear to give them a superiority over those who learnt to ride later when they were more easily able to assimilate instruction.

There can be no doubt that although riders at the top may be equally skilled, whether they come from Britain or elsewhere, there is nevertheless a much greater depth of ability in Britain. It is for this reason that there is such a remarkable reservoir of riders of potential in Britain. It is significant, too, for instance, that in any one season more than 20 different riders represent Britain in show jumping, something which no other country in the world has achieved. It is the same with eventing. This is entirely due in my opinion to the fact that as children, British riders have, thanks to the ponies which are indigenous to Britain, had the chance to learn to ride at an early age: and, if wisely advised, learnt to ride on the right sort of animal.

Riding Overseas

In the United States of America, in the Antipodes and in South Africa there is a somewhat different style of riding and, therefore, a somewhat different type of horse is required. It is estimated that there are over seven million different horses in the United States: there is no doubt that, as in Europe, riding has increased enormously in popularity. The result of this has been the considerable development in various horses such as the American Saddle Horse which was always considered ideal, in the old days, for the planters in the Ohio valley, as well as being aesthetically satisfying. It is comfortable, but not particularly fast, although it is reckoned that in Kentucky after several generations of selective breeding the ideal Saddle Horse has now been achieved, now known, indeed, as the American Saddle Horse. Equally famous, perhaps, is the American Quarter Horse, having initially achieved world-wide recognition as the most suitable cow-horse for working the beef herds in the United States. In fact, the Quarter Horse originally came from the eastern states, being bred along the coastal settlements. There is, undoubtedly, Spanish blood in their veins; they are immensely fast, compact, rather chunky, seldom more than 15 hands high, with massive muscular quarters and remarkable acceleration. At one time they were called Quarter pacers, the implication being that they were raced with remarkable results over very short distances of no further than a quarter of a mile. Latterly, with the Quarter Horse developing its protective instinct towards other animals with a quite remarkable reaction and anticipation to their movements, they have been widely used to contain cattle. They are also well-known today for the demonstrations that they give all over the world. There could now be as many as half a million Quarter Horses in the United States.

One should perhaps also mention the Albino or true white horse that has so long been extolled in song and story, and is part of many legends. The prancing white stallions and snowy mares have a great romance about them, popular in fiction over many centuries. The Appaloosa, however, is rather different. Like the Pintos, the Appaloosa's coat results from hereditary spotted genes inducing the double colouring with the white dominant; roan or off-white being almost equally common. There is no great similarity otherwise between the Pinto and the Appaloosa. The pattern of the Appaloosa's coat usually assumes an organised spotted design easily recognisable. The spots are frequently innumerable, appearing in a circle, known as a blanket, on the quarters. The Appaloosa, of course, came to America originally with the Spaniards, many of them drifting northwards, falling into the hands of the Nez Percé Indians. These were excellent horse breeders living by the Paloos river which gave them their name – animals of great quality gradually being developed. In fact the Appaloosa is extremely suitable for beginners. It is, in the opinion of many, ideal as a link between a pony and a horse having a very good temperament, jumping well and being something of a cross between a pony and a Thoroughbred in its stride. So often when children are promoted from riding ponies to riding horses they find it difficult to cope with the longer stride and the greater power of the horse behind the saddle, so that they become disconcerted and, perhaps, not enjoying it are tempted to give it up altogether. Despite its obvious suitability, however, the Appaloosa has never really become popular as a riding horse in Britain and although there is now an Appaloosa Horse Society which is doing quite well it tends to be used as a Western style of riding mount rather than as a mount for the more ordinary English style of riding. This is possibly due to the fact that Western riding is becoming increasingly popular in Britain, and the Appaloosa is inevitably associated with the West and the Western. In the States it would appear to be more or less fifty–fifty between English style riders and Western riders. In Britain, of course, the greater number of people still ride English style, but more and more people each year are taking up Western riding with the typical Western saddle, even riding in Western style clothes with a stetson – and on a Western-type horse.

The Morgan horse is also worthy of a mention. It is, perhaps, most similar to the English Hackney, but it has more substance, generally being rather thick through the neck, though this does not deny it quality. It carries its hind legs well away from it, as does the hackney, but it is a horse that has become very popular in the United States both for riding and for driving. The history of it is somewhat obscure other than it derives from a single phenomenal stallion owned by a certain Mr Morgan. The stallion, named *Figure*, was the progenitor of this type of horse that gradually became known as the Morgan. It has considerable speed and there are many people in the United States who believe the Morgan to be the best all-round horse that there is. Certainly they have a great capacity for endurance, equalled only by the Arabs. They are individualists, very strong, yet have what appears to be a happy, carefree temperament.

Finally, as far as the Americans are concerned, there is the Standard-bred or American Trotter. Its name is derived from the old custom of testing untried harness racers to determine if they could go the mile within a specified standard or time allotment. Today the standard is 2 min 20 s for the mile. At a speed at anything less than the gallop it would appear generous enough when one considers that half a century ago, when tracks were not half as carefully prepared as they are today, a horse called *Dan Patch* completed the mile in less than 2 min flat. In the same category, perhaps, is the Tennessee Walking Horse. The old saying goes that if you ride a Tennessee Walking Horse today you will buy it tomorrow. They have a soft, fluent, almost gliding gait which to the spectator appears to be half a walk and half a run, though to those who are used to this particular kind of pace it is apparently considered gentle and relaxing; but to those who are not used to it it is obviously somewhat strange. Interestingly enough the horses were at one time known as Turn-Row horses as they were used for inspecting the crops in 'rows'. Now they are extremely popular for riding and for racing, over 30000 horses in the States being raced as Tennessee Walking Horses. Indeed, their owners are so enthusiastic that at their great annual show at Shelbyville, classes attract more entries than at any other horse show in the country: indeed, this kind of horse is now spreading to other parts of the world. Generally, it is true to say that the tendency in Australia, New Zealand and Africa is to follow the influence of America as much as that of Britain.

3
What to Ride in

It cannot be denied that riding clothes can be costly. Today a pair of boots from a top-class bootmaker can cost up to, or even over, £300. A good hacking jacket costs over £100; a pair of tailor-made breeches over £100. But although it is nice if one can afford to be dressed in the best and although it may be true to say that the better the quality the longer it all lasts, nevertheless it is still quite possible to dress adequately for a comparatively modest sum.

Headwear

A hard hat is an absolute essential: indeed before very long it might become as compulsory as a crash helmet is for riding on a motorcycle. One usually wears a velvet cap or hunting cap for ordinary riding which can be obtained at most outfitters. They are comfortable and on the whole safe, though there are many people who feel it should be made compulsory that in addition a harness should be worn, ie a contraption round the chin to make sure that the cap remains in position in the event of a fall. In the case of children, especially, it is all too easy for a hat to come off leaving the head defenceless. It is also essential in choosing a velvet cap that one should choose a hat that has been properly approved so that there is no danger of the peak cutting the nose or, because of the angle at which it is set on, cutting the forehead, or even fracturing the skull. A great deal of trouble is now taken in the production of a safe velvet cap, especially for children.

Casual exercise wear – note the hard cap

Sensible, comfortable wear by Bullen children, three of whom became Olympic riders

Correct wear for hunting: top boots with red coat *(left)*, 'butcher' boots with black coat *(right)*

The bowler hat is, of course, also worn for riding. It is now, except in formal circles, a little outdated, although there are many people who still insist that in the hunting field the bowler is more correct than the velvet cap. It would be stupid to pretend that there is any protection from the bowler; it is, nevertheless, a hat that has always been associated with riding, and properly worn – not at an angle or on the back of the head – it can look smart. The bowler is obviously correct for the formal occasion, ie in the show ring (either for an exhibitor or a judge) and in the hunting field (if an adult, though not necessarily a female adult as today in many hunts females are permitted, even encouraged, to wear a velvet cap rather than a bowler hat).

Finally there is the top hat which is only worn in the hunting field with a red coat or a proper black hunting coat and top boots, or in one of the bigger shows. The

Western style

top hat, which is now very expensive – probably around £80 – is only worn with formal wear, that is to say it is never worn when the rider is in mufti or 'rat catcher', which is the description given to a tweed coat, drab breeches and brown boots.

Coats and Jackets

The coat should be essentially practical, ideally of a fairly heavy material as protection against the weather, and should be properly lined in the tail so that the material is not ruined by the horse's sweat on its flank. It should not be too waisted and should never be double-breasted, other than with a cut-away or swallow-tail coat. It can, however, have either a single or a double split at the back; it must certainly have one or the other. For hunting one can wear a tweed coat if one comes out in 'rat catcher' or mufti, or one can wear a red or black hunting coat. It is usual only to wear the red hunting coat when one has been invited by the Master to wear the Hunt Button. Each Hunt has its own Hunt Button which might be likened to a Club tie. The Hunt Button can also be worn with a black coat, though it is correct to go out in a black coat and a top hat wearing only a plain button on the coat.

For hunting one wears a hunting stock or hunting tie which is similar to an old-fashioned cravat and is invariably plain white. It is not easy to tie a stock correctly and one should be properly instructed in the art, for nothing looks worse than a badly-tied stock flowing out like a bath towel. Only in show jumping do riders wear a white shirt with a white tie, rather than a hunting stock. This is a custom which is still frowned upon by a great number of the older hunting fraternity.

Breeches and Jodphurs

Breeches, properly made to measure in a good material, can be very expensive, but there are many good outfitters who specialise in riding clothes and can provide very adequate breeches at less than half the price charged by the best tailors. Obviously if they are to be given hard use they will not last as long, but they can certainly look as smart, especially now that the fashion is to wear breeches tight at the thigh rather than bowed-out as was the fashion in the old days. One should add that the button of the breeches is always on the inside of the knee, though it is intriguing to speculate just how this came about; in old prints one invariably notices that the buttons are on the outside.

If one is wearing jodphurs they want to be neat below the knee and down the calf, otherwise they look sloppy and amateurish.

Informal

Hacking

Boots

Wearing top boots one can either have a mahogany top, which is only worn out hunting, or plain brown or black boots; brown boots usually being referred to as polo boots. Today because of the increasing cost of boots that are made to measure, excellent boots are now being made in rubber which has of course the advantage of being easily washable. They are now properly lined and can even be made with mahogany tops and are therefore permissible with hunting kit. Leather boots if they are going to last should be carefully looked after: in particular they should always have wooden trees to keep the leather properly stretched. It is also wise, in view of the initial cost, to follow the advice of leading bootmakers and stand them upside down when first purchased (before wearing them) so that they do not crease over the instep: they should also be kept well oiled before getting the proper polish on them.

With top boots, hunting spurs should always be worn; they can also be worn in the show ring but never by the judge. The spur should always sit on the top of the heel, the roller pointing downwards. The easiest strap to wear with spurs today is the single strap known as the polo strap.

There has long been a tradition that people who ride are well turned out; it is not only a tradition which should wherever possible be followed, but it is equally important that riders should look smart. Clothes should be well-cut and clean, and indeed today there are many cheaper tailors specialising in riding clothes which are well within the pocket of the ordinary rider.

Very often a rider looks unkempt because he does not wear the clothes correctly. I believe that anyone

Perfection: the complete immaculate turnout for dressage: highly polished boots, worn with spurs; tight fitting breeches; cut-away or swallow-tail coat; gloves; well-tied hunting tie or stock; top hat, with hair in hair net

taking up riding can, simply by following the example of people who are smart in appearance, look equally impressive. I remember once in the show ring seeing a girl so beautifully turned out that I felt convinced that she came from the aristocracy. It turned out that the only space in which she had to ride her pony was a half-acre paddock at the back of her house, but since a small child whenever she had gone to a show she noticed how the best riders were turned out and as soon as she was in a position to buy clothes for herself she made sure that she looked as good as them. This is an example of what can be done if someone is sufficiently anxious to appear properly turned out.

So often it is the detail that betrays the less experienced rider, not through the riding but through the clothes. For instance, if wearing top boots a garter is provided to keep the breeches from riding up over the knee. The correct way to wear the garter is with the tongue pointing outwards and the buckle nestling against the button of the breeches. If the garter is made sufficiently tight there is no problem about it remaining in this position. Unfortunately, even in the best circles one frequently sees garters sufficiently loose to have been allowed to ride round to the wrong position. Similarly, the way the tie or stock is tied can indicate how experienced the rider is, and the more experienced rider does not appear in brightly coloured gloves, though there has long been a tradition of wearing a coloured handkerchief in the breast pocket and in the old days it was invariably the sign of a dealer to have a red and white spotted handkerchief in his pocket.

The hat should never be worn at a rakish angle. This gives a musical comedy effect which betrays immediately that the rider is not very experienced. He may cut a dash in his own immediate circle of non-riding friends, but he will certainly make no impression with people who know.

As a postscript to these remarks on correct wear, it might be of interest to explain the origin of the top boot as worn with hunting kit. Up to the beginning of the 18th century it was normal for top boots to stretch right up the thigh, thus protecting the breeches or trousers worn underneath the boots from the mud resulting from the unmade up roads and tracks. At the time of the enclosures which were the result of a certain Robert Bakewell indulging in selective breeding policies for cattle and building separate enclosures, fences traversed the countryside: to follow hounds it became necessary to jump these fences. This was in fact the first time that fences were jumped by horse and rider. Up to this time it had therefore been usual to ride with a long length of leg, similar to the dressage seat of today – as can be seen in old pictures; but when fences had to be jumped it proved to be difficult to ride with a long stirrup as there was not sufficient purchase from the knee to the thigh. Stirrups, therefore, were shortened; but with the boot going right up the thigh this made it extremely uncomfortable because of the leather cutting into the back of the necessarily bent knee; thus it became the custom to turn down the top of the boot so that it hung over the calf. Naturally, the inside of the boot would not be polished, this then giving the impression of a brown, unpolished top hanging down over the polished calf and foot; hence the origin of top boot.

It may finally be of interest to give an explanation for the use of the word pink when referring to a red hunting coat. Up to the middle of the 19th century men wore coats of different colours, wearing exactly the same out hunting as they did in ordinary everyday life. The only coat, whether for riding or not, was swallow-tail, rather than the frock coat worn in town life. The only headwear, whether for riding or not, was a top hat. Towards the first quarter of this century it became the custom to wear a grey or a black coat, or at any rate a coat in a sober colour. This was to satisfy those who believed that Britain should go into mourning because of the lack of progress in the world of art during Queen Victoria's widowhood. The red coat remained only for the Hunt servants, all hunting rights traditionally being vested in the Crown, with scarlet as the Royal colour. Gradually it became the custom for everyone to emulate the Hunt servants by wearing scarlet coats rather than the dull coloured coats then *de rigueur*. By chance the tailor in the City of London who was most fashionable at this time and to whom most of the wealthy went for their Hunt coats was a gentleman named Pink; one therefore referred to a 'Pink' coat (as one might today refer to a Moss Bros morning suit). It was pure coincidence that the name of the tailor was Pink, but as the red coat worn for hunting was a subtle colour which was not quite a conventional red and had a hint of brick in it, it became popularly and appropriately referred to as hunting pink. It is generally accepted in the best circles today that a hunting gentleman wears scarlet in the field and pink in the evening, but he buys a red coat!

As with so much to do with equestrianism there is, even with clothes, much more than may immediately meet the eye, but it can safely be said that it is the person properly turned out who will be regarded as the most experienced horseman.

Variation in Dress in Different Countries

Naturally enough there are considerable differences in the riding wear in different countries. Basically, the costume is the same because in any country the kit is designed to be the most practical. Many countries, however, have, for instance, rather more baggy breeches which are less shaped than in Britain. In fact Britain was the leader in the most baggy breeches as recently as immediately after the Second World War,

Hunting

but whereas since then the British have come back to the almost skin-tight breeches similar to the skin-tight trousers ridden in the 18th and 19th centuries, most countries on the continent and overseas tend to retain the considerable bag in the breeches. It will also be noticed that coats are usually shorter in other countries, often waisted in a more exaggerated manner. Though it is easy to be smug about British tailoring, it is generally agreed that the tailoring of riding clothes in Britain is the best in the world; more than this, well tailored riding clothes have always been trend setters in fashion. It is, for instance, noticeable that what is in one generation used as sports wear, in the next generation becomes accepted wear for the ordinary person. An example is the cut-away coat already referred to: originally cut-away to make it easier for a man to sit astride a horse, in Victorian times the cut-away coat became *de rigueur* in all of the more fashionable sections of the community. In the same way the tight trousers narrow to the foot, often with an elastic under the instep, were designed for riding, but they were adopted for ordinary wear. One could even sight the present day sports jacket which has of course come directly from the hacking jacket or riding coat with one or two slits behind.

Britain, too, has been fortunate in having developed a trade of very experienced bootmakers with the result that the British top boot made to measure has always been elegantly shaped. One seldom sees a boot so elegantly shaped on the continent where they are more of the gum boot or wellington shape, more or less straight from the heel to the top of the boot with very little shaping down the calf. It may well be that this is more practical as the boot is both easier to pull on and to take off, but it is certainly less smart. However, one has to accept the criticism that in by-gone days the British have been prepared to put up with appalling discomfort to look almost fastidiously smart. Hence the tight neck-wear of the 18th and 19th centuries and in the female world, corsets.

Perhaps the most noticeable difference between riders in Britain and other countries is in the headwear. Again the velvet cap is most common, but whereas, certainly amongst top riders, the velvet cap is well-shaped and has a certain distinction, in other countries it is very stereotyped, having little character. In some countries, particularly in the Eastern block, the hat is worn with an elastic under the chin. The bowler hat, of course, originated from Britain, but although it is increasingly used on the continent – and was originally done so in blatant imitation of those who wore a bowler hat in Britain – the continental version is altogether a more lightweight hat than its counterpart in Britain, and one does not have to be a sartorial expert to appreciate that it does not come from Lock or Herbert Johnson. Paradoxically, as the bowler hat comes to be worn less in Britain so it is increasingly worn in continental countries, but it is likely that it will always be regarded as an English-type headwear. Some years ago when Piero d'Inzeo, the Italian rider, was left out of the Italian team because of one of his periodical differences of opinion with his Federation, he turned up in England at the Royal International Horse Show at the White City sporting an exaggeratedly curly-rimmed bowler hat with a rolled umbrella over his arm: if I cannot be here as an Italian then I will come as an Englishman, he seemed to imply.

It is the continental top hat that is perhaps most different to its English counterpart because it is much flatter and arguably, therefore, more practical, though this is doubtful: neither flat nor tall is really practical. The continental top hat, however, seems to lose something of the elegance that the English top hat derives from its height; at least in English eyes. In either case the top hat is not only unpractical, but an anachronism. However, it has become part of the riding wear, both in the hunting field and in the show ring and, indeed, in dressage, both in ordinary competition and in the dressage phase of a three-day event; and very smart it looks. It is interesting to note that whereas the continent has often copied the English style of riding wear as far as the top hat is concerned, an increasing number of English riders are now wearing the flat top hat so much associated with the dressage rider on the continent: as, indeed, British riders are now emulating the black breeches worn on the continent. Obviously it is a matter of opinion, but in my own opinion the flat top hat is seldom flattering, whereas the tall hat, if properly worn, has a commanding elegance.

It is also of interest that whereas Britain has so often set the fashion in riding wear the red coat was first adopted on the continent as the proper wear for show jumping. It could be that with little or no hunting there was no traditional sporting wear immediately obvious for adaption for show jumping, and so they chose the hunting red coat. Whereas in Britain show jumpers were jumping in uniform, so many of them being in the Cavalry, or in mufti, wearing soft hats or even cloth caps, the bowler was something of an exception. On the continent with the red coat they always wore the hard velvet cap which of course became the accepted wear for show jumping, though for some time many riders, especially in Ireland, still continued to wear a top hat with their hunting coat which in that particular instance was green. The top hat, too, even in the twenties was worn in point-to-points. One should, perhaps, in fairness add that Britain with its tradition of high-class tailoring

During a cross-country event it is essential to wear a hard hat with harness

always produced a red coat that all the world accepted as superior to the more lightweight less shapely coat worn on the continent and overseas. The exception, of course, is the USA and the Commonwealth countries who have understandably followed Britain's lead and very much moulded their own riding fashions on those of Britain.

One can, perhaps, be forgiven if one refers only briefly to the style of riding wear for those who ride in the Western fashion. It is, virtually, the cowboy fashion: anything approaching a hard hat is totally unknown. Yet in every other form of riding the hard hat is now considered as absolutely essential. Ironically, Western style riding is associated with something a good deal more enigmatic and hazardous than ordinary riding: yet even for hacking one is expected these days to wear a hard hat. Could it be that we are placing too much importance on the hard hat today? Or will we soon see a crash helmet obligatory under a stetson?

PART TWO
The Three Disciplines

4
Show Jumping

It is not easy to say exactly when show jumping as a sport started, but it is generally believed that in the 1860s some sort of show jumping event was held in Paris, probably connected with military training. At the turn of the century, show jumping was practised increasingly with the Cavalry Regiments, but it was really only at the first International Horse Show of Great Britain, held at Olympia in 1907, that regular show jumping competitions were organised and held for the most part for military competitors. Between the wars, show jumping became more popular, thanks largely to the rules that had been drawn up both on the continent and in Britain immediately after the First World War. These rules made the competitions more easy to understand from a spectator's point of view: they also produced better results, discontinuing marks awarded for style, as had hitherto been the case.

In 1923 the British Show Jumping Association was formed by a number of enthusiasts, both military and civilians, who felt that it was time that show jumping in Britain became a properly organised sport. The principal people involved were Col. V. D. S. Williams, who became the Secretary of the Association, and Col. 'Taffy' Walwyn, who became the Chairman. They collected a number of able and experienced people who together created an entirely new picture for show jumping in this country. The standard improved quickly, a number of names becoming well-known in the mid 20s: names such as Tommy Glencross, the Taylor brothers, the Foster brothers, and many others including the Bullows sisters. The Bullows sisters were really the first lady riders to become accepted as experts and the equal of men riders. They were extremely popular with the crowds who came to see them jump both at the big shows in London and at the County shows.

By modern day standards the rules were somewhat strange, as seen from the table showing the old points system. Today's rules are much simpler:

4 faults for a knock down
8 faults for a fall
3 faults for a refusal, 6 faults for a second refusal and elimination on the third refusal

It is not surprising that show jumping events were frequently followed by controversy, especially concerning the removal of slats and feet in the water: it has often been said that the argument at the end of a show jumping competition took as long as the competition itself. These rules were also largely responsible for the surprising fact that British riders never won international events between the two wars. This was because when the rules had been drawn up in the early 1920s no reference had been made to the continental countries who were also drawing up rules. The result was that there was one set of rules for England and one set of rules for the rest of the world – a fact which has a familiar ring. The differences were not very great, but they were important. On the continent they appreciated that in jumping a course of fences taking as long as one liked, even allowing one's horse to look at a fence to make sure that he understood what he was going to have to jump and then giving him time to properly adjust his stride, made the jumping not only too easy but too boring from a spectator's point of view. The result was that the spectators for show jumping gradually diminished. On the continent, by contrast, an element of speed had been introduced; not only did riders have to complete the course within a specified time, but in the event of equal faults between two or more riders then there was a jump-off, in which time was the deciding factor. This made the sport far more exciting and far more interesting to the spectators, in addition to being a much greater challenge to the riders. For jumping large fences at speed is obviously very much more difficult than jumping fences, taking as long as you like. It was not surprising therefore that British riders, though well-mounted and, indeed, consummate horsemen themselves, never won in international competitions, never having had any experience in jumping against the clock.

There was another factor. Federico Caprilli was born in Italy in 1868 and it was he who in the early days of the 20th century invented the Forward Seat, believing that it was better for a rider to sit forward and slightly out of the saddle when taking off at a fence, and at the same time maintaining a firm contact with the horse's mouth, then allowing the horse to balance itself with its legs arching its back. This was totally different to what had been the practice previously and, indeed, in Britain until the late 1920s where the rider sat well back, as does a steeplechase jockey, allowing the reins to slip through the hands. Caprilli initially practised his theories on military recruits in Italy until gradually his policies spread, becoming popular all over the continent. Not only was the result more accurate jumping, but when it came to jumping against the clock the rider who rode with the Forward Seat was at a very considerable advantage. Caprilli's theory could be equated with

OLD POINT SYSTEM

Faults to count as follows:

1st Refusal or Bolting	1 Fault } = 3 Faults
2nd Refusal or Bolting	2 Faults } = 3 Faults
3rd Refusal or Bolting	Disqualified from the competition

Refusals are cumulative on the entire round, that is the third refusal in any one round disqualifies.

This rule does not apply to Novice or Juvenile Classes. In these classes the 3rd refusal at any one fence disqualifies.

A Slat knocked to the Ground	½ Fault
Horse causes all or any part of the obstacle to fall with fore legs	4 Faults
Horse causes all or any part of the obstacle to fall with hind legs	2 Faults
Horse and Rider, or Horse or Riders falls	4 Faults

In the events of a Slat being knocked off with the fore feet and the obstacle being knocked down with the hind feet 2 faults to be counted.

Refusals: If in the opinion of the Judge the horse is presented at the fence and refuses to attempt to jump or runs out at the side, it shall count as a refusal, whether the fence is knocked down or not.

If the horse in attempting to refuse slides into the obstacle, pushing it down, and his hind legs cross the line of the jump, it shall count a jump and 4 faults be added.

NB If a horse turns round or be turned round after having been presented at the first fence in such a way that his hindquarters are to the fence, a penalty of 1 fault will be added. This rule does not apply to the water jump.

Water Jump: 1 fault shall be added if the horse strikes the take-off fence hard or knocks it down.

Each foot dropped in the water	1 Fault

If the horse jumps to the side of the water it shall count as many faults as would have been made had the water been wider.

Double Oxer: This fence to be counted as one as regards faults: ie 4 faults to be added if horse knocks down:

(a) ox rail on take-off side with fore legs	2 faults if with hind legs
(b) ox rail on landing side with fore legs	2 faults if with hind legs
(c) ox rail on both sides with fore legs	2 faults if with hind legs

In-and-Out: Should a horse jump into the double and refuse, he must continue to the second fence and not turn back and jump out over the first fence under penalty of 4 faults.

Should he jump out over either side he loses 4 faults and proceeds to the next fence. This fence to be judged as 2 fences as regards points and to count as 2 fences.

A marker will be found of great assistance to a Judge.

Tod Sloan's theory of a jockey riding very short enabling the weight of the rider to fall well forward thus helping a horse to go faster.

This lack of success in international show jumping by British riders inevitably led to a lack of support from the public, for the British public is notoriously fickle when it comes to sport. It likes to support its team when it is winning, but prefers to forget it when it is not doing well. So it was, that towards the end of the thirties, in the last year or two before the outbreak of the Second World War, many shows did not even bother to include a show jumping event in their programme. Even the great Royal Show itself had no show jumping event in 1939, the year that the Second World War broke out. It was felt that there was not sufficient support for show jumping to justify valuable time in the timetable being taken up with something which was of so little interest to the public.

This could well have been the end of show jumping were it not for a remarkable sequence of events that took place during the war.

As a result of Dunkirk, hundreds of thousands of soldiers, officers and men were taken prisoner of war and spent the rest of the war in camps in Germany. In one camp it became the custom, simply to relieve the monotony, for a member to give a talk on a Monday evening, the rest of the week being taken up with small groups discussing this original talk. On one occasion it was the turn of one officer who announced that he was going to give a talk on show jumping. It aroused little enthusiasm, but assisted by a fellow prisoner of war he made his talk so fascinating that a riding club was formed within the camp. Despite the fact that they lacked one rather essential commodity, a horse, they nevertheless were able to make do with a saddle made out of papier mâché, reins from string, and so on, the whole purpose of their club being to carry out research into horses jumping, something that had not previously been done. It had always been taken for granted that horses jumped – people had seen them jumping in the Grand National or out hunting, when in actual fact the horse is not a natural jumper, having a very heavy body and very delicate legs. Unable to jump vertically, like a cat, a horse can only jump a fence in the same sort of way that an aeroplane can take off at the end of a runway, depending entirely on the speed and the momentum of its run up. This and many other factors were taken into account when the prisoners of war, among whom were many young men who had been in hunt service, had ridden as jockeys, or worked in studs or riding schools, produced their final thesis. They now had a plan on which to work in designing courses which would encourage horses to jump bigger, more fluently and with less physical effort than had hitherto been the case.

When the war was over some of them got together to try to put their ideas into practice, but finding the offices of the British Show Jumping Association closed they sought out the Secretary who had retired to the West Country, and persuaded him to call a meeting. This was held in June 1945, and Colonel Ansell (now Sir Michael Ansell), the prisoner of war who had given the original talk in his prisoner of war camp in 1942, was elected Chairman. His election was of course of momentous importance.

The meeting that afternoon decided to organise a championship to be called the Victory Championship which, they hoped, would draw the attention of all those interested in equestrianism, particularly the Press, to this new style show jumping. They believed that if they could arouse the interest of the public then very quickly show jumping could be put on the map.

A course, designed and constructed at Aldershot, was finally brought up to London to be erected in the White City Stadium the afternoon before the event, which was held in 1945 on the first Saturday in September. There can be no doubt that this date is as important to the history of show jumping as 1066 is to the history of England; but initially there were considerable problems. When the riders first saw the course, consisting of some 17 or 18 fences with doubles and trebles, brightly coloured poles, no wings but narrow uprights with flags at the top, which were all so different from the figure-of-eight course of gorse hurdles and white poles that they had been used to before the war, many were reluctant to jump at all. In fact, the majority decided to withdraw their entries. Eventually, however, after much persuasion, having agreed to have a go in the competition on the next day, there was general surprise at the way their horses jumped. In fact, there were no less than 17 clear rounds from 23 starters, proving that the kind of course they were jumping obviously encouraged a horse to jump much better than ever before. The reason was that they were jumping a course of fences that had been almost scientifically designed along the lines of all the discussions and theories in the prisoner of war camp three years earlier. The end of the competition itself was something of a fairy tale. When, with no jump-off against the clock, the judges had decided that the fifth jump-off would be the last there were only two left in; one was the veteran rider of the day, then at the very height of his profession, namely Ted Williams, with a horse that had seldom been beaten called *Umbo*, while the other was Col. Nat Kindersley who had been Ansell's assistant in the original prisoner of war talk. Michael Ansell had come home to find that his wife had bought his old favourite army charger, *Maguire*, who had been such a good jumper before the war. She felt that her husband would be happier to think of his old friend pensioned off in their paddock at home, rather than sold to a complete stranger at the age of 16.

Maguire had always been a good jumper, having represented the army before the war; he now jumped as well as ever, but when it came to the final jump-off it was a clear round to win for *Umbo*, who had gone first, had had only half a fault, removing one of the slats. *Maguire* jumped as well as ever until he came to the last fence of all which was an upright white gate. Having been raised several times it now had no ground line which made it particularly difficult, and sure enough *Maguire* missed his stride and stopped. Just when it looked, however, as though he was going to have three faults for a refusal he somehow propelled himself into the air and climbed over the gate without dislodging it. Thus he became the winner of the Victory Show Jumping Championship, achieving something that had been only a dream within the grey walls of a prisoner of war camp in Germany, and turning it into a reality in the famous White City Stadium in London.

Michael Ansell had unfortunately been blinded at the time of his capture at St Valéry in 1940, but what he lacked in physical sight he more than made up for with his mental vision: if the Victory Championship had done nothing else it had convinced him that show jumping was a sport at which the British could excel and which could well be popular with the British

Col. Harry Llewellyn (GB) on *Foxhunter* (1952). Olympic gold medallist, 1952

public. Fortunately, Frank Gentle, the Chairman of the Greyhound Racing Association (GRA), owners of the White City, shared Michael Ansell's opinion and offered the White City as the venue for the Royal International Horse Show, should it be revived at the White City instead of at Olympia where it used to be held before the war. He further guaranteed that should there be any losses the GRA would underwrite them, but if there were any profits they would be equally shared. When, therefore, the International was revived in 1947 it was held at the White City.

The year after the revival of the International Horse Show the Olympic Games were held in Britain with the show jumping taking place on the last day immediately before the closing ceremony at the Wembley Stadium. Naturally, riders from many nations took part in the Olympic Games and agreed to stay on to take part in the International Horse Show at the White City. This enabled the public to see some of the most brilliant horsemen and the outstanding horses of the immediate post-war period. There can be little doubt that the greatest draw of all these was Lieut.-Col., now Sir Harry, Llewellyn's *Foxhunter*. This great and remarkable horse never disappointed his public, but probably no performance reflected more greatly to his credit nor, indeed, was to benefit show jumping as a sport in so handsome a manner, than his first winning of the King George V Gold Cup, against all the best riders and horses who had come to England for the Olympics in 1948. Indeed, *Foxhunter* thereafter almost became a cult, like a pop star, with people flocking many miles to see him when they knew that he was competing at a show.

No less popular was the young Pat Smythe who had so quickly reached the top from the most humble beginnings. Not only did she catch the imagination of the public, but she was an inspiration to countless thousands of young people who felt that if she could succeed, having learnt to ride on Barnes Common, and enjoyed no special privileges, then perhaps they might be able to emulate her. There can be little doubt that this was the start of a great wave of enthusiasm for riding that began in the late forties and carried right on through the fifties and sixties. Obviously there are many others who played their part in popularising show jumping; too many, perhaps to enumerate, though one feels it would be right to mention first Peter Robeson who so excited the public with his brilliant performances on his little mare (bred out of a cart mare), *Craven A*, who was reserve in the Olympic Team in 1952 and was still a member of the Olympic Team in 1976; also *Nizefela*, another great horse bred from a Shire mare. *Nizefela*, ridden by Wilf White, first endeared itself to the public

because of its sledgehammer kick-back. He was one of the first personality horses. Every sport needs its personalities and show jumping has been fortunate in having many great equine personalities through the 25 years of its revival.

By 1948 show jumping was well and truly on the road to success: there seemed to be little doubt that if all went well it would, within a few years, become an accepted popular national sport as Michael Ansell had envisaged.

This, in fact, turned out to be no pious hope, for in the fifties show jumping attained a popularity in Britain that it had never known in the 80 years of its existence. This was due to two factors. Firstly, the winning of the Olympic gold medal at Helsinki in 1952. Led by Lieut.-Col. Harry Llewellyn on his famous *Foxhunter* with Wilf White on *Nizefela* and Col. 'Duggie' Stewart on *Aherlow*, the British team won their medal at literally the fifty-ninth minute of the eleventh hour, the show jumping team event traditionally being the final event of the Olympic Games. Up to this moment no British athlete or competitor had won a medal of any sort at Helsinki. The show jumpers therefore came home to a heroes' welcome, to be fêted by the Press and the public in a way that show jumpers had never been fêted before: within months *Foxhunter* had become a legend.

Pat Smythe (GB) on *Prince Hal* (1963). First woman to ride in the Olympics, 1956

It was this hero worship, something entirely new in the world of show jumping, that was the second factor in the success of show jumping in the 1950s. Harry Llewellyn was not, of course, alone; there were other riders who almost equalled his popularity, either because of their horses or themselves. *Nizefela*, for instance, with his famous kick-back; *Craven A*, the little speed-merchant mare; *Nugget*, the short-tailed Welsh Cob; *Dundrum*, the Connemara pony that could clear 7 ft. Amongst the human personalities there was Donald and Curly Beard, from Yorkshire,

Seamus Hayes, from Ireland, and perhaps the most popular of all, the young Pat Smythe. With her horses, *Tosca* and *Prince Hal*, she had proved to the British public, for the first time, that if you had sufficient skill and dedication it was still possible to get to the top, even though you were not fortunate enough to have great, or at least considerable, wealth behind you. The consistency of Pat Smythe's success, the unassuming charm of her personality and the brilliance of her riding not only endeared her to hundreds of thousands of people who saw her at shows or watched her on television, but she encouraged countless hundreds of young people to take up riding in a hope of emulating her.

The success of our show jumpers in international competition, the popularity of the sport generally, meant that the public was directly, or indirectly, providing the funds to enable British teams to travel frequently abroad, all the time increasing their experience. In the late fifties and early sixties they seemed almost unbeatable as a team. At Stockholm in 1956 they won the bronze medal in the Olympic Games; in Rome in 1960 David Broome, for the first time, appeared on the scene as a leading international rider, winning the bronze medal on *Sunsalve*. Four years later in Tokyo, Peter Robeson won the bronze medal on *Firecrest*. In Mexico in 1968, the young Marion Mould, at her best, on her pony *Stroller* won a silver medal; an achievement emulated in Munich four years later by Ann Moore on *Psalm*. Meanwhile, our riders had been consistently winning the President's Cup, which is awarded for the team which wins most points in Nations Cups throughout the season. After the Munich Olympics, however, the luck of British riders seemed to decline; this was for two reasons. The first was the increasing strength of the opposition. For many years it had been dominated by Germany, Italy, and America and several great individual riders such as Nelson Pessoa who rode for Brazil and Hugo Simon who rode for Austria. During the seventies the standard of jumping in many other countries improved considerably, notably Holland, Belgium, France, Ireland (which for so long before the war had probably been the leading show jumping nation), Canada and Switzerland. Each of these nations could be relied upon to give a good account of themselves; the sport was no longer dominated by the big four.

But the second reason for the partial eclipse of Britain was the new developments in the professional–amateur situation. Prince Philip, as President of the International Federation, had felt for some time that show jumping was reaching a similar situation to that experienced a few years earlier in tennis: in other words, shamateurism. He felt that riders should come clean and admit when, in one way or another, they were earning money from show jumping. He believed

Wilf White (GB) with *Nizefela*: a veteran recalling their 1952 Olympic gold medal

that Britain should set an example and so, through the British Show Jumping Association, British riders were persuaded to admit to professionalism if they were in any way involved in accepting money for their show jumping activities. The result was that some 20 or more of Britain's leading riders immediately became professional which, of course, debarred them from jumping in the Olympic Games. It was hoped that other countries would follow suit but this did not happen, not necessarily because riders from other countries were less honest than British riders but rather because the Federations of other countries did not encourage their riders to admit to being professional; generally for a very good reason: for example, in Germany if a professional rider takes part in a show then that show is liable to substantial entertainment tax; riders, therefore, naturally enough are not encouraged to turn professional. The result of all this was that in the 1976 Olympic Games, in Montreal, the leading British riders were prevented from competing because of their professional status with the result that the team of amateurs found themselves jumping against the very best riders of the leading nations of the world, people who were probably as professional as Harvey Smith, David Broome and others, but not professional in the eyes of their own Federations. In fact, Britain still has outstanding riders who retain their amateur status, but understandably it is less likely that they will have at their disposal horses as good as the professionals. At Montreal they were only united with the good horses on which they competed a few weeks before taking part in the Olympic Games.

Above: Carol Hoffman (USA) on *Out Late*

Right: Anneli Drummond-Hay on *Harlequin*: winner of Ladies European Championship, 1968

Below: Tommy Wade (Ireland) on *Dundrum*: winner of King George V Cup, 1963

Below: Pierre d'Oriola (France), winner of Olympic gold medals in 1952 and 1964

Above: Piero d'Inzeo (Italy) on *The Rock*: Olympic silver medallist, 1960

Below: Gerd Wiltfang (Germany) on *Roman*: World Champion, 1978

Below: Marion Mould on *Stroller*: Olympic silver medallist, 1968

Nick Skelton breaking the British High Jump Record (7 ft 7$\frac{5}{16}$ in) (*above*) in 1978, after a rather disastrous first attempt (*below*)

Not surprisingly nations do not win medals in this way. As far as the future is concerned, however, the British Show Jumping Association and the British Equestrian Federation are well aware of the problems and every effort is now being made to find good horses for our leading amateur riders so that they will be able to hold their own against the best of the opposition in the Olympics. It is, of course, only the Olympic Games that are affected: yet it is the prestige of Olympic medals that still means more to a nation than any other international success. Unfortunately, by Olympic rules no one who has at any time been a professional, even if he has reverted to amateur status, can compete.

I have already mentioned the leading nations in show jumping – Germany, Italy and the USA. It might be as well to look at the history of each of these nations as far as their show jumping is concerned. After the war Germany was not in a position to take part in international jumping until the 1952 Helsinki Olympic Games. They then very quickly established themselves as one of the leading nations in the sport, if not the leading nation. This was due to two things. Firstly, the thoroughness of their training which was largely made possible by the amenities provided at Warendorf where they had their Olympic training centre, subsidised by the Government. Secondly, by the fact that in Germany horses were bred ideally suited to jumping big fences. These were in particular the Hanoverians with their great power behind the saddle, enabling the riders to take them steadily up to a fence, see a few strides away the stride they were seeking for the perfect take-off, and then to accelerate powerfully just those few strides away and still be able to jump a really big fence. The accuracy demanded by German show jumpers in many ways altered the style of jumping throughout the world. Hans Heinrich Brinckmann, their course builder and probably the best in the world, designed courses that were understandably suited to the German style of jumping: gradually, therefore, during the sixties and seventies there was a premium on accuracy; fences being built either high, straight and upright or very wide. The thoroughness of the Germans has paid good dividends and riders such as Hans Winkler, Alwin Schockemohle, the late Hartwig Steenken, Fritz Thiedemann, Hendrik Snoek and others have over the years frequently proved themselves almost unbeatable, and although their style depended so much on accuracy they nevertheless had such control, such power of acceleration that they were not necessarily at a disadvantage against the clock.

The Italians, by contrast, ride in a totally different style. Their riding has been very much influenced by the great riding master, Federico Caprilli, who invented the Forward Seat. The father of the famous d'Inzeo brothers learnt from Caprilli, and it is they,

Piero and Raimondo, who have dominated the Italian jumping scene for so long. Indeed, it is almost true to say that they have so dominated the Italian jumping scene that there has been little room for others, though it should be remembered of course that Graziano Mancinelli won the Individual gold medal at Munich and Dr Vittorio Orlandi is probably one of the most improved riders in world show jumping over the last decade.

Whereas the Germans are immensely disciplined in their riding the Italians are entirely fluent. They ride on the lightest contact, have much greater activity in the body, and to the general public are very exciting to watch. The brilliance of the d'Inzeos is accepted the world over. Graziano Mancinelli is exaggerated, but immensely effective. Vittorio Orlandi has in recent years attempted a much more classic style of riding. From the general public's point of view the contrast between the German and Italian style of riding is of great interest because it is possible for any layman to see the difference.

In contrast again, to both the Germans and the Italians, there are the Americans. Their style of riding is essentially classical; indeed, it is near perfection. This is very largely due to the training they have received over the years from the great Hungarian instructor, Bertalan de Nemethy. He achieves a pattern or a mould into which all his riders fit. It has sometimes been said that they are so perfect, so completely positioned by their trainer, that if anything goes wrong they are at a loss. Obviously one has seen examples of American riders being nonplussed in an awkward situation, but one has to remember that in Bill Steinkraus, the winner of the Mexico Individual gold medal, and in Frank Chapot they have two of the most consistent riders in the world. They are fortunate in that they are provided by generous patrons with beautiful high-class Thoroughbred horses, but unless these horses were perfectly trained and most ably ridden the horses could never have achieved the successes that they have. It is only sad that being separated from Europe by the Atlantic they are not more frequently in competition with the leading European nations.

It is worth mentioning here that while the Germans, Italians and Americans have such easily recognisable individual styles the same cannot be said for British riders and British teams. There can be no greater contrast, for instance, between the riding of Harvey Smith and David Broome. Harvey Smith is perhaps more influenced by the German style of riding, David Broome by the Italians. Harvey Smith is the more rigid in his style, while David Broome is the more fluent. Harvey Smith perhaps rides with a greater determination, while David Broome rides in a more cavalier fashion, seemingly completely relaxed.

Of the other major competing nations perhaps the

Hartwig Steenken clearing the 7 ft wall at Amsterdam

Johan Heins (Holland) on *Seven Valleys*: European Champion, 1977

Janou Lefebvre (France) on *Rocket*: Ladies World Champion, 1970

Yuri Solos (USSR) on *The Rok*

David Barker (GB) on *O'Malley* in 1960

Below: Harvey Smith on *Graffiti*: five times winner of the John Player Trophy

Above: Alan Oliver on *Sweep* in 1966. He has been an international rider since 1951

Below: Paddy McMahon on *Alcatraz*: Paddy was European Champion in 1973

most interesting is Ireland. Between the wars with riders such as Col. Dan Corry, Comdt Ahern and Col. Lewis, trained by the legendary Col. Paul Rodzianko who himself had ridden for Russia at the very first International Horse Show at Olympia in 1907, they seemed almost unbeatable, mounted as they were on superb Irish-bred Thoroughbred or three-quarter-bred horses. After the war, however, things were different. The Army which provided the team was composed of people who had had little riding experience before they joined up. They had therefore to be taught from scratch. Naturally this system produced few really outstanding riders, the chief exception perhaps being Michael Tubridy who was tragically killed in a riding accident, and Col. William Ringrose whose many successes included one of the most sought after Grand Prix, that of the Rome International Horse Show at the Piazza de Sienna in the Borghese gardens. For many years after the war the Irish selectors insisted on Ireland being represented by an all Army team. There were in fact many outstanding Irish civilian riders, notably Iris Kellet, twice winner of the Queen Elizabeth II Cup, Seamus Hayes, winner of most of the major international events the world over and Tommy Wade whose magnificent little Connemara pony, *Dundrum*, became the darling of the national audiences in the fifties and early sixties. Occasionally a mixed team of Army and civilian riders represented Ireland: finally the Irish selectors of the Irish Federation, ultimately responsible, agreed on Ireland, or Eire, as they preferred to be called, being represented by an all civilian team. During the last few years the Irish have come close to repeating their successes of pre-war days with riders of exceptional ability such as Eddie Macken, who is without any doubt one of the three or four best show jumping riders in the world, and young Paul Darragh, who for a time succeeded Eddie as the rider of *Pele* when Eddie attached himself to the Schockemohle stable in Germany. He has since proved that he can succeed on horses less outstanding than *Pele*, who is now known as *Kerrygold.*

It is interesting that during the sojourn of Eddie Macken in Germany it was not only Eddie who benefited, for many knowledgeable observers were of the opinion that Alwin Schockemohle himself became more fluent in his style as a result of working with Eddie Macken.

Holland and Belgium are perhaps the most improved show jumping nations in the world during recent years. Before the war the Belgians were of a very high standard in international jumping, but since

Capt. Mark Phillips on *Hideaway*: a successful recruit to international jumping

M. Kloess (Germany) – unconventional descent

Ann Moore on *Psalm*: Olympic silver medallist, 1972

the war it has taken them some 20 years to climb back to the top. Their success in the Olympic Games in Montreal in 1976, when they won an Olympic bronze medal, was a reward for the painstaking recovery that they had made over recent years. Holland, too, has climbed back to a position of some importance, winning both the Individual and Team gold medals in the European Championships in 1977, though the Dutch have, in fact, been consistent for a very long time without being particularly outstanding. There is little doubt that they owe this in part to the influence of Germany, and particularly, to their use of German-bred horses. Belgium, perhaps, has been more influenced by France than Germany.

France, in fact, is one of the most interesting show jumping nations. They have an Olympic record second only to Germany, yet between the Olympics, except as individuals – Janou Lefebvre, winning the Ladies World and European Championships, is a case in point – they have not shown consistent form. This is probably in part due to the fact that they compete less frequently than the other major show jumping nations, seldom going overseas. It may also be in part due to the fact that the French Equestrian Federation is answerable to no less than five different Government departments, not all of which are in complete agreement as to the right policy for French equestrianism. There is no doubt that they owe much to the brilliance of Pierre d'Oriola, who won the Olympic Individual gold medal right back in 1952 at Helsinki, repeating this achievement in Tokyo in 1964. His style and his influence have been considerable, but although there is a consistency in the style of French riding, classic yet at the same time active, there is also a considerable individuality amongst their riders. With the exception of perhaps Hubert Parot, they tend to ride lightweight Franco–Arab type horses which are brilliant and extremely manoeuvrable, but possibly lack the scope and substance to jump really big fences which tends to result in their using a rather different type of horse for the Olympics than they use for ordinary international jumping between the Olympics. This is probably a carefully planned policy: certainly it has paid off.

Graham Fletcher at the Devil's Dyke at Hickstead

Eddie Macken on *Kerrygold* at Hickstead

Anne Backhouse in trouble with *Cardinal II*: winner of Ladies European Championship, 1959

Although Hugo Simon from Austria and Nelson Pessoa from Brazil have brought their countries very much to the fore in international show jumping, one really cannot pretend that the countries as such are significant in the show jumping world. This is because both Simon and Pessoa could be described as expatriates. Hugo Simon having a passport both for Germany and Austria elected to represent Austria when he realised that because of the strength of the German team there was little chance of him jumping for Germany in the Munich Olympics. Nelson Pessoa, Brazilian born, has for many years been domiciled in Europe, jumping horses that have been bred in Europe and usually owned either by himself or other Europeans. It is only by birth that he is Brazilian.

One should perhaps mention in addition Canada, as this country sprung a complete surprise in winning the Olympic Games in Mexico in 1968. They have splendid big thoroughbred-type horses, bred on the American lines, and a small number of dedicated riders who are determined to hold their own with the best riders from the United States and from Europe. It is, perhaps, lack of international experience that debars them from doing consistently better.

The Argentinians, who always looked as though they were going to be a leading show jumping nation, have good riders and big scopy horses, but they have never performed regularly as well as one might have expected. Obviously there is Spanish influence, but again the Spaniards themselves, like the Portuguese, have had many good riders and good horses but appear to have lacked a consistent policy and so, apart from isolated incidents such as when Don Carlos Figueroa won the King George V Gold Cup for Spain in 1952, their successes have not justified their being considered as a leading show jumping nation.

Unfortunately, the appearances of show jumping teams from behind the Iron Curtain have not been sufficiently regular either to make it possible to judge them or for them to get necessary international experience to be able to hold their own in top-class jumping. There is little doubt that the USSR, East

Above: Ferdi Tyteca (Belgium), puissance expert, on *Exact* (Look, no hands!)

Below: Hans Winkler (Germany) – unconventional descent

Above: David Broome on *Philco* at the Horse of the Year Show in October 1978

Left: Harvey Smith on *Sanyo San Mar* at the Royal International Horse Show in July 1978 at Wembley

Right: Con Power in difficulty at the Hickstead Derby Bank

Germany and Poland all have potential, but it is unfortunately seldom fully realised. It may be that with the Olympic Games in 1980 taking place in Moscow, the Eastern bloc countries will make more of an effort to get the sort of international experience necessary for them to achieve success against the more experienced countries from Europe and the USA.

It remains only to mention those countries that because of distance or quarantine regulations make it impossible for them regularly to compete against the best teams in Europe, namely Australia, New Zealand and South Africa. Australian riders have always done well when they come to Europe, but the cost of appearing in Europe regularly is prohibitive. The same goes for New Zealand. It could well be, however, that horses bred in the Antipodes, if given the opportunity, could hold their own with the best in Europe. As far as South Africa is concerned there is no doubt that their riders are equal to any in the world; indeed, when they have visited Europe and ridden other people's horses they have invariably given a good account of themselves. Because of the possibly

Alwin Schockemohle (Germany) on *Warwick Rex*: Olympic gold medallist 1976

exaggerated risk of African Horse Sickness they cannot, unfortunately, regularly appear in Europe, thus denying Europeans the opportunity of jumping against a team that would, I am convinced, prove a very strong opposition.

Over the last two or three decades show jumping has become a major international sport. There is, moreover, considerable money now involved in it. The top-class horses are worth anything up to and, indeed, exceeding £50 000, a value which is very largely based on prestige for it is most unlikely that any horse could win this amount in prize money, while from a stud point of view, unless a horse is a mare, there is no chance of recovering the money in that respect. Many governments give financial assistance both in thc purchasing of the best horses for their riders and for the administration of their Federation. It is, perhaps, to be hoped that one day Britain will get the same sort of Governmental support. There can be no doubt that nations denied this support are going to find it difficult to maintain a standard as high as that of their rivals who are in a position not only to pro-

John Whitaker on *Ryan's Son*: 1980 Olympic hope

Geoff Glazzard on *Penwood Forge Mill*: *Forge Mill* was European Champion in 1973, ridden by Paddy McMahon

vide the proper training facilities, which includes travelling overseas to compete in international shows, but also can purchase the horses which will otherwise be those they are likely to be competing against. Ideally, perhaps, there should be some ruling insisting that in team events riders can only be mounted on horses bred in their own country, but with the precedent of other sports it is unlikely that this will ever come about.

Show jumping today is a clean, straightforward sport as indeed it has been ever since it's revival after the war. It gives a great deal of pleasure both to those who take part and to those who watch. It would be sad if it was at this stage allowed to be spoilt by over-commercialism.

The acrobatic Jeff McVean from Australia in the Radio Rentals Championship at the Horse of the Year Show in October 1978

Roland Fernyhough on *Automatic* at Hickstead

Alison Dawes on *The Maverick*: Olympic Reserve, 1968; winner of Queen Elizabeth II Cup, 1969 and 1973

5 Horse Trials

There can be no doubt that the three-day event is the most demanding and in many ways most spectacular of all equestrian sports. It could be argued, however, that it has never wholly become a popular spectator sport because of the confusion that arises from the various names that it has been given. It is generally referred to as a three-day event although it was originally known on the continent as Le Militaire. Later it became known as a *concours complet* (the complete test for horse and rider) and it is also referred to as combined training since there are three disciplines involved. Today, it is frequently referred to as horse trials. This is not only confusing to the public, but it suggests a sport that is complicated in itself. In fact this is not so, the basis of the whole event being simply a test of stamina. It is the cross-country phase (the second phase) which is the most important in the event. The dressage on the first day is only included to show that a horse has had proper basic training. The show jumping on the third day is included to show that a horse, despite the rigours of the cross-country phase on the preceding day, is still fit, active and supple enough to jump a small but twisty course of show jumping fences. Thus the competition is entirely comprehensive: training, stamina, accuracy.

It is alleged that this event was originally part of cavalry training, hence the name Le Militaire, and it is likely that cavalry regiments in many countries did in fact employ some sort of rigorous training that enabled the horse to have sufficient stamina to survive a severe campaign carried out over difficult terrain. Dressage was certainly added considerably later, the probability being that when it became a sport rather than a training exercise it was generally agreed that it was necessary because it could introduce an element of skill and correct equitation. The three-day event is obviously extremely demanding; it is possibly one of the weaknesses in the sport that at top-class functions, such as the world championships and the Olympic Games, there are too many horses which are not really sufficiently fit or experienced to be taking part in such events, coming as they do from countries where there is only a limited amount of eventing. An effort has been made to overcome this problem by introducing one-day events and even two-day events. In the one-day event it is usual for the show jumping to be inserted after the dressage phase and before the cross-country. This obviously is practical but it tends to ignore the purpose of the show jumping being included to show that a horse is fit and supple after the cross-country. In the two-day event it is possible to finish with the show jumping, but frequently the road and track phases are eliminated altogether, or else they are drastically reduced.

The present pattern in the cross-country phase of a three-day event is to start with a comparatively short roads and tracks phase carried out at a pace which is roughly a hand canter. This is followed by a two-mile steeplechase course which has to be covered at a proper gallop. There is then a longer phase of roads and tracks, perhaps six or seven miles, to be carried out at an average speed which is slightly slower than the first roads and tracks phase. Finally there is the cross-country course which is anything between three and four and a half miles with 30 or more different and difficult fences. Until a few years ago this was followed by a fifth phase, a sharp gallop on the flat to the finish, but this has been discontinued.

Jack Le Goff, the French rider, who coached the winner of the gold medal in Mexico in 1968 and who became the chief instructor in three-day event riding and training at Gladstone, the National Equestrian Centre in America, has recently advocated that the roads and tracks should be dropped altogether from the three-day event because he feels that the event should be a test of ability rather than stamina. He is of the opinion that horses are often too tired, thanks to two roads and tracks phases and the steeplechase course, when they arrive at the start of the most important and certainly the most difficult phase of all, the cross-country course. This has received considerable support – from, amongst others, Lucinda Prior-Palmer and Chris Collins. On the other hand there are those who believe that this particular sport should be kept as different as possible from those equestrian sports where speed is the main concern. The long phases of roads and tracks do put a premium on the judgment of the rider, at the same time preventing the whole event becoming a race.

The three-day event was first introduced into the Olympic Games at Stockholm in 1912 when 27 riders took part, representing seven nations. The gold medal was won by Sweden: the British team was eliminated, none of their four riders completing the course. The following Olympics were held at Antwerp in 1920 but the three-day event was entirely different from that of any other Olympic Games. The dressage test was eliminated altogether, there being two long-distance rides, the first of 50 km which included 18 obstacles, the other rather shorter. There was finally a jumping

Lorna Sutherland and *Popadom* about to come to grief during the World Championships at Punchestown

test. A time limit was imposed of $3\frac{1}{2}$ hr. The first test was won by a Norwegian rider who took 3 hr 5 min, the second test being won by a Belgian. Once again Sweden was the overall winner of the Team event with an entirely different team to that which won four years earlier, thus reminding us of the predominance of Swedish riders in the early part of this century. Swedish riders were in fact first and second in the overall Individual; Sweden also won the show jumping event that year. In 1924 when the Olympic Games were held in Paris, Holland which was to be a dominant equestrian nation in the 1920s and 1930s, superseded Sweden as the winners of the gold medal. An individual Dutch rider also won the Individual gold medal. Britain did not compete at all in 1920, but in 1924 Capt. de Fonblanque was sixth, the highest placing for a British rider in a three-day event so far. Another member of the British team that year was Maj. P. E. 'Bogey' Bowden-Smith who was to play such a part in the organisation of the three-day event when it was first introduced in Britain. Holland repeated their success in the Olympic Games in Amsterdam in 1928, winning both the Team and the Individual gold medals; in the Individual they also won the silver medal. Britain was not amongst the 17 nations that competed, and only three finished from the 17 teams that entered. There is little doubt that the tendency at the Olympic Games to build three-day event courses of too severe a character has provided ammunition for those who have criticised this particular sport as being too demanding on the horse, in the same way as many people criticise the Grand National for being too hazardous a steeplechase. To build a course that results in only a few of the competitors getting round must be detrimental to any sport.

Again in Los Angeles in 1932 only two teams out of the five finished. A Dutch rider again won the Individual gold medal and with the United States winning the team medal it was once again a case of the home nation succeeding. Britain did not compete in Los Angeles, but in Berlin in 1936 Britain was one of no less than 19 nations comprising some 50 riders that took part in what was probably the most severe Olympic three-day event ever. It was won by Germany with a German rider winning the Individual. Britain in fact won the bronze medal, being the third of only three teams that completed the course. Their team included Capt. Richard Fanshawe who finished last with a record score of 8754·2 penalty points, having lost his horse after a fall on the cross-country. Capt. Alec Scott, now one of the senior stewards at the Badminton Horse Trials, did best for Britain, finishing seventh.

After the Second World War when the Olympic Games were held in London, Britain had still not mounted a three-day event itself and therefore seriously lacked experience. Maj. Peter Borwick did best for Britain finishing 17th, Brig. Bolton was 27th, while unfortunately Maj. 'Duggie' Stewart's mount went lame which resulted in the team being eliminated. In the following Olympics, however, Col. Stewart, as he then was, found compensation in winning a gold medal in the show jumping team event at Helsinki, riding *Aherlow*. The Team gold medal in the 1948 three-day event was won by the United States.

In the opinion of many, Britain was unfortunate in 1952 at Helsinki in being denied the start of the run of successes that they were to experience right through the 1960s and into the 1970s. Sweden would almost certainly have won anyway at Helsinki, but it is likely that Britain would have won the silver medal had it not been for the misfortune that befell Maj. Lawrence Rook whose horse, *Starlight*, put his foot in a ditch and turned over, concussing Maj. Rook. Still in a

Jane Holderness-Roddam on *Warrior* at the Water Jump at the Badminton Horse Trials in 1978

54

Sheila Willcox on *High and Mighty*: Badminton winner 1957, 1958 and 1959

Col. Frank Weldon on *Kilbarry*: Olympic Team gold medal, 1956

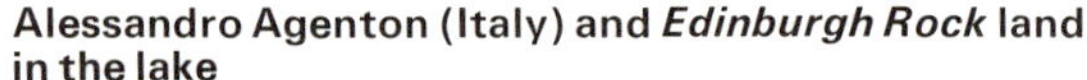

Alessandro Agenton (Italy) and *Edinburgh Rock* land in the lake

concussed condition they went the wrong side of a marker and thus the British team were eliminated. Bertie Hill, who was later to win a gold medal himself, was the leading British rider finishing seventh on *Stella*, while the team captain, Reg Hindley, finished 13th on *Speculation*. In 1956 at Stockholm, Britain really came into her own with a decisive victory for the team which consisted of Lieut.-Col. Frank Weldon on *Kilbarry*, Maj. Lawrence Rook on *Wild Venture* and Bertie Hill on the Queen's *Countryman III*. Col. Weldon also won the Individual bronze medal. Unfortunate falls in Rome in 1960 for Col. Weldon and Bertie Hill on another most testing course, with the most difficult fences coming at the end, denied Britain a medal and relegated them to fourth place. In Tokyo in 1964 at the end of the cross-country Britain was in a strong position with three members all in contention for the Individual, but, as had happened on previous occasions, show jumping let Britain down and no medal was won. In 1968, however, Britain won the first leg of a double of gold medals when, despite appalling weather conditions in the closing stages, the brilliant team consisting of Maj. Derek Allhusen, Richard Meade, Sgt Ben Jones and Jane Bullen (now Holderness-Roddam, winner of the 1978 Badminton) won convincingly with Maj. Allhusen also winning an Individual silver medal. The following year at Munich, led by Richard Meade, Britain won not only the Team gold medal, but Richard Meade himself won the Individual gold medal. Mary Gordon-Watson, also riding for Britain, riding on *Cornishman V* finishing fourth. Great hopes were held for our performance in Montreal in 1976 with Her Royal Highness Princess Anne in the British team, but tragically two of our best horses, Lucinda Prior-Palmer's *Be Fair* and Hugh Thomas's *Playamar*, went lame. The accident to *Be Fair* was particularly unfortunate in that Lucinda Prior-Palmer had twice won the European Championship on this brilliant horse. Princess Anne, when going

Richard Meade on *Bleak Hill*: Olympic gold medallist, Team 1968, Individual 1972

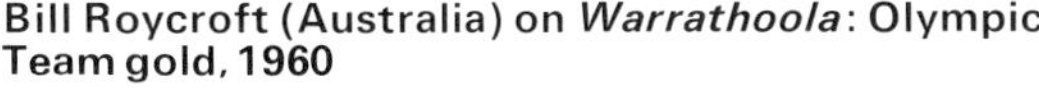

Bill Roycroft (Australia) on *Warrathoola*: Olympic Team gold, 1960

Michael Plumb on *Free 'n' Easy*: Olympic silver medal, 1976

extremely well on *Goodwill*, had an unfortunate fall which delayed her some six minutes, thus giving her too many time penalties to get into the final reckoning.

To sum up, the success of British riders in the three-day event is shown by the fact that they have won no fewer than eight Individual and eight Team European or World Championships, three Team Olympic gold medals, a record that no other nation can begin to match. That this remarkable record should have been possible is very largely due to the foresight of the Duke of Beaufort who recognised, after watching the three-day event at Aldershot in the 1948 Olympics, that although the British team was eliminated because Col. Stewart's horse went lame, this surely was a sport at which the British with their unique cross-country riding experience (the result of the 300-year-old tradition of foxhunting) could succeed. He therefore decided to make his home at Badminton Park available for the first three-day event to be held in Britain. This took place in 1949 with Col. Trevor Horn whose only previous experience of a three-day event was as a dressage official at the Olympic Games the preceding year, as Director of the Horse Trials, as they were then

Top: Jane Starkey on *Topper TOO*: World Championship Team, 1978

Centre: Lucinda Prior-Palmer on *George*: European Champion, 1975, 1977

Bottom: Anneli Drummond-Hay on *Merely-a-Monarch*: winner of Burghley 1961, Badminton 1962

Jane Bullen (Holderness-Roddam) on *Our Nobby*: Olympic Team gold medal, 1968. Winner at Badminton 1968, 1978

Lorna Clarke on *Greco*

HRH Princess Anne on *Doublet*: European Champion, 1971

Capt. Mark Phillips on *Chicago*: Olympic Team gold, 1972; winner at Badminton, 1971, 1972, and 1974

described. The event was an immediate success being won by John Shedden on *Golden Willow*, attracting a considerable crowd who thoroughly enjoyed themselves wandering around the beautiful park at Badminton watching the horses competing. The event was repeated the following year when Capt. Tony Collings, who had been second the first year, won on *Remus*. With the first foreign success in 1951 when Capt. Schwarzenbach on *Vae Victis* from Switzerland won, the event became firmly established, gaining particular popularity through the support that it received from the Queen and members of the Royal

Mary Gordon-Watson on *Cornishman V*: World Champion, 1970

Stefano Angioni (Italy) suffers total immersion

Family who enjoyed staying for the event with the Duke and Duchess of Beaufort at Badminton. For the year 1955 only, at the Queen's request, the event was held at Windsor being won by Col. Frank Weldon on *Kilbarry* who won again the following year when the event returned to Badminton. He was followed by Sheila Willcox's remarkable hat trick on *High and Mighty* (1957 and 1958) and *Airs and Graces* (1959). Only Capt. Mark Phillips has repeated the hat trick with *Great Ovation* (1971 and 1972) and *Columbus* (1974) which belonged to the Queen. The three-day event at Badminton now attracts a crowd variously

Lorna Sutherland (Clarke) on *Popadom*: winner Burghley 1967, 1978

17
B

17
B

Jane Winter in trouble on *Stainless Steel* at Goodwood in 1975

estimated at anything between 50 000 and 100 000. In 1955 a second three-day event was introduced at Harewood, near Harrogate, at the invitation of the Princess Royal. This was a great success until after the decimation of her herds of cattle through foot-and-mouth disease, the major part of Harewood became arable and therefore unsuited to a three-day event. However, the Marquis of Exeter came to the rescue of the British Horse Society, which was of course responsible for these three-day events, and offered his beautiful home, Burghley, near Stamford, with the surrounding parkland as a venue for the new three-day event. The first event was held at Burghley in 1961 when Anneli Drummond-Hay riding *Merely-a-Monarch* won, one of the comparatively few riders to have won both Badminton (1962) and Burghley. She was also one of the few riders to reach the top in both eventing and show jumping: initially on the same horse, *Merely-a-Monarch*.

With two such suitable and attractive sites for major three-day events it is not surprising that British riders were able to avail themselves of unique experience which resulted in their remarkable record quoted above. But more than this, the existence of so many one-day events for novice horses and for those at an intermediate stage ensured that there was a plentiful supply of good horses who were able, in due course, to tackle a three-day event course. With a membership in the combined training group of the British Horse Society of over 3000 there is no doubt that this new sport has become one of the most popular equestrian sports in the country. Each year many new recruits come up from the Pony Club which has its own event championship and at which young riders have proved themselves to be highly capable on more than one occasion winning the European Three-Day Event Championships for juniors.

Inevitably there has always been a certain amount of controversy about the marking and scoring in a three-day event, especially perhaps in the dressage section when at times the marks of the three judges for any one competitor are considerably at variance. This does not matter very much as long as each judge is consistent in his marking, but it would seem unfortunate that a competitor might win at the end of three days and more than 20 miles of great exertion by one small point or even part of a point in the dressage marking, when obviously that point is entirely a matter of opinion of one judge; in other words there is no exact marking of dressage.

In the cross-country it is different because although the penalties are extremely severe they are acceptable. A fall, for instance, costs 60 penalties and a refusal 20 penalties. There is, moreover, an important premium on time, the custom now being to set a very fast time allowance, penalties being added for each second over that time. There are those who think that this encourages horses to be pushed too hard and too fast to ensure that they get as near as possible to the time allowed, with the result that at the end of the course they tire and perhaps fall. Show jumping penalties are also straightforward with five penalties for a knock down, 10 for a refusal and 30 for a fall.

The popularity and successes of the three-day event in other nations is fairly widespread. As far as the World Championship is concerned when first held in 1966, Ireland won defeating Argentina which supplied the Individual Champion in Capt. Carlos Moratorio. In 1970 Great Britain won the Team and the Individual Championship, the latter bringing the first major success to Mary Gordon-Watson and *Cornishman V*. On this occasion only two teams finished. In 1974 the United States were the victors and in 1978, held at Kentucky, the winners were Canada with Bruce Davidson on *Night Tango* winning the Individual.

In the European Championships, which were first held in 1953, Great Britain won on the first four occasions, after which Germany won in 1959, the USSR in 1962 and 1965, Great Britain again in 1967, 1969 and 1971, with Germany winning at Kiev in 1973, and the USSR winning at Lumuhlen in 1975: 1977 saw another victory for Britain. There have also been Individual winners from Poland (M. Babirecki), Ireland (Maj. Eddie Boylan) and the USSR (A. Evdokimov), from which it will be seen that despite the obvious advantage for British riders, which has already been explained, Britain nowadays by no means has it all its own way, with successful riders coming both from those countries where there is hunting, such as in America, and a tradition of cross-country riding such as in Italy and the USSR where it has been a part of cavalry training, and even those countries such as Switzerland, France, and certain countries in eastern Europe where riding is largely limited to dressage and show jumping. Mention should also be made of Australia, a country which, considering the comparatively small number of people riding – certainly riding in competitive three-day events – has had a remarkable record, largely due to the great veteran Bill Roycroft who on more than one occasion has produced a team consisting entirely of his own family, and who holds the extraordinary record of riding three horses in the Badminton event which meant that on the cross-country day he covered some 60 miles: an achievement only equalled by Lorna Sutherland (Clarke).

There is little doubt that eventing is popular now both with riders and spectators; but there can be little doubt that if the test became too demanding, let alone too dangerous, with fatal accidents, then very quickly there would be a reaction against it. It would seem essential that course designers should design and build courses that are testing but absolutely fair, and never dangerous. It is surely possible to get the right result without constructing a course that can only be jumped by the very best and most experienced horses. It is probably correct to say that the ideal course for an international event can expect to eliminate one-third of the competitors, for the most part due to refusals rather than accidents; but not more. As the standard improves there must be a temptation to make the course more demanding; it is a temptation that most certainly should be resisted if this comparatively new sport of three-day eventing is to continue to be both successful and popular. It is surprising to recall that proper rules for the three-day event were only finalised in 1957, little more than 20 years ago. It should always be possible, therefore, to approach the administration of this sport with an open mind to ensure that it provides the maximum of enjoyment for the largest number of people with the minimum of danger.

6
Dressage

Unfortunately, for a long time in Britain at any rate, there has been a certain suspicion of the very word dressage. For many people it has a mystique about it, suggesting that it is not for ordinary horsemen and horsewomen such as themselves. Yet dressage is but the training of the horse, intended to improve his natural balance and movement, something that can be carried out perfectly well by any moderately competent rider. Unfortunately, many people still regard dressage as the performing of difficult high school movements; they fail to realise that in fact every rider can benefit from straightforward dressage and need have no aspirations to the more advanced movements which are involved in advanced competition. The nearest analogy is perhaps to that of dancing where a dancer can be trained to perform ordinary stage dancing very adequately, but to be able to perform ballet needs much more advanced training.

More than 300 years ago one of the most distinguished *haute école* riders, the Duke of Newcastle, attempted to introduce high school riding into England, but it never became popular for whereas the continent had become obsessed with equitation and the possibilities that it presented in the training of a horse, Britain was becoming increasingly interested in the joys of foxhunting. So it was that the continent had what amounted to a 300 year start on Britain in the field of advanced equitation. The extent of this development is illustrated by the great classical schools that existed in the courts of Europe, but few of which exist to this day, the Spanish Riding School of Vienna being the great exception; though others such as Saumur, near Paris, had a tremendous influence in their own countries for many centuries. Italy was in fact probably the leading country in equitation and advanced high school riding for most of the 18th century. The pioneer in Italy was Federico Grisone who had made a careful study of Xenophon's famous treatise on equitation and had, in fact produced a book of his own. His most outstanding pupil was Pignateli who became an écuyer – chief instructor – at the famous riding academy at Naples. The youthful Antoine de Pluvinel, who came from France to study under Pignateli, became court riding master to Louis XIII of France. His own book *Manège de Roi* was broadly based on his own Master's methods, thus the original teachings of Xenophon were carried right down to the 18th century, some 2000 years after Xenophon's death. The methods of equitation, having been accepted, were developed during the latter part of the 17th century by the great François de la Guérinière. The French Revolution was eventually responsible for much of the classical tradition being lost in France, and indeed in much of Europe, but thanks to Max Ritter von Weyrother, head of the school at Vienna, the traditions of the past were maintained while the influence of Vienna spread wide and far, as indeed it does today. Even the great French riding master, François Baucher, could do little to improve on the standards of Vienna, let alone develop them. While eventually in England a rider and instructor appeared who was to gain an international reputation. This was James Fillis who went to Petrograd to become riding master to the Czars.

At the end of the 19th century France regained something of its old glory through the Cadre Noir, a

Mrs Brenda Williams on *Pilgrim*: first British rider to compete in Olympics

unit of the French Cavalry that, riding black or dark brown horses, went some way to rival the famous white Lippizaners in Vienna. Vienna, however, remained supreme through the authority of their great commandant Col. Alois Podhajsky, through whose friendship with my father, Col. V. D. S. Williams, dressage was once again introduced into Britain in the late 1930s. There was, however, not only a great leeway to make up, but also considerable resistance to overcome, for England was still a foxhunting country. Fortunately, however, sufficient people whose reputation in the world of the horse was considerable came to believe that there was a true purpose in dressage, that it was not just something strange and foreign but

Mrs Lorna Johnstone on *El Farruco*: Olympic Team 1956 and 1968

Harry Boldt (Germany) on *Woychek*: Olympic silver medal, 1972, 1976

in fact no more than basic training which was the nearest accurate translation of the word dressage. Indeed, people came to realise that in the cavalry training at the Army Cavalry Schools, particularly at Weedon, the Cavalry Equitation School, the training that had been carried out was basically simple dressage training.

It was not, however, until 1956 that Britain was represented at dressage in the Olympic Games at Stockholm. My stepmother, Mrs V. D. S. Williams, was the first British competitor actually to ride in the Olympic Dressage. Accompanying her was Lorna Johnstone, who was to ride again in the Olympics, at the age of 70, when they were held at Munich in 1972. Furthermore, she was included in the final 12 who are called upon to do a second test. This, indeed, was a remarkable achievement, giving those in Britain who were genuinely interested in dressage great hopes, though it has to be admitted that their hopes were somewhat dashed by their poor showing in the Montreal Olympics in 1976. It has been suggested that this was largely due to the fact that they sought instruction from too many different sources while Mrs Johnstone had depended largely on her own skill and Mrs Williams had been taught solely by her husband who had learnt from Col. Alois Podhajsky.

It is, of course, an undeniable fact that there are different methods in the training of a horse at all levels. This results in there also being different fashions. A look at the results in dressage in the Olympic Games bears this out. In 1912 Sweden swept the board, winning the gold, silver and bronze medals in the Individual event as well as the Team event. In 1920 it was still Sweden that dominated, again winning all three medals in the Individual and the Team event as well. In Paris in 1924 it was Sweden again, but a French rider who was to become very well thought of, François Lesage, won the bronze medal in the Individual and the silver medal in the Team. In 1928 Germany replaced Sweden, but it is generally thought that their methods were largely identical. In the Individual a German won the gold, a French rider the silver and a Swede the bronze. France won the gold medal in Los Angeles in 1932, but only four nations competed. They also won the gold and silver Individuals, while Sweden had to be content with the Team silver medal. For the first time the United States entered a team winning the bronze medal; Mexico was the only nation that did not win a Team medal, but there was only one Mexican rider which would suggest that the USA won something of a hollow victory. In the famous, or infamous, Berlin Games in 1936, Germany won the Team gold and the Individual gold and silver medals, while France and Sweden won silver and bronze respectively in the Team event. There is no doubt that prior to the war Germany was the greatest influence in dressage at this level. In the first Games after the war in 1948, it was France that won the Team event with the United States runners-up; but for the first time a Swiss rider came into the reckoning and we had Capt. Hans Moser, winning the Individual from the famous Col. André Jousseaume. At Helsinki in 1952 Switzerland kept up the pressure, running Sweden very close for the team event, but Sweden also won the Individual with their famous rider Maj. Henri St Cyr, and for the first time we not only had a success for Denmark with a silver medal in the Individual, but we also had the first appearance of the remarkable lady rider Lis Hartel who overcame the enormous disability of polio to become one of the great dressage riders of all time. In Stockholm in 1956 Lis Hartel was again second to Henri St Cyr and a second lady rider Liselott Linsenhoff won the bronze medal for Germany in the Individual, while Sweden beat Germany and Switzerland in the team event.

Since then it is Germany and Switzerland and the USSR that have dominated the Olympics, but it is noticeable in recent times that the fluent Soviet style of riding Grand Prix Dressage, very similar to that of the French, has gone out of favour while the more correct, exact and accurate style of the Germans and the Swedes has become acceptable to international judges. In Montreal, for instance, the Swiss horse *Granat* ridden by Christine Stückelberger was immensely impressive, but in the eyes of some spectators heavy, almost ponderous; but his accuracy, due to his enormous strength and exact training, gave him higher marks for almost every movement than the freer horses of other nations such as the French, the Soviets and the Americans who due to enormous determination and dedication have managed in the last few years to reach a standard that is not far behind the great dressage nations of the world. In Mexico in 1968, the

Jennie Loriston-Clarke on *Dutch Courage*: World Championship bronze medal, 1978

Soviets with their great fluency very nearly persuaded the judges that they were as good as, if not better, than the West Germans who finally won the team gold medal with a score of 2699, the Soviets winning the silver with 2657. But few will forget the Soviet stallion *Pepel*, ridden by Elena Petuchkova, for the delightful free forward movement and lovely paces, and probably only beaten by her *piaffe* (marking time movement) which was noticeably inferior to that of the leading German riders. In the Individual, however, the USSR did manage to hold off the German supremacy with Ivan Kisimov on *Ijor* winning the gold medal. It is of interest that but for the rather indeterminate methods of scoring in the Olympic Games the Soviets might well have beaten the Germans in the team event had their scores in the ride-off, surely the most important part of the competition, been included. It was, however, for the time being the last challenge to the might of the Germanic-style riders, who without any doubt dominate the dressage scene at the moment.

Inevitably dressage is going to be controversial because it can in no way be described as an exact science. In other words it is largely a matter of opinion as to just how well any one horse goes; just how accurately any one competitor performs. It is in fact like skating

Christine Stuckelberger (Switzerland) on *Granat*: Olympic gold medallist, 1976; World Champion, 1978

when each judge is asked to make his or her own assessment; but it cannot be denied that whereas in skating, or indeed in diving, there is little difference between the marks of the various judges there are often, as has been suggested in the chapter on combined training, very considerable discrepancies between the marks of different dressage judges. Perhaps because of this lack of exact marking there will always be a certain amount of doubt as to the importance of dressage. But what really matters is not dressage from the competitor's point of view but dressage as a preparation for any form of equestrianism, whether it be showing, show jumping, combined training, or even hunting, racing or polo: though I fear that it is likely to be some time yet before this fact is universally accepted. This is a pity because there can be no doubt whatever that a well trained horse has the advantage over a horse that is untrained, simply because the untrained horse is not properly balanced. An excellent example of this was the Australian rider, Lawrence Morgan, who won the gold medal in the Rome three-day event and also won the Foxhunter's Chase at Aintree. This was almost entirely due to gaining some ten lengths at the Canal Turn because of the balance and control of his horse, *College Master*.

There can be little doubt that the great successes recently of the German show jumping team owes a great deal to the fact that they spend more time than most other countries in work on the ground; that is to say they indulge in a good deal more dressage than most international riders. The result is that their horses are more controlled, more disciplined and probably better balanced than those from other nations. It is sometimes thought that the German style of show jumping is almost too rigid, too disciplined, but there is little doubt that the rider's complete control of the horse does produce good results; it also enables the rider to approach a fence more accurately than most, thus being better assured of a good take-off. It has sometimes been suggested that a horse thus trained lacks the ability to jump at speed, but in fact this is often belied by the performances of the top-class German riders who indeed not only jump against the clock extremely effectively, but because of the training of their horses are able to go round a course in the most economic manner possible.

There are in fact three different types of dressage, though basically they are all related. The first is ordinary basic training; it is this that forms the test in an ordinary one-day or three-day event. At this level horses are expected to be able to give a good account of themselves at the three basic paces – the walk, the trot and the canter. They also have to be able to track to the left and to the right; this means going sideways as well as forward; they also have to be able to describe a small circle of some 20 m diameter which demands particular balance and collection. They have to be able to rein back, which is probably the most difficult of the basic movements in dressage particularly for horses that are not very experienced. They also are expected to be able to track at the canter and, finally, they have to be able to halt which is not of course as easy as it sounds. A horse at the halt should be absolutely steady and is expected to be completely immobile for five or six seconds. In these combined training tests horses also have to be able to move from a halt straight into a trot without an intermediary walk and also to proceed from the walk to the canter without an intermediary trot. Also included are subtle differences in each pace; for instance there is a medium trot, a working trot and an extended trot. There is a medium walk, and an extended walk. There is a medium canter, a working canter and an extended canter. To the layman it is not easy to appreciate the subtle differences though probably people will notice quite easily that at the extended trot the rider rises whereas at the medium trot the rider remains seated. In the dressage test used in one-day and three-day events the object is to do no more than to see that a horse has been properly, basically trained so that it is supple, balanced, disciplined and comfortable. In the Grand Prix Dressage there are much more demanding movements for the horse and rider. These include such things as the *pirouette* when the horse revolves, its hind feet virtually remaining in one place; the *piaffe*, when the horse appears to mark time on a single spot; and the *passage*, when the horse moves forward at a hesitant, elevated trot so that it appears as though the feet are held momentarily in suspense between each stride. Not only is great skill required in training a horse to this standard, but in the judging of them in a competition great store is set on the accuracy of the movements. For instance, at the *piaffe* the marking time must be as regular as a metronome; one, two, three, four. At the *passage*, again the forward movements must be straight and regular; and in the *pirouette* the horse must move in its circle pivoting on the hind feet in such a way that rhythm is maintained with the feet remaining close together. Any deviance is strongly marked down by a judge.

In Grand Prix Dressage there will obviously be only a very limited number of riders in each country capable of the standard demanded. Only in recent years has it been possible for Britain to field a team in the Olympic Games, simply because there were not enough riders of sufficiently advanced standard to perform the movements required. On the continent there are of course many more riders of this standard and it would be possible for Germany, say, to field three or four teams of Olympic calibre.

One of the great difficulties in persuading people of the value of good, basic dressage is that they seem unable to appreciate the difference between the kind of dressage which is no more than sound basic training that is required in the test for a one-day or three-day event and the more advanced dressage that is required in tests which are held in dressage, simply for the sake of dressage. In other words, whereas dressage in a three-day event is a means to an end, Grand Prix Dressage is very much more an end in itself.

Even more an end in itself is *haute école*. This is the most advanced type of dressage, comparable with the greatest skills that can be found in a ballet dancer. This, of course, is what one experiences at the displays given by the Spanish Riding School of Vienna. Initially there are the ordinary basic movements performed mounted or on the long rein: next, the famous exercises sometimes referred to as the airs or schools above the ground: lastly, by contrast, there is the famous quadrille when the team of twelve Lippizaners perform a series of movements which are in fact no more difficult than the basic dressage referred to earlier, but which performed in consort are extremely effective. It is the famous exercises which constitute the most advanced development in this equestrian ballet. The principle exercises above the ground include the *levade*, when the horse squatting deep on its haunches lifts its forefeet off the ground and maintains this position for a length of time. The more advanced the horse, the longer he can retain this awkward position. The *courbette*, one of the most difficult of the exercises is when the horse in the *levade* position executes several leaps forward on his hind feet. In the *capriole* the horse leaps simultaneously with all four feet off the ground and at the height of its leap, with his body horizontal in the air, kicks violently back with its hind legs. It is alleged this was a mediaeval battle technique by means of which a knight hard pressed by foot soldiers could disperse his attackers. At Vienna these exercises above the ground are frequently done between the pillars. This, in fact, is the basic schooling for these complicated and difficult movements; the horse being retained in the necessary position for the instructor to make it do the movements. These exercises done on the short rein enable a trainer to determine which of the various movements a horse is capable of.

In addition to the most established movements there are high school movements such as the *passade* where the horse turns a very small turn with the hindquarters describing a smaller circle than the forehand – this in effect is a preparation for a half *pirouette*, but is not included in ordinary tests; the *pesade* in which the horse lifts its forehand off the ground with lowered hocks, its body being held at an angle of 45° – this is the preparation for the *levade*: the *croupade*, in which the horse jumps off the ground in a position similar to the *pesade*, tucking its legs underneath its body, is

The author congratulates World Champion and Olympic gold medallist, Christine Stuckelberger

preparation for the *courbette*; the *ballotade* when the horse kicks, tucking its hind legs under its body so that the shoes are seen from behind, but does not kick back as in the *capriole*. These exercises, demanding years of training and enormous strength in the stallions which are used to display them, are the height of achievement to which it is possible to aspire in the training of a horse. This, indeed, is *haute école* or high school dressage.

It is likely that amongst some sections of the equestrian public there will always be a certain suspicion of dressage, believing it to be something rather 'foreign' that is practised by fanatics for schooling rather than by anything that is required of the ordinary horseman, let alone the cross-country rider. It is true of course that some people take their dressage very seriously and because of their dedication, which at times appears humourless and limited, tend to alienate people. Particularly in Britain, people dislike the obsessive or fanatical, but it would be a great pity, indeed it would be a disservice to equestrianism, if the ordinary rider was deflected from a proper interest of, and study of, dressage when so obviously every form of riding is going to benefit greatly if a horse is properly trained. In summing up it is worth quoting from the International Equestrian Federation's definition of the object of the dressage:

'The object of dressage is the harmonious development of the physique and ability of the horse. As a result it makes the horse calm, supple and keen, thus achieving perfect understanding with its rider.

'These qualities are revealed by the freedom and regularity of the paces, the harmony, lightness and ease of movement, the lightening of the forehand and the engagement of the hindquarters, the horse remaining absolutely straight, in any movement and

Mrs Boylan (Canada) on *Jungherr* in the John Pinches International Dressage at Goodwood in 1975

Jennie Loriston-Clarke (GB) on *Kadett* during the dressage in the 1972 Olympic Games

bending accordingly when moving on curved lines.

'The horse thus gives the impression of doing of his own accord what is required of him. Confident and attentive he submits generously to the control of his rider.

'His walk is regular, free and unconstrained, his trot is free, supple, regular, sustained and active. His canter is united, light and cadenced. His quarters are never inactive or sluggish, they respond to the slightest indication of the rider thus giving life and spirit to the rest of the body.

'In all his work, even at the halt, the horse must be on the bit. A horse is on the bit when the hocks are correctly placed, the neck is more or less raised according to the extension or collection of the pace, the head remains steadily in position, the contact with the mouth is light and no resistance is offered to the rider.'

It has been said that a rider is as good as he rides, but a method is no better than the man. In other words, it is up to each and every rider to get the most benefit that he can for his horse and ultimately for himself from his basic dressage.

There can be little doubt that Britain has much to learn and, indeed, a long way to go before it can claim to be of a comparable standard in dressage to that experienced in so many other countries; but the fact that dressage is now so popular in Britain with some 3000 members belonging to the Dressage Group of the British Horse Society is extremely encouraging. Moreover, the fact that in 1978 the World Dressage Championships were held in Britain at Goodwood was indeed proof of the fact that it is now accepted, even in the most dressage-conscious countries, that dressage is at last being taken seriously in Britain. The result of this can only be to the benefit of British equestrianism.

Even more important is the fact that Jennie Loriston-Clarke, with *Dutch Courage*, by a brilliant fluent performance won the bronze medal, second only to Christine Stückelberger with *Granat* and the German Schulter Baumer with *Slibovitz*, and this must be an immense inspiration to British riders. Such is the innate ability of Jennie Loriston-Clarke that it is not impossible to see her influencing international judges away from the German accuracy and exactness that has so dominated the dressage scene. There must surely be a place for aesthetic pleasure in the highest level of international dressage. It was discernible with both the French and the Soviet riders not so long ago. If it can become acceptable again then Britain, if developing along the lines so brilliantly pioneered by Jennie Loriston-Clarke rather than slavishly following the existing German insistence on accuracy, so often at the expense of fluency, then British riders could well find themselves near the top much sooner than expected.

PART THREE
Sports and Pastimes

7
Driving

The popularity of driving is surely one of the strangest phenomena of our age. Anyone would have been forgiven for thinking even at the end of the First World War, certainly at the end of the Second World War, that there was no further use for the harness horse in a modern, mechanised society. In fact between the wars a certain amount of driving survived; there were, of course, the classes still held at one or two of the major shows for coaches, but this was really little more than an exhibition employed to promote a certain amount of nostalgia – and, indeed, there is nothing more magnificent than to see a stage coach drawn by four fine horses. There were also the harness classes that happily survived between the wars, mostly because, being so much part of the tradition of the International Horse Show held at Olympia pre-war and the Great Richmond Royal Horse Show, there was enough enthusiasm to maintain a limited number of classes at the show. During the Second World War there was a slight, but noticeable, increase in the amount of driving resulting from the shortage of petrol. People discovered that they had old traps and carriages in their yards or old coach houses, so they trained a horse to work to harness, many people who had never driven before being persuaded to take it up. With the return of peace and the availability of petrol there was of course little demand for the harness horse, it being virtually true to say that it only survived because of the use by the major brewery companies of heavy horses to pull their drays, principally as an advertising project. There was also a limited number of people who kept ponies and carriages to perform at shows where they still had a driving class. But not surprisingly the standard of driving and, indeed, the

Mrs Cynthia Haydon with *Marden Little Swell*

T. L. Vestra (Holland) at Royal Windsor Horse Show in 1978 driving a team of black geldings

enthusiasm for it was steadily declining until a vital development occurred in 1957 which was very quickly to completely change the whole situation.

At the Royal Windsor Horse Show in 1957 Col. Arthur Main of the old Coaching Club, which was still in existence, and Capt. Frank Gilbey were judging the private driving marathon. There were few entries and what there were were not very impressive. The judges remarked on the poor standard in the hearing of one of the stewards, Reg Brown, who was then Secretary of the British Horse Society. He remarked that it was a pity that there was no club or society in existence which could help those who were still anxious to drive, despite the fact that horse-drawn vehicles were now a luxury. Col. Main, an enthusiastic and impulsive person, immediately suggested the forming of a club, and suiting the action to the word gathered together a few people who were on the showground arranging to hold an initial meeting in the near future. Those supporting Col. Main were Sanders Watney, Geoffrey Cross, who is the Chairman of Windsor Show, Frank Haydon, Capt. Frank Gilbey and two or three others. An advertisement was put in *Horse and Hound* announcing the meeting and Reg Brown circulated those members of the British Horse Society who he thought might be interested. On 23 September 1957 the meeting was held at the old British Horse Society offices in Bedford Square and no less than 60 people turned up, the majority of whom forthwith filled in membership forms. Sanders Watney was elected President – an office that he still holds – and a Committee was appointed to draw up rules, regulations and objects. The working committee consisted of Sanders Watney, Col. Main, Capt. Frank Gilbey, Mr Elhurst and Reg Brown, with Mr L H Chandler, as Secretary.

After a series of talks and demonstrations had been arranged for the winter months, Geoffrey Cross suggested that the first official meet of the Society should be held at the Royal Windsor Show. To everyone's surprise some 50 turnouts paraded, thus starting a tradition of a meet, now attended each year by something like 100 members, being held in the Home Park at Windsor. Interest spread rapidly and meets were held at Shotover, near Oxford, at Cirencester, Woburn and in the New Forest. A leading show, the British Timken Show, held just outside Northampton, suggested that an official meet should be held there as it would be particularly convenient for drivers in the Midlands and the North. Transport obviously provided a considerable problem for however great enthusiasm might be it is hardly practical to take a horse-drawn conveyance very far along the main roads. Not only is the traffic extremely discouraging, but there are few hotels or inns on the roads these days which are equipped to provide accommodation for horses and ponies. It is necessary, therefore, to provide motor-driven transport to convey vehicles to meets unless the meets are very local. In fact, something like 100 meets are now organised annually on a regional basis so it is always possible for at least some of the drivers to get to meets under their own steam.

By 1964 the Society had its own show which is obviously the highlight of its year. It is usually held on Smiths Lawn, Her Majesty the Queen frequently being present on these occasions. In 1970 Princess Anne agreed to become the 1000th member and in fact drove herself in the *concours d'élégance*.

It would be foolish to pretend that this was not a recreation that was costly, though such is the enthusiasm of many members of the Society that little labour is employed, the looking after of both the ponies and carriages being carried out by the owners. It is not easy to say exactly what it is that has so attracted people to driving. Up to a point there is no doubt that like riding it is a reaction against the tempo and pressures of the times. But with driving I believe there

Mrs Janet Kidd with her Norwegian Fjord ponies, driving through the water obstacle at Hickstead

Mr J. P. G. Runciman's famous team of Hackneys, driven by Mrs Haydon with her husband, Frank, beside her

is a certain pride in appearance. Drivers take enormous trouble to see that both their vehicle and their harness are in first-class condition, spending hours cleaning the tack, and taking no less trouble with the horses or ponies between the shafts. Indeed, there must be something very satisfying in driving a smart turnout, taking one back, as it must, to a more spacious and leisurely age when the horse played a much greater part in life than it does today. Fortunately, although a certain amount of skill is needed in driving, it is an art that can be very quickly and easily acquired. It is only when one comes to competitive driving that a much greater skill is demanded.

One should perhaps mention the outstanding driver, or 'whip', of present times, namely Cynthia Haydon, who, with her husband Frank, has completely dominated the competitive driving scene ever since the war. That Cynthia Haydon is a brilliant driver there can be no doubt, but it should also be recognised that she puts in an enormous amount of hard work; indeed, there are no two people more dedicated than Frank and Cynthia Haydon. Not only have they succeeded in Britain, but they have played a major part in developing and improving the standard of driving in the United States and in Canada where, as in Britain, it has become increasingly popular over the years.

On the continent, in Germany in particular, driving has always been a part of the equestrian scene: at most major shows some magnificent equipages superbly driven can often be seen with teams of six or even more horses. It is, however, perhaps true to say that on the continent it is still an occupation chiefly connected with the aristocratic families and the large estates, whereas now in Britain, people from all walks of life are driving with enthusiasm and with considerable expertise.

It was inevitable that with the increase in the popularity of driving a competitive element should very quickly creep in. Not only were there classes for turnout and general performance at many shows, but in 1970 it very much came to a head when the International Equestrian Federation under the Presidency of the Duke of Edinburgh held a meeting in Switzerland with the object of encouraging the art of driving. After much discussion, rules and conditions were produced, in many ways not dissimilar to the rules and conditions of a three-day event. The first phase in fact was presentation and dressage – presentation meaning general turn-out and appearance. The second phase was the marathon, that is to say a course of considerable length with a certain number of hazards; and the third phase, the equivalent of show jumping in a three-day event, was obstacle driving; that is driving through tricky obstacles in a comparatively small area. This, of course, took place in the main show arena. The scoring was also very similar to that of a three-day event. Later in 1970 an event under these new rules was held at Windsor, being won by Douglas Nicholson who narrowly beat the Queen's team driven by the Crown Equerry, Sir John Miller. Shortly afterwards, international competitions were introduced, the first one being held in the spring of 1971 when a Hungarian team won from a German team, with the Queen's team in third place. By the following year no less than 16 teams took part in an international three-day event, thus showing that international driving had now become part of the equestrian scene. By this time the Duke of Edinburgh had become immensely enthusiastic himself and was before long to be selected to represent Great Britain. As with so much else in which he has been involved he not only threw himself into the sport with immense enthusiasm, at the same time acquiring very considerable skill, but he was also a considerable inspiration, encouraging many others to take up driving, just as a few years earlier he had encouraged many people to take up polo.

It could be said, therefore, that there are three types of driving; there is the driving in the show ring when for the most part hackneys are exhibited. Although there are classes for amateurs as well as for professionals this is basically a professional sport, and highly professional and skilled at that. Secondly, there is the driving which is exemplified by the meets arranged by the British Driving Society, those who take part doing it very much more for love than for money. Thirdly, there is the competitive driving now organised under the aegis of the Combined Driving Group which is a branch of the British Horse Society. Each of these facets of driving is equally and increasingly popular and it would seem that the popularity is likely to continue to grow for some years yet, despite the cost of transporting vehicles. It is not only

HRH Prince Philip, Duke of Edinburgh, driving the Queen's team of part-bred Cleveland Bays to a Balmoral Dog Cart

Cross-country in the World Driving Championships provides excitement for:

***Top Left*– Gyorgy Bardos (Hungary), World Champion; *Bottom Left* – T. L. Vestra (Holland);**
***Top Right* – George Bowman; *Bottom Right* – Alan Bristow**

3

the individual enthusiasm that attracts people to driving; there is also the companionship of meeting and competing with people with a similar interest. This, of course, encourages them to do as well, if not better, than others whom they meet driving.

As far as the British Driving Society is concerned a very great debt is owed to Sanders Watney who for so long has been President and as such an inspiration to the membership. For him nothing is too much trouble, while it is still a joy to see him handling a coach and four as he frequently does at many of the major shows.

While it is obviously true to say that there is a certain old-worldliness about driving which inevitably creates a certain nostalgia, the element of competition, even in private driving, has resulted in an enormously improved standard of both the horses and ponies used between the shafts and of the vehicles themselves over the last few years. Judging driving events is now a very serious business, and although there certainly is not now and probably never will be the money that is available in other equestrian sports, nevertheless driving is finding sponsors who generously not only provide the prize money and the prizes but contribute in a considerable way both towards the expenses of running the main events and even the expenses of individuals. It is not, perhaps, too easy to see what return they get for their generous investment. One likes to think that many firms are genuinely interested in helping something to survive which without financial assistance would have difficulty in doing so: and surely it is worth doing everything possible to ensure the survival of driving, for it is basically a genuinely amateur sport and not only gives great pleasure to many people who, for one reason or another, are not able to ride but have a deep affection for the horse and everything to do with the horse, but it also helps to permeate something that is very much a part of our heritage. Indeed, the very names of the vehicles are both romantic and evocative: Phaeton, Barouche, Brougham, Landau, Gig, Curricle, Cabriolet, Cocking Cart, Ralli Car, Sulky, the Sociable, the Milord, the Hansom, the Victoria, the Post-chaise; Scurry Cart, Norfolk Trap, Parisienne Wagonette, French Convertible, Spindleback. How charmingly they conjure up a bygone age, when life was more leisurely and elegant: though one cannot help feeling that roads before the use of macadam must have made a safe arrival at the end of one's journey anything but predictable. It was, however, for the mail and stage coach and for the private drag which was used for long distances, that the journeys must have been so hazardous.

In recent years, driving for the disabled has been introduced: similar to the enormously successful riding for the disabled. There can be no doubt whatever that this can be of enormous value psychologically to disabled people, perhaps of even greater value than riding where there are obvious limitations, whereas such limitations are considerably reduced in driving.

Of all the developments in driving none, perhaps, is more important than the competitive combined driving (driving in teams). It has internationalised the sport: it demands a quite exceptional skill that can only be compared with the brilliant ability of the coachman of 100 years ago. As far as Britain is concerned we are comparative newcomers to this new equestrian discipline. Although Britain, under the inspiration of the Duke of Edinburgh and encouraged by the successes of George Bowman, Douglas Nicholson, Alan Bristow, Cdr Parker and others, has achieved considerable success, the British have still some way to go before they can consider themselves in the same class as the Germans and those in Eastern Europe. The countries from behind the Iron Curtain seem to have an exceptional skill in driving, combining speed with great accuracy, yet at the same time retaining the freshness, the suppleness and the manoeuvrability of their horses. They have a long tradition of skilled driving in these countries, and although down the years there have been great British whips going back to the days when coachmen on the stage coaches and the mail coaches achieved remarkable feats of timing over long distances when roads were appallingly bad, yet competitive driving of the standard that it is today is a target which British drivers are going to take some time to achieve. Nevertheless, with such keenness and enthusiasm amongst so many there is no reason to believe that Britain will not be able to equal the best in the foreseeable future.

Such is the enthusiasm for combined driving, it is inevitably going through a period of assessment when not everybody sees eye to eye or necessarily agrees. This situation, however, must on the whole be regarded as healthy, there being little doubt that the Combined Driving organisation which in such a short time has collected nearly 600 members, already almost as many as in the British Driving Society, can only go forward. Competition is always healthy even when it is between two groups of people who have slightly differing views. As experience increases so will a common policy evolve, resulting in top-class performances from the very talented whips now revealing themselves.

The overall strength of driving in Britain is due to its variety and depth of interest; at one end there is simple competitive driving of the 'ride and drive' variety, which in reality is little more than a gymkhana event. In the middle there is the highly skilled driving as symbolised by Cynthia Haydon, driving not only horses and ponies in single harness but also pairs, tandems, four-in-hands and possibly the most

Above: The Coaching Marathon finishes at the Royal International Horse Show

Below: Young's magnificent team of eight Shires

Hickstead Water makes an attractive driving obstacle

difficult and certainly the most effective of all, the Unicorn, which is two wheelers and one in front: then at the top there is the highly demanding and very competitive Combined Driving Three-Day Event. In short, there is something for everybody and something to suit all pockets, hence the increasing support for a sport and recreation that can give satisfaction on so many fronts.

It would be a mistake not to conclude this chapter without a description of the British Driving Society's Silver Jubilee Drive in 1978 as this seems to typify both the spirit associated with and the opportunities provided in driving in Britain today. It was Mrs Parsons who first conceived of the idea of a relay drive right across Britain to finish at Balmoral where greetings could be handed personally to the Queen. It was Mrs Parsons who also organised it. Everyone approached welcomed the project, promising their support; each area was therefore provided with a pennant to which their county's emblem was attached, these pennants in turn being handed on to neighbouring counties. Departing on 1 May 1978 from Brockenhurst, in the New Forest, Sanders Watney, the Society's President, accepted the flag from the Earl of Malmesbury, the Lord Lieutenant of Hampshire, who then accompanied him in a four-wheeled dog cart followed by nearly 50 turn-outs. This was the first stage of the long journey north. The next check-point was Blenheim Palace in Oxfordshire, where the Duke of Marlborough presented the flag for its next stage. The third stage was at Sandbeck Park, the home of the Earl of Scarborough. The fourth was at Holker Hall in Cumbria, the home of Mr R. E. Cavendish. The fifth was at Gretna Green; Balmoral finally being reached on 2 October 1978.

To give just one example of the efforts people were prepared to go to make the Silver Jubilee Drive a success. Mr and Mrs Roger Page and Fred Tamplin departed from their homes, near Southampton, a month in advance with two Cobs, one vehicle and a horse box which towed their caravan, thus enabling them to drive the entire distance from Southampton to Balmoral on the hoof. Another example of enthusiasm was the party of eight who set out from Northern Ireland crossing the Irish Sea and proceeded all the way to Balmoral: but even for those who only made the last stage it was a unique experience with no less than 60 turnouts finally completing the last stage of the Jubilee Drive. Appropriately when the cavalcade arrived at the gates of Balmoral, the Queen herself drove up, not in a Barouche or a Landau, but in a dog cart drawn by a pair of Fell ponies with the Duke of Edinburgh himself taking the reins. The

Chuck wagons at Calgary

Queen spoke to all those who took part and finally watched a drive-past of all involved. What was particularly interesting was that this drive was sponsored by *Harper's and Queen*.

Interestingly, a Jubilee Drive also took place in America on 26 June 1978 following an obstacle competition at the end of the Myopia Combined Driving Event. A procession of vehicles which ranged from a Myopia shooting brake to nothing less than a 1929 Rolls-Royce Coupé, assembled at Acwila Farm, the home of Mr and Mrs Pirie. Mrs Pirie herself led the drive with her team of hackney crossbreds, while Mrs Pulsifer drove an Arab to a gig and carried the pennant and the American flag, accompanied by Mrs Moore from Canada. *Harper's and Queen* were also associated with this drive and had a shooting brake, decked with banners, driven by Charles Kellog, the Editor of *The Whip*, America's Driving Society's own publication. Some twelve turn-outs took part. This drive which took part through most attractive country round Bradley Palmers State Park raised $85 (approx. £55) for the benefit of driving for the disabled in England. The pennant was later taken to the Combined Driving Trials at Lowther, thus providing an interesting and, indeed, most welcome link between driving on both sides of the Atlantic.

As has so often been shown in the past, sport can provide a link and a companionship between two different countries, which could only risk being spoiled where there is too much emphasis on professionalism and commercialism. It is hoped that this comparatively new development of an ancient pastime will long remain an activity that can give immense satisfaction to the amateur who can benefit from the experience of the professional: and could well, before very long, compete on equal terms.

8 Foxhunting

Foxhunting has long been considered the premier equestrian countryside sport, though it is possible today to make out a case suggesting that, at any rate in certain parts of the country, shooting now takes precedence. Certainly one has to admit that it is extraordinary that hunting should have survived right through to the end of the 20th century. Considered in relation to the materialistic mechanical age in which we now live and appreciating the enormous step forward in agricultural science and transport, one must accept that foxhunting is something of an anachronism; yet strangely it would appear to be more popular than ever before with more than 200 packs of foxhounds in Britain and many hunts experiencing too large rather than too small fields. Despite the costs, the strong feeling in certain quarters against foxhunting on ethical grounds, and possible legislation, foxhunting not only survives but flourishes. Those who enjoy it, however, would indeed be unwise to be complacent.

The development of foxhunting over the centuries makes interesting reading. There has, of course, been hunting of one sort and another in every country since the beginning of man, Britain being no exception, but until the 17th century packs were not bred or used specially to hunt one particular quarry – hounds hunting the fox, the hare, the boar or the stag; furthermore, all rights of hunting were vested in the Crown which resulted in hunting only being carried out on large estates of the great landlords who hunted by permission of the King. It was in the middle of the 17th century that gradually a particular interest in hunting the fox as opposed to any other quarry developed as it was appreciated that the fox had greater stamina and, therefore, went straighter than the hare. It also had a less strong scent than the stag, or presumably, the boar, and so it presented a greater challenge to the hounds and the huntsman in following and eventually catching the quarry. It was further recognised that the fox was perhaps the most wily, crafty and cunning of all wild animals: to outwit and catch it demanded not only great perseverance on the part of the hounds, and steadiness which means that the hounds keep to their work, being neither fainthearted nor distracted, but also exceptional intelligence, even if it is an almost instinctive animal kind of intelligence, on the part of the huntsman.

Towards the end of the 17th century, the second Duke of Buckingham, with his great estates in Yorkshire, caused something of a sensation when he declared that he would willingly exchange a flock of his finest sheep for a similar number of foxes, such good sport he believed being provided by foxes. Indeed, he was eventually to die waiting for a fox to be dug out from one of his Yorkshire coverts. At about the same time the fifth Duke of Beaufort, still then in his teens, found a fox in Silk Wood which provided a hunt so good that the Duke decided then and there to steady his hounds from hunting deer and to encourage them only to hunt the fox. It is generally agreed that the first pack of foxhounds was the Charlton Hunt based at Chichester in Sussex, the Masters of which were none other than the Duke of Monmouth and Lord Grey of Werke. In neighbouring Hampshire Lord Arundel was also hunting the fox, eventually selling his hounds to Thomas Boothby, the first Master of the Quorn. It was descendants from these hounds that went to Hugo Meynell, the first Master to indulge in scientific foxhound breeding. From this time onwards it became more and more fashionable to breed hounds simply to hunt the fox and no other quarry.

In the 17th and 18th centuries the packs of foxhounds in existence hunted vast territories. Lord Berkeley's territory stretched from Bristol to Kensington; Lord Darlington's from Raby Castle (Durham) to Doncaster; the Duke of Beaufort's from Bath to Oxford; the Duke of Grafton hunted both south of the river and in his estates in Northamptonshire and Suffolk. It was indeed he who was responsible in the 1740s for introducing a bill into Parliament for the building of a bridge across the Thames which would facilitate transporting his hounds when the Croydon Ferry proved unsatisfactory.

A further important development at this time which was to have very considerable influences on foxhunting was that gradually the scrub and woodland were being replaced by cultivated land. A certain Robert Bakewell, responsible for many experiments in the breeding of cattle, started dividing his land into enclosures so that different herds could be kept separate. The result of this was that to follow hounds it became necessary to jump fences. This was the beginning of jumping in Britain and very much changed the style of riding. In order to jump fences it became necessary to ride with a shorter stirrup. The British aristocracy very quickly found that jumping fences provided a great deal of fun; they also found that the type of horse which they were used to riding was not entirely suited to jumping and so gradually the British Hunter was bred which can fairly accurately be described as a three-quarter Thoroughbred, retaining the quality, speed and activity of the Thoroughbred whilst possessing the substance, solidness and stamina of the draught horse. Mr C. J. Appleby, well-known as the sporting journalist Nimrod, was very largely responsible for the introduction of the Hunter as we know it today, popularising this type of horse particularly for hunting in Leicestershire.

Towards the end of the 18th and the beginning of the 19th centuries the whole style of hunting was very quickly to change. In the old days, as one can read from contemporary diaries such as that which exists in the history of the Charlton Hunt, hounds drew up to a fox's overnight drag with great perseverance, working up to it so that a hunt could then last anything up to six hours; but never at a fast pace. The Master, usually the great local landlord, and his few invited friends would ride after the hounds, taking a great interest in their performance, which at that time was referred to as venery. It has even been suggested that in the middle of the day the followers could pause for a meal while new horses were fetched and then, an hour or so later, carry on, hounds still being within earshot in the forest or in the scrub-covered moorlands; but with the enclosures all this was to change. There were now open spaces and naturally the fox, who it has always been said, never goes faster than the fastest hound, now had to cross the open spaces at speed to keep ahead of the hounds. Only good scenting conditions could force it to hurry, instinct normally enabling it only to go as fast as it had to while it twisted and turned to confuse the hounds. It is possible that when travelling faster the fox leaves more scent, but this is pure surmise as it has to be admitted that very little is known about scent which, of course, is part of the fascination of hunting. It is, however, a fact that in the latter half of the 18th century the whole speed of hunting increased, something that the majority of those who followed hounds found very much to their liking. A certain Duke of Rutland,

The Grafton Meet at Stowe School

Moving off in the Park

however, did not agree. He is alleged to have preferred what he called 'cunning hunting', condemning 'racing down the quarry with fast packs'. For him, therefore, it was still the hare that was king of all venery; but for the majority the faster hunting conditions were preferred and, indeed, came to be encouraged, the whole system of hunting thus being altered. The venue or meet as it came to be called, was carefully chosen at a place where it was known that the country was open and a fox would be quickly found. Understandably this kind of hunting made a greater demand both on horses and hounds and a greater area was covered. All this greatly increased the cost of hunting with the result that towards the middle of the 19th century the great landowners were finding that it was too expensive to hunt their countries privately at their own expense, and so with considerable reluctance they agreed to accept subscribers, that is to say people who lived in the neighbourhood and were prepared to pay something for the privilege of hunting with his lordship's hounds.

This, of course, coincided with the Industrial Revolution. There were, therefore, many wealthy and able people who wanted to hunt with their local hounds but whose knowledge was limited and whose background was not always considered desirable by his Lordship. Nevertheless his Lordship had no alternative but to accept their subscriptions and, indeed, was tempted to admit more and more people of this background into hunting to help him meet the enormous costs of running his hunt. Not surprisingly, these wealthy, able, if not wholly acceptable, people very soon wanted a hand in running the pack. As they saw it they were putting up the money to make the hunting possible and, therefore, they wanted a say in how the hunt should be run. This resulted in the Master, who was also the landowner and the owner of the hounds, finding himself at loggerheads with what one might refer to as the paymasters. One of the results of this was the splitting up of Hunts into smaller areas. Not only was it impossible at this time effectively and efficiently to run a hunt that stretched for over 100 miles, but those who were now subsidising the Hunts wanted more hunting in their own areas so that they could get proper value for their money. During the latter half of the 19th century, therefore, there were many new Hunts covering much smaller areas. This was fortunate in that with the Industrial Revolution becoming so influential more and more people found themselves able to afford to hunt; more than that it became the 'in' thing to hunt and people would go to any lengths to be able to follow their local hounds. The fields became enormous; it was not unusual for a fashionable hunt to have a field of 600 or even 700. Fortunately most of the land was still owned by the great landlords, so the farmers, whether they were tenants or managers, just had to put up with these huge fields going over their land. There was, of course, the advantage in that all these people's horses had to be fed and the local farmers provided them with their forage which was frequently their principal source of income. Moreover, they needed horses which their young sons broke and schooled and then sold to the many people who were looking for horses on which to follow hounds. Paradoxically, therefore, it was a prosperous time for the farmer who during the 19th century was having a very lean time. It could even be said that but for the hunting many of them would never have survived.

Famous names in foxhunting history in the 20th century

Above: **The Earl of Lonsdale, Master of the Cottesmore (1915–21)**

The Duke of Beaufort, Master of the Beaufort since 1924

As we can see from the old prints, galloping and jumping was all that mattered. A huntsman had to provide sport. Regrettably the result of all this was that a bad element crept into hunting in the providing of artificially produced foxes. Indeed, in the third quarter of the 19th century there was such a shortage of foxes because of the value of their pelts that many hunts had to buy them at the Leadenhall Market in London. Bagged foxes thus became known as Leadenhallers.

Many people imagine, erroneously, that the second half of the 19th century was the great heyday of hunting. That it must have been enormous fun cannot be denied, but it had some very disreputable features. These were the hunting of bagged foxes, riding roughshod over farmers' precious land and arrogance from the field which must have been very offensive to those not involved. There was also a very real element of cruelty, especially amongst those who were considered the fashionable trendsetters of the day; the young 'nobs', 'blades' or 'bloods'. They would happily boast of how many horses they had got through in a season, for it was not rare for a horse to drop dead of exhaustion in the middle of a hunt, many others never surviving to hunt another day. The reason for this was partly because horses in those days were unclipped and would consequently gallop in winter coats: it was also much easier in those days to cross the country without interruption. There were no main roads, no main railway lines; there was little arable land; there was no barbed wire. In the more popular hunting countries where there were only small woodlands rather than large forests, the fox had no option but to run absolutely straight. It was, therefore, a straight steeplechase as long as the fox could survive or find a hole. From a riding point of view it must have been very exhilarating, but with many of the *nouveau riche* who had little knowledge of horsemastership there was no attempt to conserve the horse, only to gallop it flat out from the start and, furthermore, to do all that one could to cut down one's rivals. In those days the great thing was to 'stump' or 'pound' other members of the field by jumping something that nobody else could jump; or, of course, by riding another rider off so that his horse was bound to run out or fall.

It is easy to write in condemnatory fashion of those days, but one has to remember that it was in keeping with the times in so far as the upper classes were concerned: just as heroism in war was a quality that was respected, so the great man across country was looked up to by everybody. Indeed, how one went out hunting played an important part in both one's social life and career.

Towards the end of the 19th century with the emergence of what one might almost refer to as professional Masters, people who really understood hunting and the problems that modern hunting

Lord Daresbury, Master of the County Limerick since 1947

Capt. Ronnie Wallace, 25-years Master of the Heythrop

presented, there was better organisation and smaller fields. It is probably true to say that it was the few years prior to the First World War that was the real heyday of hunting. After the wild rampage when hunting first became a 'free for all' in the middle of the 19th century, it was now well organised, with a proper set of rules drawn up by the new Master of Foxhounds Association, rules which were strict and which were strictly enforced. It is worth quoting the rule that has always been number one in the Master of Foxhounds Association's Code of Conduct.

'Foxhunting as a sport is the hunting of the fox in his wild and natural state with a pack of hounds. No pack of hounds of which the Master or representatives is a member of this Association shall be allowed to hunt a fox in any way that is inconsistent with this precept.'

One of the first results of this was the improvement in the breeding of the foxhound. Whereas in the days when foxes were provided, put down in front of the hounds, and then scorched at racing pace across the country, hounds virtually had to run straight. They were therefore developed very much as greyhounds with little consideration given to the nose, that is to say their ability to use their nose in following the trail of a fox, with the result that hounds not only had very little of what is the hound's greatest and most essential quality – nose – but they tended also, because of the speed at which they hunted and because there was no need to inform others in the pack that they were on the line, to run mute, that is to say without using their voice. At the beginning of the 20th century, however, great trouble was taken with certain kennels to improve the hound in these vital senses, and so over the last 80 years one has had a number of suitably bred packs with proven lines; the English Foxhound Stud Book is today something of which those involved in the sport can be very proud.

Many thought that hunting would not survive after the First World War, but in fact it was back in its stride very quickly: moreover, those not old enough to remember hunting between the wars may be surprised at the lavish scale in which it was carried out and how popular it was throughout the length and breadth of Britain. Although the First World War had been such a calamity, followed by slumps and depressions, nevertheless there were still many people who while they might not have been able to keep up an establishment in the style of the great Lord Lonsdale for instance, they could, nevertheless, live very comfortably with plenty of labour, both cheap and reliable, available. Even in the middle thirties, when the economic crisis had followed the general strike, many people who went hunting had second horses and second horsemen and a yard with anything up to twelve horses in it.

Stanley Barker, 25-years Huntsman of the Pytchley

George Barker, 30-years Huntsman of the Quorn

Again, after the Second World War, it seemed doubtful if hunting could survive. This time it did take longer to get going again, but it managed to do so, and though post-war hunting has never regained the style of pre-war hunting, and although the country has certainly become very much more difficult to hunt with big estates broken up into smaller farms and much more intensified agriculture and economic problems, hunting would appear to be in a thriving state. That this is so is due to three things: firstly, more people can now afford to hunt than ever before because money is more equally shared round; secondly, people find that the countryside – and there is no better way of enjoying the countryside than in the hunting field – is an antidote to the pressures of industrial and commercial life; thirdly, many hunts today are fortunate in that they have supporters' clubs. These supporters' clubs have a membership varying from 100 to 1000 members. Their great value is not only in their contribution in cash and kind to their local hunt, but also in the indisputable fact that the members act as ambassadors for foxhunting, coming as they do from every walk of life. When on Monday they go back to their factories or offices or shops or businesses others may say that they have had a great day at the football on Saturday, but the supporters can say how much they have enjoyed their day's hunting.

It would be foolish to pretend that foxhunting is a cheap sport; far from it. A good hunter today is going to cost a minimum of £1000; the keep of it can be as much as £12 a week, though if the horse is kept at livery with all forage and labour provided the likelihood is that the charge will be no less than £30 a week. There is then the cost of kit which can amount to anything between £300 and £500 if one is going to be properly turned-out from head to toe, though as described in an earlier chapter it is perfectly possible to be presentably turned out at very much less. The subscription to the Hunt varies in different parts of the country, but it is probably true to say that it is anything between £100 and £400, some of the more fashionable hunts charging very much more, though they prefer to be somewhat secretive about the actual charge they make. If one wishes to go and hunt with a Hunt of which one is not a member then one is asked to pay a 'cap', certainly £5 and more likely £10, occasionally even more. Each day at the meet 'Field money' is taken, this varying between £1 and £3. Children who are members of the Pony Club are as a rule allowed to hunt for a very much reduced Hunt subscription, or more commonly on the payment of 50p or £1 a day. Labour, of course, is expensive which means that if a person expects a groom, male or female, to look after his horses, it can cost anything between £30 and £50 a week.

One might well be forgiven for thinking that all this cost would preclude people from hunting, but as said

The Quorn at their famous Opening Meet at Kirby Gate, Leicestershire

at the beginning of the chapter the fact of the matter is that more people are hunting than ever before. In one way and another many people find it possible to cut down on their expenses, others just prefer to spend their money in doing something which gives them so much enjoyment. It is, of course, the same in all sports, there are more than enough people willing to pay £500 for a gun in a good shoot with which only ten or twelve days shooting and all the additional expenses makes the sport no less expensive, apart from the kit, than hunting itself. Similarly people are prepared to pay large sums for a short stretch on a famous river. In Britain, sport has invariably dominated people's pockets; this is a characteristic of the British which would appear to be changing only slowly, if at all.

Foxhunting, of course, is not the prerogative of Britain. Indeed, for many people the very word foxhunting is synonymous with Ireland where there are still more than 30 packs of hounds showing consistently good sport, though it has to be admitted that hunting in Ireland is not quite the same as it was for similar reasons to those in Britain. More young horses are sold early, fewer young farmers are in

Top: The Whaddon Chase, led by Joint-Masters, D. J. L. Wyatt and Dorian Williams, leave Winslow, their Boxing Day venue

Centre: The Whaddon Chase arrive at their famous Opening Meet draw, High Havens

Left: Albert Buckle, Huntsman of the Whaddon Chase for 25 years, leads a large field with his hounds in North Bucks

farming just for the breeding of horses and, as in Britain, there is more serious agriculture, more barbed wire and more roads. Nevertheless, as long as hunting is talked of there will always be famous hunts remembered with affection, the names of which are part of hunting history: the Blazers (County Galway), the Kildare, the Limerick, the Meath, the Tipperary; these names and many others still provide wonderful sport for the visitor and seem as much a part of Ireland as the Irish brogue itself. The landscape is surely a foxhunter's paradise with so much vivid green pasture, every type of fence and bank and, compared with Britain, very few towns. Hunting in Ireland is a very much less lavish and, therefore, a less expensive sport than in Britain. Indeed, there are fewer wealthy people able to run a pack of hounds in Ireland and it is not uncommon to find Masters who have come from Britain or even from the USA.

It takes all sorts: correct gear all round

Owing to the almost non-existence of foxes in Northern Ireland there was little hunting until 1948. There is now plenty of good hunting, though the conditions are not as ideal as in the south with considerably more plough. The three hunts that exist in Northern Ireland today are the East Down, the Dungannon and the Strabane, and Donegal. The packs of foxhounds in Ireland and Northern Ireland have their own Irish Masters of Foxhounds Association and registration.

In America there is also hunting which is extremely popular though carried out on a rather lavish scale; in fact, it has been said that hunting in America is more like hunting was in Britain 100 years ago, except that they do not have very large fields. Hunting has in fact existed in the USA for upwards of 200 years. Foxes are more scarce in America than they are in Britain and there is little doubt that considerably fewer foxes are actually caught, but many countries provide first-class sport over stiff fences, particularly stiff timber fences. The most popular districts for hunting are in Virginia and Pennsylvania. There also hunts in

Different aspects of hunting in England

Tennessee, Alabama and Georgia. It would, I think, be true to say that hunting in America is still mainly the preserve of wealthy people, certainly those who follow hounds are invariably beautifully mounted; the turn-out, too, leaves nothing whatever to be desired.

There is a limited amount of foxhunting in Australia, the fox not being indigenous to the Antipodes, but introduced in the early days of settlement appears to have become acclimatised. The main Hunts are the Melbourne, Oaklands, Findon, Yarra Glen and Lilly Dale. There is also hunting on a limited scale in Tasmania and in a rather more advanced state in New Zealand. In Canada there is the Montreal Hunt that has been in existence since 1826 and generally claims to be the oldest surviving Hunt in North America. The Toronto Hunt dates from 1843, but is now known as the Eglinton and Calendon Hunt; the London Hunt was formally established in 1885, but has records going back 40 years longer, while the Ottawa Valley has existed since 1873. In all there are some 13 Hunts in Canada, stretching from Quebec in the east to British Columbia in the west. The season is necessarily a short one, lasting from August until the freeze-up which is round about December. Occasionally the hunts start again in April and May.

Since 1835 there has been hunting in Italy, namely the Rome Hunt where for so long Count Cigala Fulgosi was Master; the Kennels being on the Appian Way, eight miles from the centre of Rome. The Rome Hunt is very much a part of Roman society, but good sport is enjoyed with the limited number of foxes that are to be found, very few of which are killed. Finally there is a pack of foxhounds in Portugal, but it is, perhaps, rather more of a drag hunt than a fox hunt, nevertheless giving pleasure to those who follow once or twice a week, not more than 30 in number. Most overseas packs use English blood extensively in the breeding of their hounds.

Obviously Britain has the ideal terrain for foxhunting, but the enthusiasm of those who hunt, experienced by visitors from overseas, has proved infectious with the result that attempts have been made in different countries to run Hunts along British lines. As suggested earlier, foxhunting may today be something of an anachronism. It cannot be denied, however, that it is a great part of the British heritage. That it will come increasingly under attack is obvious: one can only hope that common sense will ensure its survival for some time yet. For hunting to disappear would leave the English countryside in winter strangely silent and empty: and cause much distress amongst countrymen.

9
Point-to-Point

Point-to-point racing is the natural progression from steeplechasing. More than 100 years ago it was suggested that in addition to flat racing which had taken place over the centuries at such centres as Newmarket, Goodwood and Doncaster, there should be a race over fences, not over an organised course, but literally from a certain point to the nearest church tower, hence steeplechasing: early steeplechases included the Vale of Aylesbury steeplechase, the Northampton and Liverpool Grand Steeplechases. They soon became more organised and were to settle down as National Hunt Racing. In hunting circles, however, there remained a desire and, as it transpired, a need for rather more informal racing, and so a pattern was developed along the lines of the original steeplechases, a race from one point to another, to become known as point-to-point racing, but with fewer rules and regulations. Naturally this racing soon became better organised, although well into the thirties it was usual for these races to be the prerogative of owners riding genuine hunters and, what is more, riding them in proper hunting kit. Indeed, there was then, as there is today, an insistence that horses could only be entered for point-to-points if they had been 'well and truly hunted' with a registered pack of foxhounds. After a short time it became the custom to limit these races to

Josephine Bothway, David Turner's sister, on *Pennyman*, winning in Hampshire

a three-mile course, to be contested at level weights of 12 st 7 lb.

It is only since the Second World War that point-to-pointing has so strongly developed. It is a short season, a bare 16 weeks; though it is now true to say that each year the season gets a little longer. It is not unusual, and is indeed permissible, for a point-to-point to be held in the second week of June, and, weather permitting, the first point-to-points are held at the beginning of February. Obviously this is a sport which is particularly attractive to the hunting community, though over the years it has attracted an increasing number of people who look upon it as a cheap and enjoyable day's racing – no one can be charged entry for a point-to-point, only for the car: and crowds of 10000 are not unusual at the better organised point-to-points, especially if large fields can be guaranteed. There were more runners in point-to-points in the 1978 season than ever before, which suggests that as with foxhunting there is no decrease in its popularity.

When in the early 1920s the Master of Foxhounds Association decided in their wisdom to limit the prize money to £20 for first prize there were many who thought that this was being unnecessarily severe, since before the war there had in fact been considerably larger prizes in point-to-points. The purpose of the Master of Foxhounds Association Committee was to keep the sport as amateur as possible. It was hoped that people would then continue to ride their hunters which had been 'regularly and truly hunted' throughout the season. Their objective was to discourage people from keeping horses just to point-to-point, it being appreciated that the point-to-point could in fact be a good schooling ground for potential steeplechasers, and indeed at that time in particular, though rather less so since the war, many good horses migrated to National Hunt racing from point-to-pointing. Now it is almost true to say that the reverse is happening. One finds in point-to-points many good horses that have spent several years in National Hunt stables running in high-class races. It is not in the least unusual nowadays to see an ex-Grand National horse running in a point-to-point. In 1978 there was even an example of an ex-winner of the Cheltenham Gold Cup winning a point-to-point. One reason for this is that today, with training expenses so high, many people feel that they cannot afford to keep a 'chaser in training once he is past his best. On the other hand, a horse may not be ideally suited to hunting, and indeed he may still possess considerable ability. The point-to-point seems therefore the ideal compromise; to continue racing but in less exalted company.

There are many who think that this situation has proved a fillip to point-to-pointing, a public which perhaps does not often go to a proper race meeting being given the opportunity of seeing good horses racing in point-to-points. On the other hand, it has to be said that the presence of such horses both discourages people from running a horse that really is a genuine hunter and no more; and also encourages people to keep a much higher class type of horse for point-to-pointing. It is true to say that there are now several point-to-point stables where the main interest throughout the year is the production of top-class point-to-pointers. There is nothing particularly wrong in this; good horses appear at meetings each week, well, almost professionally, ridden, and give the punters a good run for their money, but it cannot be denied that it is shifting the sport from its original purpose in no small way.

As regards the prize money, there is in certain circles a strong feeling that this should be increased. Indeed, it has been very considerably increased during the last two or three seasons, though with a first prize of only £60 or £70 it is still not likely to be the prize money that attracts people to run horses in point-to-points.

Recently a Point-to-Point Owners Association has been formed which obviously hopes to bring pressure to bear on the Jockey Club – Master of Foxhounds Liaison Committee, which is the advisory body responsible for the running of point-to-points. There is no doubt that this association consists of people who are closely concerned with the sport and, more than that, are enthusiastic patrons. It could be said, therefore, that they have a slightly less than detached interest; nevertheless, their views are well worth considering. For instance, they are anxious that a weight for age allowance should be introduced. This has been agreed to as an experiment as it has been felt for some time that for a five-year-old to be expected to carry 12 st and more round a three-mile course is asking rather a lot. They particularly want to increase the prize money until it makes point-to-pointing viable. It is doubtful whether this will ever get any strong support as almost certainly the Jockey Club, which is always a little wary about where point-to-pointing is going lest it should be a rival to National Hunt racing, will give it scant support. The Owners Association also wants to consider the qualification and suitability of officials as they feel that they are better qualified than existing bodies to pronounce on that. But here again it is generally agreed, as it is in most sports, that it is better for the governing of the sport and the making and enforcing of rules to be carried out by a detached body of people who are not actively involved in the sport. It is of interest that in show jumping there is now a Professional Riders Association, but this association works in conjunction with both the National Federation and the International Federation and is of an advisory nature. It is to be hoped that the Point-to-Point Owners Association

David Turner, on *Hardcastle*, winning at the Bicester Point-to-Point

will remain content to act in an advisory capacity, rather than to try and take over the running of the sport.

On the vexed question of prize money, which one feels is really the *raison d'être* for the Point-to-Point Owners Association's existence, one cannot help feeling that there is a certain contradiction in terms, in that in 1978 there were well over 3000 point-to-point horses registered with about 12000 runners, all apparently quite content to run for the existing prize money. In other words, there is little justification for believing that point-to-points will only survive if the prize money is increased. Indeed, there are those Hunts embarrassed by enormous entries now suggesting that the opposite would be more effective: reduce the prize money and you will reduce the fields.

There is no doubt that the point-to-point is a very attractive feature of the countryside in spring and early summer. Not only is it the gathering of the clans when all the countryside meets up enjoying a good day out, but increasingly it is enticing people from the ever-spreading towns and cities to a day out in the country. They meet country people, seeing something of the country way of life; hopefully they learn that without hunting there would be no point-to-pointing at all. It could also be that some of their prejudices are reduced because they have been actively participating themselves in what for the countryman is just a way of life; this can only do good. In addition, of course, point-to-point meetings help to swell a Hunt's income, many Hunts becoming increasingly dependent upon the money made at their point-to-point. This enables them to keep the subscription low and helps them to recover some of the ever increasing costs. Unfortunately, with the additional cost of running a point-to-point and the undeniably overcrowded calendar in the brief three or four months of the point-to-point season, takings are not always as high as they used to be: in many cases profits are today drastically reduced. This is unfortunate, not only because it would be a great pity if local Hunts decided to give up their point-to-points and because every Hunt needs the money, but also because Hunt Committees might turn their glance towards a new kind of sport that is becoming increasingly popular in the countryside; a sport that is less trouble to run, is growing in popularity and would appear to be a good way of raising money. This is cross-country riding. It will be dealt with fully in the following chapter. Suffice it to say here that it would be tragic if cross-country riding were ever permitted to replace the point-to-point as the countryside's, in general, and the local Hunt's, in particular, own sporting day out.

A day out is what point-to-points are primarily about. They were originally conceived as a way of entertaining local farmers over whose land the members of the Hunt had enjoyed their sport during the season. This was the Hunt's way of expressing their gratitude to the farmers: a day out which they could enjoy and during which they could relax. Frequently they were entertained to a sit-down lunch. Even today most Hunts, apart from giving them free access to the meeting, entertain their farmers at least to drinks, often to some kind of a meal. It is essential that farmers should feel that this is the occasion on which the Hunt entertains them.

It is this that is largely responsible for the atmosphere of a point-to-point. It is quite different to that of an ordinary race meeting. It is all much more informal, friendly, and intimate in that, in theory, everybody knows everybody. It would be sad if this feeling should ever disappear, if the whole amateur aura of the point-to-point should be allowed to evaporate.

It is something of a paradox that, just as there seems to be a boom in the point-to-point scene with more runners than ever before and record attendances, it should be threatened by the new sport of cross-country riding which has that same appeal to the amateur that was once the hallmark of the point-to-point.

Hopefully there is room for both. There should be if those responsible for each sport are realistic and prepared to consider their sport in as detached a manner as possible. Time will tell. To jeopardise one at the expense of the other would be short-sighted indeed.

The Surrey Union Point-to-Point

10 Cross-Country, Long-Distance and Trekking

Cross-Country Riding

In 1974 at Hickstead, Douglas Bunn first conceived of the idea of a team cross-country event. He was already used to preparing a drag-line (ie laying a trail of aniseed) on his farm: and there was therefore no great problem in preparing a two-and-a-half mile course with some 20 to 25 fences, wide enough to be jumped by a team of five. For many years there had of course been the Melton Hunt cross-country ride, but this was for some 60 or 70 riders all going from A to B (a course of about three-and-a-half miles), the winner being the first one home. The Hickstead idea was something quite different. This was for teams of five, the time being taken from the start to the fourth one past the post; in other words, the team could lose one member, but still qualify. Very quickly it was discovered that the best way to succeed in a cross-country of this nature was to have a pathfinder, someone really experienced in front who could blaze a trail which would be followed by the others. In the event of more than one falling, or refusing, then obviously the leaders had to stop since there was no point in their getting home on their own: those at the back, moreover, might not get home at all unless they had a reliable lead from those in the front. At the first Hickstead cross-country event in 1974 the going was rock hard and there were many people who thought that there would be some bad falls and some badly injured horses and riders. The second fence, which was a kind of Becher's, was formidable indeed with a big drop and a wide ditch behind an already wide enough fence. Not surprisingly this did take its toll and there was one horse fatality. Immediately afterwards there was an 'In-and-Out' of very solid rails, which surprisingly caused remarkably little trouble, as did a fence later on in the course which was preceded by a really wide ditch.

All in all the event was judged a great success. The teams certainly enjoyed themselves coming as they did from every walk of equestrian life; jockeys, show jumpers, event riders, dressage riders, Hunt teams, farmer teams and army teams. In particular it made first-class television on that Good Friday morning in 1974. Within days any number of Hunts had been in touch with Douglas Bunn or other equestrian organisations with a view to arranging something similar themselves. Some of the first to follow were the Zetland Hunt in the north of England, the Pytchley Hunt in the Midlands, and in the West Country the Heythrop. These and the others that followed were all deemed highly successful. Not only did they attract large numbers of entries, but they also attracted very large crowds which made useful money for the Hunt running the event.

The difference between the Hickstead event and the others was that almost invariably the Hunt events limited the teams to four with the third home to count for time. It was felt that teams would have a problem in raising five members, though this certainly would not appear to have been the case at Hickstead which each year is over-subscribed.

There can be no doubt that this new country sport has caught on and is now very popular. Nevertheless, there are obvious risks which should be considered and are now being taken very seriously. The British Horse Society arranges informal conferences twice a year for those involved in cross-country events in order that experiences can be shared and the events improved. The main danger it would seem is always going to be speed. If this sort of event is really designed for genuine hunters, rather than one-day eventers who do the cross-country and also dressage and show jumping, then it has to be recognised that the ordinary hunter is not used to jumping fences at the speed at which these events are inevitably run, the fastest team being the winner. This obviously can lead to tired horses at the end of a course having bad falls. In an effort to ensure that the team gets home, riders feel that there is an obligation to finish whereas out hunting they would pull up.

It is absolutely vital that the fences should be well constructed because surprisingly enough it is the small, badly constructed fences that invariably produce the falls. Horses tend to ignore them or not take them seriously enough. The bold, solidly built fence will always be treated with greater respect than the flimsy fence. It is interesting to see in the Grand National, the Topham Trophy or the Foxhunters at Aintree that once a horse has realised after the first fence that the Aintree fences cannot be treated in a cavalier fashion, then they jump bigger and bolder than they jump on any other course. So it would seem to be that the better the fences are built the less falls they have at these new cross-country events.

It has been suggested that there should be a minimum weight as it would seem unfair for a young girl riding at under $10\frac{1}{2}$ st on a big horse to be competing against men. Indeed, some of the events stipulate that there must be at least one rider weighing less than so much while others stipulate that there must be one rider over such-and-such an age. The idea is always to keep the sport as amateur and natural as possible. Already, unfortunately, there is a certain professionalism creeping in and there are certain teams which will travel the length and breadth of the country to go to one of these events; indeed, it has been known for them to persuade organisers to pay their expenses to go to an event, such is the draw of the public of one of the top-class teams.

This brings us to prize money. At present there is no limitation in prize money; there could not be simply because there is as yet no official organisation responsible for the administration of these events. But it does seem questionable that a first prize of £1000 should be permissible. Presumably, the prize goes to the Hunt entering the team, if it is a Hunt, although this is not always the case as there are now more and more independent teams entering who presumably share the prize money amongst themselves. As it is not impossible for a team to be taking part in one of these events as often as once a week, both in the spring and the autumn, it can readily be appreciated that very quickly people will enter for the prize money, if prize money remains so high.

As things stand, there would be nothing to stop a team consisting of Harvey Smith, David Broome, Graham Fletcher and Paddy MacMahon, calling themselves the Show Jumpers, from entering an event. Already there are teams made up of such experienced three-day event riders as Richard Meade, Capt. Mark Phillips, Princess Anne, Hugh Thomas, Toby Sturgis. To compete against such a team presents an almost impossible task for an ordinary Hunt team, mounted on horses that far from going round Badminton have just been involved in a little genuine hunting during the winter months.

The danger is not only that this will very quickly make the sport far more professional than it was ever intended to be, but even more that it could very quickly result in the sport becoming a rival to point-to-pointing where the prize money is so strictly controlled: a rival even to eventing where the prize money is not so great and in which riders have also to perform a dressage test and complete a show jumping course, both of which involve much extra training. At present it has to be admitted that, despite the big prize money, despite the incredibly quick growth in both the popularity and the promoting of the sport, there is no real evidence of it losing its amateur appeal. This is largely due to the efforts made by the various organisers to see that the ordinary rider is still catered for, either by having novice events or by insisting on one novice being in each team. It is hoped that this will continue to be the case.

The local South Hill team taking part at the Heythrop Cross-Country Event

Above: The Hunting Farmers at the famous drop fence at the Hickstead Event, which they won

Below: A 'dressing' fence in a cross-country event, riders being penalised if they are not close together

The second danger with this new sport is the reaction of the Jockey Club. Understandably they guard very jealously their racing responsibilities. Anything that infringes on these would be quickly frowned upon. It is absolutely vital, therefore, that the element of racing in cross-country riding should be kept to as low a profile as possible. It is equally essential as I see it, that this new sport should have as little interference as possible from the Jockey Club. The less the element of racing creeps in, the better.

In 1978 Douglas Bunn introduced at Hickstead another good rule which, it is hoped, other organisers will follow. This was to insist that on two fences on the course the team had to jump together, so many seconds being added to their time for each length they were adrift. This effectively stops the 'follow my leader' technique that had been generally adopted with a 'pilot' out in front setting the pace, the rest of the team following in single file behind. Now the team cannot become too spread-eagled. Another advantage of this rule is that it tends to steady the pace and match it to the slower members of the team. There is no point in the leaders being half a field ahead if when they come to the relevant fence they have to wait for the others.

If this new sport is developed with intelligence and common sense, with the experience of those who have run such events previously shared out with the newcomers to the sport, then it is likely to grow into a sport which can give a large number of people who are never likely to ride in a point-to-point or an event a great deal of pleasure and enjoyment.

Long-Distance Riding

This is in fact the latest discipline to be introduced by the British Horse Society. The Long-Distance Riding Group came into being at the beginning of 1976 and now has a membership fast approaching 1000. The climax of the long-distance riding year is the Golden Horseshoe Ride on Exmoor which takes place each May as the climax of a number of qualifying rides held all over the country. There are also shorter rides which are organised mostly for pleasure, and there are team relay rides which have become extremely popular. Long-distance riding is certainly now of international interest, and each year an international rally of long-distance riding enthusiasts is organised somewhere in Europe. The one at Lucca, in Italy, in 1977 was particularly successful.

The Golden Horseshoe Ride is 75 miles in length. It is held over two days, and a number of stops are included for veterinary inspection.

The famous Golden Horseshoe Ride on Exmoor

The attraction of long-distance riding is very largely, as someone once put it, the excitement of hunting without jumping fences. This in fact over-simplifies it: considerable skill is needed in preparation for a long-distance ride and, during the ride itself, in timing and conserving of the horse's strength and stamina. The building-up of fitness in both horse and rider is something that is a considerable challenge. The skill involved is in timing oneself against the clock; the ability comes in meeting the veterinary requirements.

Naturally long-distance riding requires a great deal of organisation. It is fortunate that the British Horse Society has formed a group with experienced officers and a team that can provide the necessary knowledge to promote such an event. As a sport it is becoming increasingly popular, and is likely to do so as hunting becomes more difficult in many parts of the country. There is no doubt that one of its attractions is that it is being developed in a parallel manner in different parts of the world with the result that just as there is a bond between show jumpers the world over, so there is now a bond between long-distance riders.

Increasingly, people tend to specialise in long-distance riding as their particular form of equestrian sport. Indeed, they take it very seriously. People who have never been involved may think of it as something for the amateur. This is not the case at all. Before the British Horse Society accepted responsibility for long-distance riding in 1975 no less than seven horses had died in rides during the three previous years: more than had died in three-day and one-day events. It is reassuring that there have been no disasters since 1976. All of which underlines the fact that long-distance riding demands considerable skill and ability, proper organisation and a sympathetic understanding of a horse's ability.

The whole atmosphere of the long-distance ride is something very unique. I do not think that I can better convey this atmosphere than by describing my own experience in taking part in the Golden Horseshoe Ride in 1978, which I hope not only gives one the idea of the pleasure derived in riding through beautiful country, but also shows the amount of planning and organisation required.

I was fortunate in that this year the Golden Horseshoe enjoyed marvellous weather, which made it a pleasure in itself to be riding over Exmoor. But this was not just a pleasure ride. Long-distance riding, though a comparatively new equestrian activity, is taken very seriously and if one is to succeed, demands a properly professional approach.

To ride 75 miles in two days over terrain that is always varied, often rough or trappy, demands not only fitness on the part of both horse and rider, but considerable intelligence; especially when the whole distance has to be covered at a rate of something between 8 and 10 mph by those seeking gold awards. Horses do not, like cars, carry speedometers.

Some 45 riders gathered in the auction field at Exford at 8 am and were issued with combined-training-like number sheets. Groups of three or four set off at four-minute intervals.

My mount, kindly supplied by Trevor Ball, was a lightweight chestnut hunter called *Derby Express* who was 14 years old and extremely experienced.

He had had some 70 days' hunting that season and was very fit, but his manners were exemplary. He had the lightest of mouths and quite a turn of foot as I discovered on the few occasions when we could get into top gear. He was also extremely sure-footed.

At the first check-point, below Dunkery Beacon, I was introduced to Cdr Collins, the National Park Warden, who had been responsible for planning the course. He kindly suggested that I might care to ride with him, his mount being a really useful grey mare who had on the previous day become a grandmother. So, with a young friend of his, Annette, we became an extra group.

The next four miles took us through really glorious country, following a coombe flanked by towering trees, the whole area belonging to the Devon and Somerset Staghounds. There was not a cloud in the sky and every yard was a delight; on one side a mist of bluebells beneath the shade of the trees; on the other clusters of violets nestling in shy clusters on the bank; birds singing contentedly; some fine Devon cattle grazing equally contentedly; the occasional snug cottage or farm in the folds of the hills. It was a joy to be riding through such scenery.

But there was no time to linger. We had to press on to the second check-point at Pit Bridge where we were greeted with the welcome sight of my horse's owner and his wife with refreshment, both for the horse and myself.

The next leg included a long and very steep climb up to the top of the moors, a stretch on which I noticed many riders dismounted. I felt sorry for *Derby Express*, but followed the advice of my companion who told me that I would be all right as long as I followed the Exmoor custom of walking up hill and trotting down.

However, we made the third check-point where we caught up with a rider whose horse had had the misfortune to cast a shoe. Fortunately, due to good organisation, a farrier was waiting at Horner Water.

There now followed one of the most lovely parts of the ride when we followed a coombe some three miles down a wooded valley, crossing and re-crossing it.

The Atherstone Team over the first fence at Hickstead in 1978

5

This was followed by another really steep pull up to Wilmersham Common.

Here we were fortunate enough to pass quite close to a large herd of hinds: some 30 or 40 of them. A lark hovered above, as earlier a great buzzard had circled low over us.

I was enjoying every minute of it, and by the time we galloped across Exford Common, cheered on by a carefree cuckoo across the coombe, traversed without incident a bridleway which I gathered had sometimes caused trouble, and safely reached Exford, I was sorry that it was all over.

But I had also learned that to ride the full 75 miles is extremely demanding. I can only congratulate all those who completed the course, especially those who earned Golden Horseshoes. To do so is a real achievement.

Having now taken part I do feel that this new activity is fulfilling a most useful purpose in the horse world. It is giving large numbers of people who for one reason or another are not likely to event, show jump, show, point-to-point, or even hunt, the chance to indulge in something competitive that is a real challenge and something in which by one's own efforts one can demonstrably improve one's performance.

There is, moreover, an extremely pleasant atmosphere generated among the sport's competitors – serious, yet very friendly. It is a sport that is going to give people a lot of pleasure and a lot of fun, and an increasing opportunity to learn about getting horses fit.

The Golden Horseshoe Ride, the climax of the season, is exceptional in its length of 75 miles. The qualifying rides are usually 40 miles for horses over 5 years old and at least 14 hands. To win a gold medal one is expected to average between $8\frac{1}{2}$ and 10 miles an hour: by no means easy to achieve, as explained above.

Britain has come comparatively late to this sport. The most famous ride in the USA is the Trevis Cup, the horses travelling 100 miles in 24 hours to commemorate the famous Wells Fargo days. (In the late 1870s Lloyd Trevis was President of Wells Fargo.) There are also rides in Florida, North Carolina, Virginia and Vermont. The conditions are far more severe than in Britain, but it may well be that in the course of time, as we extend our courses, conditions will become equally severe in Britain.

In the USA it is generally conceded that the Arab horse is particularly suitable for this sort of event.

Australia has also long enjoyed long-distance riding with 100 miles such as the Tom Quilty Ride in the Blue Mountain country in New South Wales. In 1966 it was won by *Shalawi*, an Arab stallion ridden bareback by Gabriel Stecher. To commemorate this remarkable performance there is now a 50-mile ride held annually at Yarra Valley, near Melbourne, Victoria.

The Endurance Horse and Pony Society Surrey Competitive Ride, 1977

With virtually no hunting in Australia the popularity of this sport is not surprising and it is likely that it will be developed in more and more countries where there is no hunting. That it should succeed in Britain where there is so much hunting proves that it is fulfilling a very real need for the many people who are now taking up riding, but who have neither the money nor inclination to hunt.

Trekking

Over the last few years trekking has become very popular in Britain, having originally been practised all over the world, especially in South America. It has now become a recognised equestrian holiday with trekking centres set up all over Scotland, Wales, the West Country and the Lake District. Indeed, it is fast becoming one of Britain's major tourist attractions. No great riding ability is needed, although at some of the better centres a good guide or instructor does accompany the trekkers so that those taking part can acquire a considerable amount of useful knowledge if they wish. At the majority of centres, however, ponies or quiet, experienced, well-mannered horses are provided. The riders under escort are taken for rides over considerable long distances in very beautiful countryside. As can be imagined, a holiday such as this has the advantage not only of riding, but also of joining a community of people in much the same way as one might at a holiday camp.

Trekking centres multiplied very quickly as the idea caught on, but now they are strictly supervised and inspected. Most trekking centres can be relied upon to provide good, well-kept ponies and horses which are easily manageable. Trekking is entirely a holiday activity and should in no way be confused with long-distance riding. Most local authorities now provide lists of trekking centres within their areas. The Ponies of Britain Club has pioneered the proper inspection

Trekking on the Yorkshire Moors

Trekking in Canada

of, and provision of information about, trekking centres. The British Horse Society is also involved, which is important as it would be very easy for an inexperienced, unqualified person to set up a trekking centre with the minimum of proper supervision, providing horses and ponies either unsuitable or in poor conditions. Naturally, those taking part frequently, indeed, more often than not, have the very minimum of knowledge, and can therefore, all too literally, be taken for a ride. Fortunately, the majority of trekking centres are sound and reliable. Those intending a trekking holiday should make sure that they go to a reputable centre. They can be assured of an extremely enjoyable and interesting experience: a holiday with a difference.

The launching recently of the English Riding Holiday and Trekking Association under the joint auspices of the English Tourist Board, the Sports Council and the British Horse Society, working closely with the Ponies of Britain and the Association of British Riding Schools, can only be warmly welcomed. The idea is to provide guidance on facilities, and through proper inspection of riding schools and centres to ensure that the holidaymaker gets a square deal in such matters as welfare of horses and ponies, proper standards of safety and instruction, and good accommodation.

Trekking on Bodmin Moor

11 Imported Sports

Polo

Polo probably originated in Iran where it was known as 'chaugan', meaning a mallet. The word polo in fact comes from pulu, the Tibetan for a ball. It was in India, however, that the game developed its present character. Played by the Indian Princes it was passed on to the British in the early part of the second half of the 19th century. The British then introduced the game into the Western world in the late 1860s, largely due to the efforts of John Watson who might be called the father of English polo. Twenty years later it was introduced into America, the first famous Westchester Cup, the match between England and America, being played in 1886. The game was soon introduced into South America, particularly the Argentine for whom the game might have been invented as not only were they natural ball-game players, but they had the ideal pony in their little ranch 'crillos'. (The 14·2 hands height limit was introduced in 1899, but in 1916 this was increased to 15·3 hands.)

Considered by many to be the fastest game in the world, with the exception of ice hockey, a change of pony is needed for each 'chukka' which is only of $7\frac{1}{2}$ min duration, such is the strain on the pony, galloping as it is from beginning to end. The number of ponies needed by a serious player is therefore considerable, yet during the last decades of the 19th century and at the beginning of the 20th century polo became the 'in' equestrian sport of the summer months. Polo at Hurlingham, Ranelagh and Roehampton was an important part of the London social season.

Polo was actually included in the Olympic Games in London in 1908, but only three teams competed, two of them coming from Britain – consequently Britain won two medals for polo. Polo was again included in the first Olympic Games held after the First World War at Antwerp in 1920. Again there were only three teams, Great Britain, Spain and the USA; they finished in that order. In Paris in 1924 Britain came third out of five teams competing, and in Berlin in 1936 Britain came second out of three

Right: **HRH Prince Charles, the Prince of Wales, with Capt. Watt, taking part in the Silver Jubilee Trophy: another Royal enthusiast**

Below: **HRH Prince Philip, Duke of Edinburgh, largely responsible for polo's revival**

Fast play on the beautiful grounds at Cowdray

Aspects of play: spot the ball!

Action shots in the world's fastest game

teams competing. That was the last occasion on which polo was included in the Olympic Games. It is, however, interesting to note the number of well-known names associated with top-class polo who appeared in the various Olympic teams: names such as Humphrey Guinness, David Dornay, Fred Guest, Thomas Hitchcock, Victor Luckett and Pat Nicholls.

It was mainly in the Services, between the wars, that polo was a regularly played game: including of course the Navy, Lord Mountbatten being one of the most outstanding polo players of his generation, even more famous perhaps for his book entitled *Polo by Marco*. Shortly before the outbreak of war it was players such as Humphrey Guinness, Gerald Balding, Alec Harper, Peter Dollar and John Lakin who were the great names. After the war it was largely these players who were responsible for its revival, helped enormously by Lord Cowdray, who not only provided grounds but also frequently provided ponies. New names quickly came to the fore, in particular the Beresford brothers, Gerard Leigh, Ronald Ferguson, Archie David and, of course, the Duke of Edinburgh. Indeed, it is very largely due to the Duke of Edinburgh that polo became so popular in the late fifties and sixties. A great stimulus to the sport at that time was the annual invasion of players and ponies from Argentina. Not only did they prove to be delightful people to play with, but they brought an exciting new element to polo in this country. Equally important, they were prepared to sell their ponies at the end of the season, and this gave a very valuable infiltration of Argentinian blood into the polo ponies in Britain. Perhaps the most famous names associated with the Argentinian invasion were the Alberdi brothers, Charlie Menditeguy, Juan Carlos Harriott, John Cavanagh and Alec Mihanovitch. Players coming from the Argentine quickly instigated a fashion, teams soon following from New Zealand, Chile, Columbia, India, Jamaica and the USA. There were also the Gracida brothers from Mexico who frequently played for the Rothschild team, while also playing in England were such players of international calibre such as Sinclair Hill from Australia, the Maharajah of Jaipur, and Hanut Singh from India. Enthusiasts playing for British teams at this time included Harold Bamburg, David Brown, John Lucas, Mike Holden-White and Evelyn de Rothschild.

At the base of the whole structure of polo lies the handicap system, which was introduced by the Americans in 1909, and the tournament fixture list. The problem is not so great as regards individual handicaps, but the team handicap limits produce a good deal of argument. Generally speaking there are three levels, the low goal tournaments for teams between 0 and 8 goals, medium goal tournaments for teams up to 12 goals, and high goal tournaments for teams up to 20 goals. The problem is that if one puts up the limits one gets a better standard of polo, but if one puts them down one gets more teams. Naturally, the good players want the better polo but the less good players want as many tournaments as possible. There is also the necessary limitation in the number of entries that can be accepted for any tournament as the number of grounds is still comparatively limited: each ground is 200 × 300 yd with goals 24 ft wide. The maximum number of teams that can be accepted therefore for a knock-out competition is probably 16 and these are of course the tournaments at the big grounds such as Windsor and Cowdray. Clubs with two or three grounds can probably only accept eight, or even only four, teams. It would be a mistake to think that only the big grounds are really suitable for, and popular with, polo enthusiasts. In fact there are delightful smaller grounds such as Kirklington, Wolmers Park, Toulston, Tidworth and Cirencester; though Cirencester is probably now regarded as being in the top league.

Prince Philip is quoted as saying that there seems to be a greater opportunity in polo for dramas than in any other sport. There may be something in this, though most sports seem fraught with dramas. In polo, however, as Prince Philip points out, the team consists of only four players, therefore if one defects then a quarter of that team disappears. And if by chance that player owns most of the ponies, then the remainder of the team is in real difficulty. There is also the system of handicapping which works in the opposite way to golf. Thus, endless permutations and computations go into getting a team together which is made even more difficult when handicaps are changed in the middle of a season. Prince Philip also makes the point that since polo is a game which is played on ponies there is an additional worry and cause for drama by ponies going lame, probably through being overplayed. All of this can put a great strain on even the oldest and strongest of friendships. Having made the point that polo is a game in which wives often like to take part and are known frequently to have very firm views, both about the way their husbands and other players conduct themselves on the field, Prince Philip points out that female participation is becoming increasingly popular, though as will be remembered by those associated with polo over the years, ladies have in fact been playing for a long time.

It is particularly satisfying today that there are very real nurseries for up-and-coming young players. The Pony Club has produced leading talent even to the extent of providing British players in the Hipwood brothers, and many clubs up and down the country do a great deal to encourage young players. One of the problems facing the young player is that he is frequently forced to play in a game that is really above his standard. Club polo inevitably limits tournaments to the eight goal standard which means that in the

Polo at Cowdray

leap of a young player into the sixteen goal tournament there is almost inevitably a difficulty in adjustment, both for himself and his pony. The Stewards of the Hurlingham Polo Association have long been aware of this and in 1978 introduced a new idea. The medium goal classic tournaments remained for teams totalling 13 to 16, but there is a new group of tournaments for teams of 8 to 12; players not being allowed to play in both of these divisions of medium goal polo. This is a most interesting experiment, and one which will be carefully watched.

Today, as in so many sports, professionalism has come to stay in polo. Most polo professionals, however, have in all probability another job as well: either running a stable or a farm or even being a horse-dealer. To be a professional at polo one has to be very good indeed, and also be a brilliant horseman and something of a diplomat. For the most part, however, polo is still a game for amateurs. Most who play probably enjoy it more than anything else they do in the whole of their lives, but they do it for fun: as the well-known player Alec Harper once said, it is surely a game which should go with sunshine, champagne and lots of pretty girls. For let's face it, he said, without all that it would be for most of us a lot less fun. It is expensive because of the ponies: it can take up a lot of time. It is for most people a hobby, but then again most people who play would admit that it easily becomes an obsession. Quoting Alec Harper again, 'Professionals set a standard of play for others, and often a standard in manners, too; but if it is true that someone once said war is too serious a matter to be left to the Generals, it is probably true to say that polo is too serious a matter to be left to the professionals. At present not only in Britain, but anywhere in the world where polo is played with the possible exception of the Argentine, the balance seems just right to keep the game happy, exciting and progressive.' The Argentine of course, is a different story for, as few people appreciate, something approaching 4000 people play in the Argentine, whereas in Britain the number is more like 600: in America this number is around 1000.

Prince Charles's involvement in the game has continued the fillip that his father gave the game. Far from cheap – a schooled pony will cost at least £1000, £3 or £4 just to hire for one chukka, and £500 to keep for a season – yet as is the case with so many other equestrian sports, it is increasingly popular with most clubs in a very flourishing position, but it should certainly not be regarded as solely a rich man's sport, especially now that it is possible for pony clubs to hire out ponies for a modest fee to keen polo members.

Action at Smith's Lawn, Windsor

Gymkhanas

Every weekend all over Britain, from the early spring until the autumn, there are literally hundreds of gymkhanas being held; many thousands of children and ponies taking part. For many it is in fact probably true to say that the gymkhana is the highlight of their riding life. The gymkhana caters for the ordinary young rider who, perhaps, has not the talent nor indeed the required pony to indulge in show jumping, showing or one-day eventing: though it should be recognised that frequently the gymkhana is the schooling ground for the able young rider to be accurate and supple and quick thinking; to develop a rapport between horse and rider.

The gymkhana as the name suggests, came from India where mounted games were an energetic and an amusing adjunct to the life of a soldier. In those early days, polo ponies were the usual mounts for gymkhanas; particularly suitable because they were so handy. Mounted games have in fact been played for as long as men have been riding horses; some of the very oldest mounted games originating in South America, and the pampas ponies, who are so quick and agile, being ideal for these sports.

The gymkhana's status has been enhanced since 1957 when the Pony Club Games were introduced to the Horse of the Year Show. This was suggested by Prince Philip who felt that there must be many young people who would enjoy something rather less formal than ordinary showing. No longer is just any old pony good enough for a gymkhana: in fact during the last two decades a particular gymkhana-type pony has developed; something that is handy, obedient and quick. The particular charm about the gymkhana, from the ordinary rider's point of view, is that it is still possible to buy a comparatively cheap pony at one of the New Forest sales for instance, and develop it into a really good gymkhana pony. Obviously the gymkhana pony must never be nervous or excitable; it must be easy to break and to school and have the sort of temperament that will put up with a lot of shouting and excitement, although even the best and most experienced gymkhana pony will become somewhat excited by the atmosphere of an exciting event.

Today the proper training of the gymkhana pony is as important as the training of a show jumper. He has to learn to accept nothing stronger than a snaffle bit, going freely forward with a nice even stride, and to be properly balanced. To expect a pony to compete in gymkhana events before being properly trained is a great mistake. Indeed, a pony will soon become bewildered and unbalanced if it is hauled about in such a way that it loses confidence in itself, very quickly losing its liking for the gymkhana. Training should start at the walk, getting the pony used to every sort of hazard and all manners of objects, such as balloons, umbrellas, even washing lines. Gradually one can proceed until all these things are accepted at a full gallop. Although a gymkhana at a show is good experience, the wise gymkhana enthusiast puts in a lot of practice at home before ever taking his or her pony to a public gymkhana.

The Pony Club Games at the Horse of the Year Show have become one of the most popular features of the show, so much so that teams from the Pony Club have been invited to many other countries to take part in games staged at their shows, with the result that gymkhana events are gradually becoming popular in other countries. They are still, however, very much associated with Britain, descending as they do from the old days of the British Raj in India, with the gymkhana as the principle means of relaxation for the Cavalry.

Not surprisingly there has always been a criticism that the rough-and-ready style of riding required in a gymkhana has little or nothing to do with equitation and therefore cannot be good for young people who are not yet very experienced. Obviously children can become very rough in their handling of a pony and, regrettably, sometimes these rough methods are effective. The Pony Club is of course in a position to check any rough riding in its members though it has been known for a Pony Club, unfortunately, to encourage rough riding in its determination to qualify for the Prince Philip Cup. By and large, however, rough treatment of ponies can be controlled, and usually is, by vigilant gymkhana judges. It is also a fact that frequently ponies roughly and harshly treated will lose their zest for entering gymkhanas and so will be abandoned as potential gymkhana ponies.

It is on the whole generally accepted today that the gymkhana can do nothing but good for young children and although it is principally for fun it nevertheless has a genuine equitation value because it helps to make a rider independent; the independent

One of the new games at an early round of the Prince Philip Cup – with a useful bit of advertising thrown in

Lap of honour for the winners in the final of the Horse of the Year Show: the Eglinton

seat being the vital quality in all forms of equitation. Over the years many amusing, testing and interesting games have been devised for the Pony Club and it is worth describing some of these.

Team Relay Bending Race

A relay race in which the riders have to weave round a line of bending posts.

The Potato Picking Scramble

The riders have to collect potatoes, one at a time, from the centre of the arena and drop them into their team's buckets. Two members of each team ride for a stated time, followed by the other two members of each team. The team which collects the greatest number of potatoes in the time allowed is the winner.

The Sack Race

No. 1 has to ride to the centre lines, dismount, get into a sack, lead his pony to No. 2 at the other end of the arena and hand the sack to him. No. 2 has to gallop to the centre line carrying the sack, dismount, get into the sack and lead his pony to No. 3. Similarly No. 3 and then No. 4 have to complete the course. The winning team is the one whose No. 4 is first past the finish in the sack and leading his pony.

Uncle Tom Cobley Stakes

No. 1, carrying a pint pot, rides bareback round bending posts to the end of the arena where he picks up No. 2 on to his pony and they both ride back to the start. Here they hand the pint pot to No. 3 who similarly rides to pick up No. 4. The winning team is the one whose No. 3 and No. 4 are first past the finish, mounted and carrying the pint pot.

Sword Race

On the signal to start, the first member of each team gallops to one of the posts, picks up the ring on his sword, gallops on and passes the sword to the second member of the team. Each member of the team completes the course in the same way, up and down the arena successively. When the fourth member crosses the finishing line he must have all four rings on his sword.

Sharpshooters' Race

The riders are mounted bareback, two on each pony. They ride to the centre line where one rider from each pair dismounts and shies at Aunt Sallys until their heads are broken. The riders then remount and gallop back to the start. The winning team is the one whose two pairs are first past the finishing line.

Stepping Stone Dash

In this event the competitor has to ride to the centre line, jump off and dash across six stepping stones leading his pony. He must be back in the saddle before he crosses the finishing line and hands over to the next member of the team.

Over 150 teams enter for the Mounted Games Championship, some six teams finally qualifying for the finals at the Horse of the Year Show at Wembley.

Mounted Games (Gymkhana) flat out at the Horse of the Year Show, 1978

Hearing the tremendous applause and excitement generated by these games it is hard to believe they started in Britain just as something of a side-line run at the end of a small country show after most people had gone home. It is very much thanks to the Pony Club itself that the gymkhana has remained well organised and properly controlled. It could so easily have got out of hand, in which case it could very quickly have become a sport that could well be detrimental, both to the ponies themselves and also to the good of riding generally.

Perhaps one of the most fascinating and indeed charming aspects of riding today is that it absorbs so many different interests and approaches, from Grand Prix Dressage to the gymkhana. For each participant there is a different level of enjoyment, and something that is enjoyable to one is often far from being enjoyment to another. It is all these different interests and activities that add up to make riding the remarkably complex comprehensive scene that it has become today.

It is significant and interesting that the success and popularity of these imported sports should each owe so much to the enthusiasm and inspiration of Prince Philip. It is, surely a tribute to his breadth of interests and ever open mind.

PART FOUR
National and International Riding Centres

12 The British National Equestrian Centre

The British National Equestrian Centre only came into being in 1967. For many years both the British Horse Society and the British Show Jumping Association had been organised from offices in London. In the early 1960s it was decided to consider the possibility of a move to the countryside, and in 1965 a decision was taken to accept the offer of a site on the showground of the Royal Agricultural Society of England at Stoneleigh in Warwickshire. The problem was to finance the enterprise. The availability of a certain amount of money would be available from the sale of the lease of the British Horse Society's offices at Bedford Square, but it was finally decided that it was better to get the landlord's permission to sub-let thus ensuring a certain income for the years remaining in the lease. The money needed to build the offices and the school was eventually raised as follows: 50 per cent through a grant from the Sports Council, £30 000 raised by 300 Founder Members who each subscribed £100, the remainder through loans from the British Show Jumping Association and the widow of a senior member of one of the Societies: the total came to about £120 000.

In 1967 the National Equestrian Centre was opened, immediately attracting a great deal of support and a certain amount of comment, some of which was inevitably critical. There were, as were to be expected, certain teething troubles, but not only were most of these ironed out during the first years of the centre's existence but it achieved the remarkable in paying its way. This was largely due to the very hard work of a small and regrettably underpaid staff which I was fortunate enough to have working for me as Chairman and Director; and also to the very full usage of the school which was considered both exceptionally functional and refreshingly modern in its amenities. Refinements had been made possible by generous donations in kind – for instance, each Pony Club gave a seat to provide the seats in the gallery with some 400 seats – resulting in a number of certain sophisticated special features. These included the Whitbread Lounge where the bar was situated, the Horse and Hound Library, the Martini Lecture Room, the Margolin First Aid Room and the Diamond Bar – an overflow bar only used on special occasions and now converted to an extra lecture room or conference room. In addition some 25 or 30 firms took display stands in the long gallery at the entrance to the school; the different Breed Societies mounted blown-up pictures of their own particular breed to form a frieze under the gallery; Spillers provided a full length mirror at the side of the school, and a VIP gallery was provided by my father, my stepmother, my wife and myself intended as appreciation of the part my father had played in building up both the British Horse Society and the British Show Jumping Association. The trustees of the Stoneleigh estate made available the land for a cross-country course and cross-country practice area; the Royal Agricultural Society made available a jumping arena. During the last ten years a new stable block has been added, generously provided by the Worshipful Company of Saddlers; a Hostel, donated by Sir Hugh Fraser; a farriery; a second indoor school; additional stabling made available by the Royal Agricultural Society in the form of some 60 new boxes, and various other refinements.

In a material sense, therefore, Stoneleigh is more than adequate for a national centre and can certainly compare with the less well-endowed national centres throughout the world; but there are inherent disadvantages. Firstly, the site is not independent in that it is part of a much larger site and it is therefore not easy for the National Centre to have an identity of its own, though this is increasingly being overcome as, thanks to the cooperation of the Royal Agricultural Society, more and more is being made available to the National Equestrian Centre. Secondly, the Centre lacks a full-time national coach of such calibre that his doctrine and policy are accepted throughout the riding world in Britain. Since the beginning the National Equestrian Centre at Stoneleigh has been fortunate in having three first-class national instructors; the first was Col. W. Froud, the second was Hilary Payne and the third was Maj. Monty Mortimer, but admirable as each of these was in his or her own respect much of their time was of necessity taken up travelling all over the country organising courses. In addition, the riding world in Britain being what it is, none of them was accepted as of sufficient calibre to be able to dictate to all the other instructors in this country. Indeed, one is tempted to say that it would be difficult to find anyone in the whole world who would be considered entirely acceptable. It may be that at the very beginning those responsible should have appointed some equestrian personality, either from home or overseas, as the national instructor, backed him to the hilt, accepting the inevitable criticism that would come from many sources, but disregarding it in the hope that in the end their confidence in their choice would have been justified: gradually an accept-

Above: The front of the British Equestrian Centre offices

Below: The Indoor School

Top: Entrance to the Saddlers' Stables

Bottom: The new RASE boxes

able doctrine – acceptable to everybody – would have been satisfactorily established. I am inclined to think that this would never have been more than a pious hope.

Since the closing of the famous Cavalry School at Weedon there has been no accepted style or standard of equitation. Gradually the Weedon products have died out. Nevertheless, down the years certain firm precepts have been accepted, it generally being agreed that the one who perhaps contributed most was my father, Col. V. D. S. Williams, who was in the opinion of Col. Handler, the late Commandant of the Spanish Riding School of Vienna, 'the one who has so long been successfully the pioneer behind all the activities of the British horse world and its progress'. Col. Handler's own predecessor, Col. Alois Podhajsky, referred to my father as the one who is entirely responsible for the development of dressage in England and to whom England owes an undying debt. He was, in fact, responsible soon after the war for founding the St George's School at Winkfield which it was hoped might become the national centre. Unfortunately, it was ahead of its time and unable therefore to muster the necessary funds and support, lasting only a few years.

It may be relevant to set out the precepts that were produced by my father and his fellow administrators at St George's in the late forties, as these are the precepts which have been followed in British equitation ever since:

'The purpose of training a horse is to be able to go where one wants, and how one wants, with a minimum of exertion and effort on the part of the rider and with a maximum of ease and, therefore, of preservation on the part of the horse.

The degree of training depends on the end which the rider wishes to obtain and the work that he requires from his horse. For example, the military horse must be trained to carry different riders under a variety of circumstances; they must go in formation or singly; they must be able to carry a heavy weight for many hours and they must be able to go across country. For economic reasons they must be trained so that they will give useful service for as many years as possible. With the hunter, however, the main thing most people require is that he should be able to gallop and jump; that he should have courage and constitution. The former, therefore, must go through a course of physical and mental training, whereas with the latter it is more a development of innate qualities than actual training that is required.

The high school rider wishes to train his horse to do all the classical school movements in complete harmony between horse and rider, whereas the circus rider wishes to show to a public that does not understand too much about riding a number of effective and brilliant tricks and movements.

The Whitbread Room

Background of pictures of British Pony Breeds at the side of the school

The former (the high school horse) can only be obtained by a comprehensive course of training, whereas the latter (the circus horse) can be obtained much more quickly by artificial movements which, for the sake of sheer display, sacrifice that harmony between horse and rider which is so essential in the former. But no matter what the destination, where time and good riders are available, a proper course of training can only be of advantage to the horse, besides proving a great source of pleasure to its eventual owner. On the other hand, if the training is done in haste and by riders who do not understand what they are doing, more harm than good is done.

Before discussing the training of the horse, it is necessary to discuss the training of the rider. In the practical teaching of riding a number of important problems cannot be handled owing to lack of opportunity. Yet it is important for the pupil to understand these problems in order that he may understand the difference between theory and practice and avoid the difficulties that arise from trying to obtain the impossible from himself and his horse.

The Correct Seat

The three principles of a good seat are: balance, looseness and the ability to follow the movements of the horse. To tell the rider how to hold his limbs or to copy a stereotyped seat is inclined to lead to stiffness, which is the one fault which we wish to avoid. Nevertheless, the rider must sit well down in the lowest part of his saddle with the weight of his body resting vertically on two pelvic bones and the fork – the three points of support. The seat should be maintained chiefly by balance, grip only being resorted to when balance is lost, or to prevent the loss of balance. Arms and legs have nothing to do with balance and should be left free so that they can apply the aids correctly.

Exercises for Bracing the Back

In foreign schools great importance is paid to the use of back muscles. The correct use of the back muscles must be thoroughly understood: it is just the reverse of sticking out the buttocks and hollowing the back. On a swing the back is braced for the forward swing and slackened for the backward swing. If you sit on a chair, leaning against the back, you can slide your buttocks forward by bracing the back. If you straddle a stool and sit right on the edge, you can tilt it forward by bracing the back muscles, but to do this, the legs from the knee downwards must be behind the perpendicular and to the sides.

Bracing the Back on Horseback

The same movement as practised on the ground must now be practised on the horse's back. It is essential for the rider to thoroughly understand this movement in order to be able to stick to his horse – sit down in the saddle – following the movements of the horse – and "feel".

Feel

From the beginning, the rider must be taught to "feel" the movements of his horse with his seat. When the horse stands unevenly on his hind legs, the rider shifts in order to lever himself up. He must be taught to realise why. Trotting on different diagonals is a good exercise in feeling.

The Centre of Gravity

The rider must always keep his centre of gravity directly over that of his horse. By this the rider is able to control the movements of his horse with as little exertion as possible and the horse is best able to deal with the rider's weight. A good example of this: the porter easily carries the heavy trunk on his shoulders when its centre of gravity is directly above that of his own. The law of balance can best be explained in terms of a juggler. When he stands still he holds his staff vertically, when he moves forward he inclines the staff forward and the faster he moves the more he inclines it.

The Balanced Seat

When the horse moves forward the rider must move his centre of gravity forward so as to remain in balance. At the same time he must maintain his seat on the three points of support. To combine these two movements is difficult: if the rider leans his trunk forward he must raise his pelvic bones from the saddle. The critical moment is at the beginning of the movement, when there is a danger of being left behind.

If the principle of bracing the back is adhered to, the rider presses his horse forward by pushing his buttocks and, therefore, his whole centre of gravity forward. The result is a very close contact with the horse and the rider avoids being left behind or raising his pelvic bones from the saddle.

As the pace increases, the difficulty of maintaining both the seat of the three points of support and the centre of gravity in harmony with that of the horse increases, until in the extended trot the rider is forced to "post" and in the gallop the rider abandons his seat in the seat and takes his support on the knees and stirrups, resting his hands on his horse's neck.

Position of the Hands

Generally too much importance is paid to the position of the hands. The movement which the hands execute in order to give the aids should be slight and be confined to almost imperceptible twists of the wrists. All aids, even those for turning, should mainly emanate from the seat. It is utterly wrong to attempt any change of direction by the reins alone. This is driving not riding.'

These simple precepts, agreeably free from technical jargon and pedantry, form the basis of the British style of riding.

It would be idle to pretend that all interested in equitation in Britain accept such a simple, straightforward doctrine. Indeed a characteristic of British equestrianism is the amount of independence and individuality. There is, in fact, no proven right way and wrong way in the techniques of riding. For some, one method will work, for others another, but it is generally agreed that what one might term the common denominators are the points contained in the above, which are in the official manuals of both the British Horse Society and the Pony Club.

Finance is the other problem, proving over the years to be a handicap that could ultimately prevent Britain, for so long a front runner in the world of equitation, especially in the competitive field, from maintaining a standard equal to that of other nations who are fortunate enough to enjoy heavily subsidised national centres. It may be that in due course sufficient funds will be forthcoming, either directly from the Government or by the Sports Council, to enable Britain to run a viable centre. At present Stoneleigh has to be content with the Sports Council grants for instructors and development officers, but must find the running expenses of the centre through its own efforts and resources. Fortunately, money has been available for essential capital expenditure, indeed, the Sports Council itself has been most generous in its contribution, usually amounting to 50 per cent of the cost of each project. But if a national centre is to be national in every sense of the word, providing a service for all riders at all levels all over the country, then obviously the cost is going to be a great deal more than the British Horse Society is ever going to be able to provide itself, even with the help of the British Show Jumping Association, now limited to some £2500 a year.

Perhaps the greatest lack is the absence of horses owned by the centre. In any serious instruction it is vital for the instructor to be able to provide different horses for a rider on which to learn. Firstly, this is because a rider needs to experience the difference in riding different horses and secondly, because a rider can only learn the best by riding the best horse. In other words, a trained horse is an adjunct to training; it will be seen that many national centres were in a position to provide students with three or four horses each. In Britain, however, not only is there not the money available to buy good school horses of different levels, sound and temperamentally right for the sort of work that would be expected of them, but, an equally real problem, there is not the money to provide their keep. At Stoneleigh the problem is to a certain extent, but only in a very minor way, being overcome by the employment of students or working pupils who bring their own horses with them. This means that at least the working students have the opportunity to ride each other's horses, thus getting the experience of riding different kinds of horses, but understandably it is not possible to make available to all the students at all the different courses at Stoneleigh the working pupils' own horses. The tendency, therefore, is to give instruction to students on their own horses. This is valuable in so far as it goes, but the student would learn a great deal more if he were able to ride strange horses, thus learning how to get the best performance out of a horse with which he is not familiar and which is not familiar with him.

The Riding Foundation has already been mentioned; it is hoped that funds raised by the Foundation will be made available to improve the amenities at the National Equestrian Centre; the amenities, of course, including the provision of horses. Other projects are also in hand to increase the Centre's income. In 1978 a lottery was started which, if and when it gets going and proves successful, could well provide the Centre with a sum of money each year of anything between £15000 and £50000; though probably one should accept the fact that this could well be comparatively short-lived in that the popularity of a lottery may not last.

In Britain every horse show in the country gives a percentage of its prize money to the Olympic Fund. With some 2000 to 3000 horse shows in the country and with the prize money increasingly large a very considerable sum is realised in this way. Shows do not complain of this levy because the organisers are fully aware that the best stimulus to show jumping in this country, or in any other country, is for British riders to have international success. They are therefore glad to support the Olympic Fund knowing that they will indirectly benefit. It could be said, however, that the time is coming when our riders will not succeed internationally because there is not a sound thriving national centre as in other countries, and that therefore it could be argued that just as a small percentage of all prize money should go to the Olympic Fund so a small percentage of all prize money should go to the Foundation, or the Fund responsible for maintaining the National Centre. This already happens in many countries with the result that they are inevitably far better off financially than Britain. (The best example is the ten pfennig levy in Germany.)

It would be a mistake to paint too gloomy a picture of the prospects of the National Equestrian Centre in Britain for, in fact, in the few years since it was started in 1967 it has made quite extraordinary progress. More important, perhaps, is the fact that its existence has without any doubt enormously increased the membership of the British Horse Society. If this could be increased still further then the additional income through the membership of the Society would go a long way to solving the financial difficulties of the Centre. Having visited many, if not most, of the national centres in Europe I have little hesitation in saying that the British National Equestrian Centre at Stoneleigh has a potential equal to most centres, particularly in the activity and atmosphere: that is, student usage and public interest. Obviously Stoneleigh can never rival Saumur or Warendorf, let alone Vienna, in the purely physical sense, but Stoneleigh puts on a variety of courses that might well be the envy of other countries. Not only are almost all the courses fully attended, but many of them also attract a full house of spectators. Indeed, when the Centre is fortunate enough to present a world famous expert such as de Nemethy, Bachinger, Boldt or Klinke, then there is no difficulty whatever in selling every available seat for upwards of £3.

There are still varieties of approach, almost endless differences in method. Each country brings to its training programme slightly and subtly different techniques and doctrines; yet frequently these differing methods and doctrines appear to achieve virtually identical results: all of which only underlines the fact that the horse is the most remarkable of animals in that it adapts itself to the rider whatever the style of the rider might be. The horse is always anxious to learn and is prepared to do so by almost any method. Different experts will produce different theories, each one convinced that his theory is right. One day it may be universally agreed just what those basic common denominators are; and one day, possibly, there will be general agreement as to what is the most successful way of developing from those basic principles. One cannot help feeling, however, with the accepted independence of all who train horses that that day is still a long way off. Meanwhile, each country through its national centre is developing its own doctrine, spending more and more time and money on experiment and research. At this stage who is to say that one doctrine is more successful, let alone more correct, than another? The following chapter outlines detail and comparison of some of the leading international riding centres.

13 International Riding Centres

Austria

Obviously the riding school situation in Austria is dominated by the famous **Spanish Riding School** in Vienna. This is a unique tradition that has existed for some 300 years providing the highest form of equitation in the world, with its concentration on *haute école*. It is possible for a limited number of students from outside Austria to be accepted for a year's training at the school, but it is only very few people who are fortunate enough to have the opportunity of going to Vienna. However, such is the influence of those students who have been that many others are gaining an indirect benefit, and members of the school itself, such as Ernst Bachinger, are also now holding courses at certain times of the year in other countries.

So many books have been written about the Spanish Riding School in Vienna that it would be superfluous to go into very much detail. Suffice it to say that the magnificent, baroque palace, designed by Emanuel von Erlach with its crimson and gold, its magnificent royal box and its superb chandeliers, creates a splendid atmosphere in which both the schooling and performances take place, and which are open to the public. The schooling exercises are of the greatest fascination, giving the spectator an idea of the years of patient training required to bring these famous Lippizaner stallions to their remarkable standard in high school movements. Only Lippizaners, from the stud at Piber, are used and except for the odd brown or bay, traditionally part of the performance, they are all grey. Strong, sturdy, with short legs and possessing ideal temperaments, they are seldom more than 15 hands.

France

Since 1969 **Saumur** has become the official national institute of education. The famous Cadre Noir – the French equivalent to the Spanish Riding School display – is still the centre of it, and in conjunction with the French Equestrian Federation does much to ensure that the famous spirit, tradition and expertise associated with Saumur for over 200 years survive. The transitional stage during which the military establishment developed into the national centre has been carried out smoothly and efficiently. The role of the famous Cadre itself has naturally changed under the new organisation, it now being the instructors of the overall committee who teach the students and the potential instructors while the Cadre acts as a consultant body and is responsible for public displays. For the Cadre Noir there is a rigorous training programme. The Écuyer en Chef is responsible for the instruction of the Écuyers for one hour each morning after which they work on their own, each officer having four horses. A senior Écuyer is responsible for the training of the Maîtres and Sous Maîtres who also have four horses each.

The Cadre Noir, Saumur, France

For the civilian students the programme is rather different, being drawn up by the office of instruction made up of the two Écuyers responsible for the training facilities. Courses for civilians start in October, the instructors certificate being awarded in July. The course is not very different from that for the military instructors, consisting of:

1 improving the seat and balance through use of cavalletti, jumping without reins, riding with and without stirrups;
2 two-track work, basic dressage;
3 jumping instruction, riding over fences, studying combinations, work on the flat; and
4 competitive work.

Each of the four horses is at a different stage in its training and is used for the four different levels of instruction. Students are also expected to teach a class. In addition, of course, there are conferences and lectures.

There are also eight refresher courses held each year, each lasting twelve days and attended by ten students. Again each student has four horses at his disposal and three full-time instructors. Finally, there are a number of dressage courses for six students at a time.

The set-up at Saumur is very fine with stabling for 450 horses and accommodation for 50 civilian students. There are three open arenas for dressage and show jumping as well as two exercise grounds and a show jumping arena, a cross-country course and a 500-metre steeplechase course. Sited by the Loire in delightful country, Saumur is entirely financed by different ministries of the French Government; namely the Army, Agriculture, Education and Sport: responsible, also, for breeding activities in studs all over France. This, understandably, is an enormous benefit to riding, with the not surprising result that France is once again gaining eminence in the international competitive field.

Though now a civilian centre the basic doctrine and present methods of training at Saumur are founded on and developed from the original teaching there in the 18th and 19th centuries when it was considered to be the leading military academy of equitation in Europe. Its particular advantage over other national centres is the very generous subsidy it gets from the Government. It probably amounts to over £7 million a year.

Germany

Not surprisingly Germany has the most thorough and in many ways the most sophisticated of all the national riding centres in Europe. In fact there are three centres or schools in Warendorf, a small town near Münster in Westphalia, a flat but not particularly beautiful area with large coniferous forests and wide stretches of pasture land creating opportunities for dairy and beef farming on a large scale and also for horse breeding which has long been Westphalia's greatest tradition. Warendorf was therefore a natural choice for a national centre.

The oldest of the three schools is the **Deutsche Reitschule** (the national riding school); the second is the **Military Riding Academy** occupying a barracks with stables and training facilities used at one time for the training of Olympic teams; the third school is the new **Olympic school** which was produced after the army had taken over the old school in the 1960s. West Germany is probably the only nation in Europe that has had the foresight to build a special training school for potential Olympic riders, while it has at the same time developed a national riding school devoted to improving the standard of riding generally, but more important, to produce top-class instructors. This is a policy which has surely paid off as is evidenced by the success of West German riders in all three disciplines – dressage, show jumping and eventing.

The Deutsch Reitschule is situated near the centre of Warendorf with stabling and offices which are partly modern, but also include old buildings that were allegedly once part of a monastery. Somewhat austere brick buildings flank the manèges but these give the school an air of permanence and dignity. The facilities for schooling are spacious with a sand manège, a covered area for schooling horses on the lunge, and an outside show jumping ring. There is also a parade ground, a cross-country course and, some way off, tracks for hacking facilities. The Director of the school is Gunther Festerling, a man of considerable vision and great ability with a reputation that extends far beyond the boundaries of Germany. In the academic area there are well-equipped classrooms with models illustrating anatomy, all types of show jumping fences, course design and modern visual aids. The larger indoor school is 25 × 85 m with a grandstand for spectators. In addition to the stallions which are traditionally housed here there are between 50 and 70 horses accommodated in 19th century stabling which is first-rate with lofty ceilings and spacious centre aisles. The loose boxes are constructed of heavy timber with iron railings. Although a little old-fashioned in appearance everything is spotlessly clean.

The national school does not specialise in any one particular branch of equestrianism, its main goal being to produce instructors trained equally well in all subjects. Instruction revolves round comparatively short courses lasting between two and eight weeks for students who come from every background. The only level that is not catered for at Warendorf is children.

The Olympic school is separate. The Head of the Olympic school is Alfonso Doneckhoff who has three senior instructors under him, one for each of the three main disciplines. Herr Brinkmann is chief instructor for show jumping and is perhaps the best known show jumping course designer in the world today. For eventing the chief instructor is Herr Habble. The third instructor is a visiting teacher for dressage who usually comes from Vienna. In all there is a staff of about 15 which, considering that only the top 20 riders or so in the main elements of competitive riding are eligible for the school, is a remarkably, and indeed enviably, high ratio of staff to students. The Olympic school runs properly organised courses only in the autumn and for the rest of the year students come in all groups with their own horses to courses lasting three or four weeks.

Entrance to the Olympic School, Warendorf

There is stabling for 43 horses at the Olympic school, the majority of which belong to the riders or to the West German Federation. The large indoor school has seating for 300 spectators with sophisticated lighting, an excellent sprinkler system and windows which are opened and closed by remote control. The stables are all on ground-floor level, some of the horses being entirely indoors, and have sliding doors with metal bars forming the top half and dividing walls with non-slip tiled floors leading to small, but well designed, tack rooms. The stables are surrounded by attractive lawns and paddocks backing on to woodlands; hostel accommodation is available in the complex. At the Olympic school there are also first-class facilities for outdoor training with a large dressage manège, grassed areas for show jumping with a great variety of fences and an event training course all accommodated in one large paddock with artificially constructed slopes and gradients. In this there is a formidable array of practice fences of the Coffin and Normandy Bank variety, with spreads and drops and water jumps.

At the National school some 60 horses are provided by the Government. The vital personality, as far as the National school is concerned, is Dr Specht who is a man of great energy and a brilliant administrator. His specification for a typical programme at Warendorf suggests that a candidate for an examination to be an amateur instructor must be 19 years old, have acquired a third-class groom's medal of the German Horse Society, and had sound basic training. The medal proves that he has the ability to ride dressage or take a jumping test with good results. The student is also expected to have taken part in more than one preparatory course before he comes to take the examination. These preparatory courses are held at schools all over Germany.

In the examination the rider has to prove his ability to ride dressage up to elementary standard, to pass a jumping test up to Class A standard and must be able to give a lesson in which he teaches one or more riders both dressage and jumping. He is also expected to be able to lunge correctly and take part in something that is very popular in Germany – equestrian acrobatics. He also has to take a theoretical examination showing that he understands the science of riding, of horse-management and of grooming. A certain veterinary knowledge is also required and he must be fully familiar with the whole organisation of riding in Germany.

For a training centre to be recognised in Germany it must have an indoor riding school of at least 20×40 m and a properly equipped outside school. To become a professional rider a student takes a course that lasts three years with examinations at the end of each year. The training programme is specifically approved by the Government.

The source of finance for Warendorf is particularly interesting: a levy of 10 pfennigs is taken from everyone attending any horse show or equestrian event in Germany. This amounts to some £50000 per annum. There is also direct Government support and as has already been stated horses are supplied by the Government. The result of this is that there is a steadily increasing number of people taking up riding seriously in Germany, probably today 250000 come from all sections of the community since personal wealth is not necessary for a person to become a professional rider.

As one would expect, the whole structure of riding instruction in Germany is highly and efficiently organised: indeed, Warendorf with its three separate national establishments must be the envy of the horse world.

Holland

Not so very long ago the **National Riding School** was opened at Deurne, north of Brabant, in an area where there is a flat stretch of moors and woods not far from the outskirts of Eindhoven. It has typical Dutch charm and is essentially practical and functional rather than beautiful or exotic. Nevertheless, the buildings themselves have a pleasing unity and although utilitarian in design have a certain aesthetic appeal. The school took eighteen months to be built and was officially opened in July 1969 by Prince Bernhard of the Netherlands. The running costs at Deurne are about £250 per pupil per month, for which the pupil can keep his horse and himself at the school. Of this sum the pupil pays about £25 per week, the rest coming from the Government where it is raised by a levy on gambling. This Government support certainly sounds generous, but the general opinion in equestrian circles in Holland is that it is still not enough to allow less well-off people to attend the school. The school has no horses of its own, the students being compelled to bring their own. Attached to the school are four instructors and two veterinary surgeons. In addition to courses in straightforward equitation, courses are held in the management of riding schools, book-keeping, veterinary work and stable management, all of which creates an excellent comprehensive programme. In all, including the part-time teachers, there are some ten instructors but no grooms since students take care of their own horses.

Students are expected to stay for one year, there being an average of 35 full-time pupils. Before being accepted a pupil has to have had one year of practice in a riding school and must be 18 years old. The first part of the course lasts three months and is followed by a further nine months at a riding school anywhere in Holland for practical experience. A second three months at the centre brings the young student to the level of assistant instructor. This is followed by a further period of nine months of practical work at an outside riding school. The student then returns to the centre for the Instructor Third Class qualification, which involves book-keeping, etc. Only the most talented people in this final phase are selected to stay at the centre for a further year for the Instructor Second Class certificate. To reach the Instructor First Class certificate the course extends to five years.

The main feature of the whole complex is the spacious, airy indoor school, which is 65 × 25 m. It is cleverly designed to ensure good shadow-free lighting and has a gallery which runs the full length of the school where more than 200 spectators can be comfortably accommodated. The bar at the top end, not unlike the Whitbread Room at the British Equestrian Centre at Stoneleigh, overlooks the school and includes a self-service cafeteria. The hostel and stables block are physically attached to the school and are both well-equipped, cleverly designed and give the impression of cleanliness and being properly functional, eg the stables have non-slip floors. In all there are 46 boxes, all of them of generous proportions. The inspiration behind Deurne has been Col. Schummelketel who showed enormous determination at the beginning when it was not easy to get the plan accepted or, having been accepted, to get it started, many people believing that it was not wholly necessary. The present Director is Tjeerd Velstra, 38 years old and an ex-international show jumper and the winner of the 1978 International Driving Event at Windsor. Thanks to Government support it has now been firmly established. It is noticeable that there has been an overall improvement in Dutch equitation during recent years and this is without doubt due to the fact that there is an increasing reservoir of good young riders becoming available for international competition. It is significant that as well as winning the Team event in the European Show Jumping Championship in 1977 they were also first and second in the Individual.

In addition to the school and the dressage manèges, there is a well designed cross-country course in the surrounding woodlands with a great variety of fences. This is not only used for training purposes, but also for the first-class one-day and three-day events organised at Deurne.

There appears to be a greater similarity between Deurne and the British National Equestrian Centre at Stoneleigh than any other national centre. This is largely because both at Deurne and at Stoneleigh it has been necessary to start from scratch with a minimum of Government support and a need for immense enthusiasm, even dedication, on the part of those who have brought the centres into existence. It would appear that the Dutch enthusiasm and dedication has been rewarded.

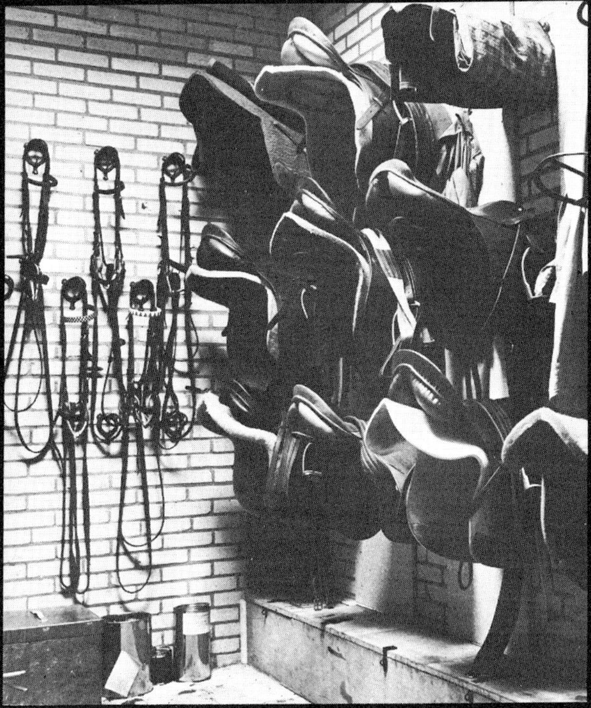

Above: Col. Schummelketel, the Founder, greeting the first course

Left: A model tack room

Below: An unusual hack

Ireland

As yet there is no national centre in Ireland, but there is an increasing number of good schools which have an international as well as national flavour. The most famous of these is **Burton Hall** which was started after the war by Col. Joe Dudgeon. He was assisted in the early fifties and sixties by an outstanding horsewoman with a most competent teaching ability, Penny Morton, who was succeeded by Sylvia Stanier. On the death of Col. Joe Dudgeon the school was taken over by his son, Ian, and in 1973 moved to a property some 20 miles outside Dublin in County Meath near the famous Fairyhouse racecourse. There are excellent amenities, with a large indoor school 60 × 25 m, a good outdoor arena, jumping paddock and cross-country course. There are more than 20 loose boxes in an excellent stable yard, some 20 horses and ponies being kept for pupils; horses are also being taken at livery.

Burton Hall has always had a strong link with America and many of the students attending come from the USA. The aims of the school are to give a really thorough basic grounding in equitation on the lines originally laid down by Col. Dudgeon. Pupils are prepared for the various British Horse Society's examinations and there is a concentration, not surprisingly, on show jumping. However, there is also a high level of training in dressage which is made possible by the fact that the pupils are learning on well-trained animals, which must always be a vital aspect of teaching. The rider is always going to learn far more if he is riding a properly trained horse.

The Irish themselves would be the first to admit that Burton Hall is very different to the Spanish Riding School of Vienna, Saumur, Warendorf or Strömsholm, but it has an important part to play and is, perhaps, better suited to the Irish and the Irish temperament than the other schools mentioned. Vienna caters for the specialist in one particular aspect of equestrianism, but Burton Hall is being developed in a simple and unsophisticated way to cater for the ordinary rider who, nevertheless, wants to improve his equitation. It is the all-round horseman that Burton Hall is trying to produce. There can be little doubt that the improved performances in the international field by Irish riders is largely due to the policies of Burton Hall and other progressive establishments in Ireland today.

Italy

Italy has never had a national centre as such. It is also probably true to say that of all the countries in Europe, riding in Italy still tends to be somewhat exclusive, although these two facts do not necessarily have a bearing on each other. The various riding establishments are, nevertheless, for the most part for well-to-do people. The equestrian sport in Italy is, however, generally sponsored and subsidised by the Government and this is largely due, in all probability, to the international reputation of the d'Inzeo brothers, and to the success that Italian three-day event riders had during the sixties.

The inflatable tent that makes an additional riding school at Castellazzo, Italy

The **Centro Ippico di Castellazzo**, run by Graziano Mancinelli just outside Milan, is the nearest approach to a national centre. Situated on the family estate of the President, Donna Cravelli's mother, Guistina di Agliate, it is extremely beautiful with a concrete and timber façade, flowering and climbing plants creeping up the walls, and two first-class indoor schools which also house a gallery, bar and restaurant. There is good stabling within the complex, and a few hundred yards away a club house which boasts over 200 members, who have use of the indoor schools. One of these is 30 × 60 m, the other 40 × 20 m, and in the winter when most of the riding takes place a third arena is added in the form of an inflated tent. There is also an outdoor area with a sand surface, a good supply of easily portable fences and a cross-country course with what are now regarded as standard obstacles – coffin, banks, timber and brush fences; though due to lack of usage these are in a certain state of neglect: indeed, it is difficult to realise that this was the site of the Italian Jumping Derby which took place in 1969. There are over 80 boxes, all filled by horses belonging to the Club or to members who pay in excess of £80 a month for livery and use of the various facilities which includes the use of a blacksmith who is permanently in attendance. The members pay an annual subscription of £100 and the Centre is entirely financially independent.

There is a full-time director, Dr Gian Boverie, a full-time instructor, Guiliano Fantarelli, and a staff of 30 grooms. The stables are extremely well kept. Young riders are particularly well catered for, their special instructor being Mario Tome.

The style of Mancinelli himself, which many international riders criticise for its over acrobatic tendency, obviously has a considerable influence on the way the young students ride, but according to Dr Boverie any over-activity on the part of Mancinelli is counteracted by his remarkable sensitivity with the horse, his patience and his ability to obtain the maximum possible from any horse that he rides. The principle at Castellazzo is very much to concentrate on work on the ground. They do not do much training over permanent fences and believe that it takes at least four, possibly five years to bring a promising pupil up to international standard. Their main precept, an interesting one, is that the horse is never wrong, only the rider. Moreover, no one is ever allowed to thrash a horse or to be cruel in any other way.

As is the case with other countries, Italy is very short of top class instructors. In an attempt to solve this problem the National Equestrian Federation in Italy attempted to start a top class training school in Rome, but this project unfortunately never got off the ground. There are no forms of instructors' exams, diplomas or, indeed, any form of licensing in Italy since down the years it has depended exclusively on the old riders from the Cavalry Regiments who were, of course, inspired by the great Caprilli himself, the inventor of the 'forward seat', one of whose pupils was the d'Inzeos' father. As in Britain the disappearance of the top-class Cavalry instructors with the disbanding of the Cavalry has left a vacuum.

Riding in Italy is therefore conducted essentially on a club basis, and while there is no doubt that business is booming at this level in the Italian equestrian world with endless new clubs boasting excellent facilities, nevertheless it would seem that equestrianism in Italy is going to be at an increasing disadvantage unless the Government, or failing that, the Federation can find ways and means of subsidising instruction and providing good schools with a high level of instruction.

Spain

Spain necessarily is going through something of a transitional stage. For many years the heart of equestrianism in Spain has been the famous **Club de Campo** at Madrid which is financed by the wealthy families of Madrid and the surrounding areas. The Club was in fact opened in 1918 and although virtually in the centre of the city there is a feeling of spaciousness about the whole set-up. Indeed, there is an almost timeless quality. The Club is so popular that it has attracted over 30000 members, each of whom is expected to pay as much as £2000 to join, although the annual subscription is only £6. Members not only have the use of the riding facilities, but can also use the golf course, tennis courts, and innumerable other amenities which include a first-class restaurant. There is also a magnificent show ground, dressage arenas, gallops, cross-country courses, polo grounds and a magnificent indoor school. There are over 300 stables at the Club and between 250 and 300 horses, the majority of which belong to members who permanently stable them there. The stable staff consist of more than 40 grooms, each responsible for six or eight horses, with a ground staff of over 60. Instruction at the Club de Campo is in the hands of three full-time instructors who concentrate for the most part on beginners; more experienced riders, as a rule, have their own trainers, either for dressage or for show jumping. For many years the senior international team trainer was the highly thought of Señor Manero.

The Club de Campo outside arena, Madrid, Spain

The indoor school, which is the principal feature of the Club, was completed in 1968 and opened by Gen. Franco in the presence of Don Jose Luis Rivas, the Minister of Sport. The Director of the Club is Don Carlos Kirkpatrick O'Donnell. The floor in the school is of light sand which provides an ideal surface; but although it is possible for 500 or 600 people to watch what is going on in the school there are no seats but only tiered standing room.

The atmosphere at the Club de Campo is different from any other national centre because the emphasis seems very much to be on the social side: indeed, Sunday is always the important day when the whole Club becomes a hive of activity. There is comparatively little serious instruction, though it should be pointed out that there are many other schools, or clubs, as they are usually designated, such as the **Club Deportivo las Lomas** about 60 miles from Madrid and the recently-opened magnificent international riding centre at Jerez, owned by the Domecq family to which young British riders are fortunate enough to be invited.

Sweden

Strömsholm has a history going back more than 400 years. It has always been associated with equitation, becoming in the 19th century the Army Riding and

Strömsholm, Sweden

Equitation School which it remained until the Army left it in 1968. Since then Strömsholm has followed the examples of other schools in other countries, where formerly there was a flourishing Cavalry, and turned its military establishment into a civilian establishment. In Sweden it is run by the Swedish Equestrian Federation and the Swedish Horse Society. It is situated on the north coast of Lake Mälaren, 120 km west of Stockholm, the nearest town being Västerås. Since the school became a civilian establishment the Director has been Hans Ernmark, the Secretary General of both the Swedish Horse Society and the Federation, though, surprisingly, he himself was never in the Swedish Cavalry, nor has he taken part in competitive riding. But in addition to being interested all his life in horses he is a brilliant organiser and administrator, having tremendous enthusiasm for all the possibilities associated with a comparatively new venture such as the civilian Strömsholm. The chief instructor is Maj. Hans Wikne, an ex-Cavalry Officer who received his training at the Spanish Riding School of Vienna, he was in fact a senior instructor at Strömsholm in its Cavalry days. As in other countries in Europe riding is very much on the increase, now being a sport at which a wide cross-section of the population join in enthusiastically. The Swedish Horse Society boasts some 60000 members – twice as many as the British Horse Society – of which 50 per cent of the riding population are members. But interestingly 90 per cent of the riders are under 25 years old and 80 per cent are female.

Oddly enough despite the great popularity of riding in Sweden there is comparatively little competitive riding. For the most part riding is purely for pleasure and leisure; in fact, there are only 20 national shows a year at which show jumping competitions are held, and there is only one major Swedish horse show a year. As yet there is no sponsorship and consequently there are very few national riders of top calibre. Today only big prize money attracts international riders, contact with whom in top-class competition turns good national riders into passable international riders. It is interesting to note that the new World Champion Cup event is to be held in Sweden.

The school at Strömsholm comprises 500 acres of open land with woodland which is also utilised. In this area is a racecourse, where in fact the Swedish Grand National is held, and a museum, all belonging to the State which demands an annual rent of something approaching £20000. The main buildings form a large square with stable blocks: on two sides running down the centre of each a long passage is flanked by stalls and loose boxes. Each block can house 60 horses with facilities for food stores, tack rooms and rest rooms. There is stabling for an additional 20 horses which is used in the summer months. As a rule about 60 horses are permanently there for school use. At either end of the complex are two riding halls, the smallest being 20 × 40 m, used for the schooling of young horses. A little less than a mile away is the old Cavalry School Commander's house, now used as an office block and conference centre with excellent accommodation for students. Opposite the training school is an imposing building designed for dressage, with a jumping hall next door; each are 80 × 35 m. A feature of the jumping hall is an ingeniously fitted lane on a steel frame with pulleys which enable it to be raised or lowered easily. There is also a saddlers and farriery block, lecture rooms seating as many as 50 people, staff accommodation in bungalow-type blocks in which the students have single rooms. Although essentially a national centre, students from other Scandinavian countries are welcome, as indeed are students from all over the world. Between 500 and 600 students attend each year.

The basis of all training at Strömsholm is dressage; the main courses being the three parts of the riders/instructors course, aiming to produce straightforward, competent and knowledgeable horsemen. Frequently there are three courses running at the same time, Stages I and II in the Instructors Course and perhaps an eight or ten week course for grooms. For the first part of the Instructors Course, which lasts eight weeks, a student has to be over 19 years old. At the end of eight weeks the students go to another riding school, which is State subsidised, for one year, returning to complete Part II of the Instructors Course which lasts six weeks. If he wants to be a Director of a riding school he then has to stay for Part III which necessitates six months in residence at Strömsholm. At the end of this he is allowed to take part in school competitions and to compete at the Malmö Show. If a student wishes to be a fully authorised riding instructor – one capable of running a district as well as an individual school – he has to be over 23 years old. Each year the top student is invited to stay for a further year in order to get the experience of riding top class school dressage horses.

In order to attend an instructor's course a student must have ridden for at least five years and have had six months under a qualified instructor, he also must have had a further education course which includes economics and veterinary science. Students who wish to receive instruction but not necessarily to become instructors may attend these courses, but they must complete each course. Students may bring their own horses, which will only be used in the school if they are considered suitable, and in addition to looking after their own horse will be expected to attend to three or four other horses. The students' day at Strömsholm starts at 7.30 a.m. and finishes at 5.00 p.m. The evenings are free, though occasionally there are lectures.

More than 150 riders apply to take part in these instructor's courses each year, but only 50 are admitted. The cost, which has to be borne by the student, is about £15 inclusive per day. The whole of Parts I and II of the instructor's course therefore costs about £240, while overseas students have to pay £500. The advance courses cost twice this amount.

Of particular interest is the fact that driving, both of two and four horse vehicles, is included in the curriculum. Hans Ernmark, the Director, hopes that before long Sweden will be a leading competitor in driving sport. He hopes very much that eventually Strömsholm will be known as the Swedish University of the Horse. Negotiations have been going on with the Department of Education in the hope that they will take over the costs of the School. At present all finances for the sport in Sweden are administered by the Central Sports Organisation which receives some £7 million each year from the Department of Agriculture which is then divided among all the sports that the Department considers worthy of support. All money received by the horse societies goes into the running of Strömsholm rather than providing facilities for competition or international travel, as is the case with the Sports Council grant to the British Equestrian Federation in Britain which now comprises the British Horse Society and the British Show Jumping Association. Should the Department of Education take on the responsibility of Strömsholm, then nationwide facilities can be improved and the number of students increased. Inevitably this would ensure Sweden a high place once again in the international scene.

Right: Paul Weier, Olympic rider, head of the Swiss Centre at Elgg

Switzerland

In Switzerland there is an association of professional instructors and riding school owners which for several years has organised instructional programmes and examinations under the patronage of the Swiss Department of Agriculture. It is organised as follows:

On leaving school young people who are starting in an equestrian profession sign up for a three-year apprenticeship with a school recognised by the association. Each of these schools has a riding Master who holds the Swiss Riding Diploma. During these three years apprentices are gathered once a year for one week to take courses organised by the Swiss Association of Professionals so that there is a unity of doctrine. At the end of three years there is a written

and practical examination at the Federal Stud at Avenches, enabling the candidates to attain the title of Groom which can in fact be awarded after only two years; or that of Stable Manager or Apprentice Instructor which can only be obtained at the end of three years. It is then possible to do a further two years at a recognised centre – not necessarily in Switzerland – at the end of which a further examination with a more intensive practical side, can be taken, enabling the student to obtain a second class instructor's certificate. The student can then choose to do a further two years in order to become a first class instructor, being then expected to know all the disciplines thoroughly; or alternatively be trained at a recognised institution for the instructor's diploma with final examinations spread over four weeks at the Federal Army Horse Depot at Berne. This final examination is seldom taken before the age of 25.

Surprisingly, despite this excellently organised plan, there is no national centre as such in Switzerland, though probably many would accept that the establishment called **Elgg** run by the well-known show jumper, Paul Weier and his wife, previously Monica Bachmann the leading lady rider in Switzerland, is to all intents and purposes the national centre of Switzerland. During the winter at Paul Weier's school there are training courses similar to the 'Clinics' run in other countries, lasting two, three or four days, after which the riders return home having learnt their ground work at which they then work by themselves before returning a month later. At the end of the winter all the riders are filmed and these performances are then watched and later discussed in detail with commentary and criticism by Paul Weier and other instructors. It is at Elgg, too, that the Swiss international teams meet as a rule for preparation before major international events.

An attractive feature of Elgg is the accommodation provided for those taking part in the courses. Run in conjunction with the riding school is a comfortable old inn built right in the middle of the village. Those taking part are naturally extremely happy and comfortable in this charming accommodation.

With the good organisation, the excellent amenities and facilities one cannot help feeling that if the Swiss had an official national centre, at Elgg or elsewhere (such a centre is, in fact, now planned), and were prepared to finance it properly, Switzerland could very quickly be in a position to make a greater contribution to international equestrianism.

USSR

Despite the Revolution and two world wars riding is increasingly popular in the USSR with some 50000 Soviets now riding regularly and more than 30 important competitions being staged to establish each year the champion rider of the USSR. Back in the mid-thirties two clubs were set up in Moscow each associated with trade unions, Spartak and Stroitel – 'builder' – the forerunners of the **Burevestnik Societies**. The Society is based on the edge of Izmailova Park where there was for many years a Cavalry Station. This very fine site, surrounded by woodlands, is situated near the entrance to the Park, but at the time of formation of the Burevestnik Societies there was only one summer house available. In a comparatively short time the summer house was refurbished and improved, and ten horses (they were all army cast-offs), four of which were draft horses, were given to the Society. With funds so short capital could only be raised by hiring out the draft horses, a move which surprisingly proved extremely popular. People from all different walks of life joined the club, rolling up their sleeves in preparation for the hard work ahead, finally providing the labour needed to build the school. By the end of the 1930s the school was completed and in 1937 a second riding club was formed in Moscow, this one connected with the food industry and its trade union. The following year, 1938, Stroitel acquired its first thoroughbred horses, a turning point in the history of the school which now felt that it was in a position to begin to train riders and horses together: the beginning of what proved to be a typically technical, even scientific, attitude towards training.

There was a set-back after the second world war in that the whole site was in a bad state and the school had to be built again, with the Society once more desperately short of financial means. Within ten years of the end of the war, however, the demands were so great and the approach to equestrianism so much more sophisticated that the requirements were considerably in advance of what had been sufficient before the war. All this coincided with a general reshuffling of the existing sports clubs which now included the Universities. Stroitel became part of the Voluntary Sports Society, which in turn attracted great support from students, today Burevestnik being almost totally associated with students. Unfortunately, such is the demand for places that it is necessary to be highly selective in choosing students who could take advantage of the courses. Naturally riding has to take second place to study, but those who show talent stand a good chance of being considered for international events: far more, obviously, than those who just pay their roubles at the local hippodrome for 45 minutes in a paddock with a dozen or so other riders, in other words, in establishments similar to the ordinary suburban riding school in Britain.

Another national school, Nauka, now has 70 boxes and an arena 180 × 70 m with a second arena of 60 × 20 m. Not surprisingly the competitive element is very strong, particularly with students playing so large a part in the riding scene in the USSR. There are not only competitions in dressage and show jumping, but even jousting; push ball is also popular at Izmailova, a sport which requires not only considerable skill on the part of the rider, but also a very bold pony since the ball is extremely heavy, though soft. As a result of this emphasis on competition much has been done to select the right kind of horse for training for international competition, great emphasis being put on matching the horse and rider. In the early days it was not easy to achieve these vital partnerships, but today with the universal use of the thoroughbred in the USSR it is possible to select horses for their suitability in training and performance, and then find the riders best fitted to ride them. It is interesting that James Fillis, the Englishman, who became chief Écuyer in St Petersburg and had such a profound influence on Soviet equitation once stated that he preferred thoroughbreds because 'anyone who has ridden a thoroughbred will never want to ride anything else'; a remark that the Soviets have taken very much to heart. Today Mikhail Ivanov, the presiding genius behind Burevestnik, likes to use a medium-sized horse – you seldom see Soviet horses over 16 hands – which is strong and able to stand up to the pressures of competitive riding and the typical terrain where their events are held. Interestingly, he also prefers horses which have had racing experience as he finds them more adaptable. All the horses are owned by the State farms or studs, which have to be persuaded to allow them to go to Burevestnik.

Ivanov himself is a traditionalist, both in his riding doctrine and the purpose to which he feels the riding of horses should be put. Frequently he refers to Burevestnik as the Moscow School of Vienna, so it is not surprising that dressage plays an important part.

Izmailova is a most suitable setting for Soviet equestrianism with its romantic background and great historic importance. Equestrianism in the USSR has had to overcome great difficulties, but thanks to the Burevestnik club and others of a similar nature now in existence it is making great strides forward, as is shown by the success of its riders in international competition. It is just unfortunate that they do not more frequently compete internationally since international competition is essential if a nation is to remain at the top.

USA

The best known and certainly the most important of equestrian organisations in the United States is the **US Equestrian Team Centre** at Gladstone, New Jersey. The estate of Hamilton Farm, some 50 miles (80·5 km) west of New York, is owned by the family of James Cox Brady, Chairman of the US Jockey Club. The main house on the estate which was built in 1907 still being occupied by members of the family.

Gladstone is not in fact officially a national centre, nor is it wholly independent. The National Federation delegates all responsibility for international training to the United States Equestrian Team Association (USET) whose charter simply states that the objects are to train horses and riders for international competition and the Olympic Games. The Government in fact has no interest in it at all, all the money needed being raised by private subscription. The Chairman is Whitney Stone, without whom and without whose generosity the USET would not be in the sound position it is today. The President is Bill Steinkraus, an Olympic gold medallist and a regular rider at the Olympics since 1952. But the person who has probably done most to establish Gladstone is Bertalan de Nemethy, Coach to the United States show jumping team. This brilliant Hungarian was a Cavalry Officer, receiving the Diploma of Riding Instructor in Hungary in 1937. He was in training for the 1940 Olympic Games which of course were never held; he emigrated to the United States in 1952, being appointed as Coach to the USET in 1955. For many years his partner was the former French Olympic rider, Jack Le Goff.

The programme at Gladstone is of a very high level. In order to find riders with the greatest potential screening trials are held regularly and in particular every post Olympic year. At these trials, which anyone can enter, de Nemethy, assisted by one or two others, watches very carefully those who have been nominated, finally selecting a limited number to enter a course at Gladstone. Despite the success of this scheme over the years, in 1973 the scheme was extended, a panel of selectors visiting more big shows all over the country having announced their schedules in advance hoping, thereby, to discover good riders and good horses that had not necessarily voluntarily put themselves forward, or been recommended for the screening trials. In 1973 over 100 candidates were screened, anything between 20 and 30 attending each trial. From these, just eight were chosen to attend Gladstone. Not necessarily everyone who is selected for training remains with the squad for the full length of the course; only those whose promise is fully proven are invited to become permanent members of the team.

Riders do not necessarily have to bring their own horses because many horses are generously lent by wealthy and enthusiastic patrons, but each rider has two or three horses for his use, though these are interchangeable.

As the programme at Gladstone has but one aim, which is the training of USA equestrian teams, the work at the school is not carried out in classes but rather in individual training sessions in which a particular rider is drilled in some aspect of international competition. Much of this training naturally takes place in the main indoor school or riding hall as it is called, though its official name is the Nautical Hall after the famous show jumper ridden by Hugh Wiley, winner of the King George V Gold Cup in 1959. The school is 60 × 26 m with a small gallery at each end and a jump store. The school is particularly well lit. Adjacent to the riding hall is an outdoor sand ring 130 × 57 m, the base is clay with river sand and a top layer of first grade sand to a total depth of 6 in. There is also another large outdoor schooling ring which has an Irish bank situated in the centre, a Devil's Dyke and a water jump. In another area of the park there are numerous permanent fences.

The stables are about 50 m from the Nautical Hall in a somewhat old-fashioned building built on two levels with a loft above the second level. Each box is 10 × 10 ft; on the ground level there are 23 boxes used by the three-day event horses and on the first floor there are 24 boxes used by the show jumpers. A gentle ramp links the two levels. Each floor has its own feed and tack rooms; the floors are paved with herringbone tiles and there are central gangways some 14 ft wide. Another stable block is 250 yd away where nine horses can be accommodated in slightly smaller stables. Everything in the stable area is highly efficient and there is a high standard of spit and polish. The staff is on the small side, but appears to be absolutely dedicated.

Adjoining the stable block is a building which houses the offices, the trophy room and the lecture room. On the opposite side of the trophy room passages lead to the accommodation quarters; there are eight separate bedrooms for male riders with a living room, kitchen and bathrooms; on the other side there are five separate bedrooms used by the stable staff. There is a large recreation room and rest room. Girls are housed in separate accommodation where there are six bedrooms, living room, bathrooms and kitchen. By sharing rooms it is possible to accommodate up to ten girls. The stable staff live in cottages on the estate.

The Indoor School, Morven, USA

Mention should be made of another important equestrian centre in America at **Morven Park** in Virginia's Loudoun County, about an hour from Washington. Morven Park was only set up in 1968 to fill the void in top riding instruction left by the phasing out of the American Cavalry schools which had, as in Britain, played such an important part in the training of international riders. The first team instructor was Brig. Dick Hobson, who based his philosophy of instruction almost entirely on that of the equitation school at Weedon. He was succeeded by Maj. Lynch who, sadly, was killed in a road accident shortly before his retirement in 1978.

At Morven there are two branches of instruction; the main course which lasts nine months from September to June, and a summer session of three four-week courses which can be taken separately or as a single unit of eight or twelve weeks. The short courses are open virtually to anyone, but the real business of the school, the longer course, is only open to those riders who have demonstrated a sufficient equestrian ability or have reached Pony Club B standard. The feature of this course is that it can result in a Bachelor of Science Degree at Springfield College, Massachusetts. Divided into sections the better to put into practice Major Lynch's description of the school programme in their brochure 'to teach people to teach after they've been taught themselves', the first half is devoted to the latter part of this proposition, students receiving instruction in riding and schooling, while the second half puts the emphasis on teaching; there is also a thorough grounding in stable management, veterinary medicine, farriery, etc. All feeding, grooming, mucking out and maintenance of tack is done by the students. This is really an economic necessity brought about by the considerable operating deficits during the early years of Morven Park's existence. The majority of students live in, either in rented quarters in the nearby town of Leesburg, or in the school dormitories which consist of single-storey white cottages with several small bedrooms. There are two outdoor manèges close to the cafeteria where the students have all their meals. Lectures are held in the main lecture hall. There are three blocks of stables which are well built with rows of loose boxes and a small, but impeccably kept, tack room. There are some 80 horses, all Thoroughbreds, some lent to the school, others given and a number purchased. The whole complex is surrounded by lush paddocks, adjacent to which there is an excellent cross-country course.

At the end of the nine-month course all students must have satisfied their instructors that they have learnt all that the school has tried to teach them: only then are the students awarded their instructor's certificates at Grade A, B or C.

Where Gladstone concentrates entirely on international riders, Morven is devoted to the training of top-class instructors. The influence of Morven will eventually, it is hoped, be as great as the influence of Gladstone.

It is probably true to say that with such excellent privately provided Centres as Gladstone and Morven – and there are others throughout the USA – there is really no need for America to have a National Equestrian Centre as such.

From the descriptions of the administration of riding and the provision of courses both for individual riders and instructors all over the world it will be seen that the British National Equestrian Centre at Stoneleigh still has a long way to go before it can emulate some of its more fortunate counterparts with their generous Government support. What is important is the fact that Britain now has a National Equestrian Centre which has been making steady progress since it was founded in 1967 (see Chapter 16). It would be far from the truth to suggest that other centres even Vienna itself or the heavily subsidised Saumur, have no problems of their own. Indeed they have, but their problems have perhaps been of a rather different nature to those of the British National Equestrian Centre.

Dressage at the new Equestrian Centre at Vilamoura

APPENDIX
INTERNATIONAL SCHOOLS

Austria
The Spanish Riding School,
Hofburg Palace, Vienna

France
National Equestrian Centre,
Saumur, Loire

Germany
Deutsche Reitschule,
Warendorf, Westphalia

Great Britain
National Equestrian Centre,
Stoneleigh, Warwickshire

Holland
Nederlands Ippisch Centrum,
Deurne

Ireland
Burton Hall,
Herbertstown, Dublin

Italy
Centro Ippico di Castellazzo,
Milan

Spain
Club de Campo,
Madrid

Sweden
Ridskolan,
Strömsholm

Switzerland
Reitsportzentrum,
Elgg

USA
Gladstone,
New Jersey (International)

Morven Park,
Virginia (National)

USSR
Burevestnik,
Moscow

PART FIVE
Horse Shows, Fairs and Exhibitions

14 Horse Shows in Britain

Horse shows have become such a feature of the equestrian world that it is difficult to appreciate that they only came into being in the early part of the present century. The first major show was the International Horse Show staged at Olympia in June 1907. It was in fact financed with American money and was principally a harness show, though there were a few jumping competitions. The whole show was mounted in a most lavish manner with the Earl of Lonsdale – the Yellow Earl – as President and also, in effect, the Director. Olympia, as it was then generally known, was one of the highlights of the London social season; most performances were in the afternoon and it was as important to be seen at one of the gala afternoons as it was to be seen at Henley or Wimbledon, or the Polo at Hurlingham or Ranelagh.

The standard of exhibits was extremely high, exhibitors taking an enormous amount of trouble not only in the preparation of their horses but also in their own turn-out which would match the magnificence of their horses. Everything about Olympia was essentially opulent and elegant. That it lost a great deal of money was comparatively unimportant, its backers never expected to make money; indeed, it could be described as a major promotion exercise in attracting the attention of the public to the harness horse.

One of the great features of Olympia in the old days was the association with Lord Lonsdale who managed, at no cost to himself, virtually to make the show his own. The livery worn by all the Stewards or, as they would now be called, the Arena Party, was the famous yellow of Lord Lonsdale. Liveried postilions rode the horses that brought in the wagons with the jumps on: all round the arena were great banks of flowers, in particular hydrangeas, azaleas and carnations: hung from the ceiling were vast, magnificent chandeliers draped in pink silk; at one end of the arena was an enormous backcloth depicting Lowther Castle, the home of Lord Lonsdale. It was in every way a superb addition to the London social season, but it was also a very valuable shop window for the horse. It also did much to popularise show jumping, the prize money attracting many riders from overseas.

After the First World War the International was revived at Olympia, continuing to run with the same success associated with its pre-war days until the outbreak of the Second World War. After the Second World War there was talk of reviving it yet again at Olympia, but this time the generous American sponsors were no longer forthcoming. With the success of the Victory Show Jumping Championships that had been organised at the White City in 1945 the Greyhound Racing Association suggested that the International should be revived at the White City. At first there was considerable opposition to this since the International had always been an indoor show; there were many who thought the White City was something of a barracks, lacking the atmosphere needed for the International Horse Show. Fortunately, however a group of enthusiasts were brought together under my father, Col. V. D. S. Williams, who acted as Chairman of the Show Committee, and between them they raised enough money, or more accurately they were able to provide sufficient guarantees, to launch the International Horse Show at the White City in 1947. That it was such an outstanding success at its new venue was very largely due to the organising ability of Col., now Sir, Michael Ansell who was appointed by my father as the Show Director. With his flair for organisation, his energy and ability and his wide knowledge of the show scene, particularly that of show jumping, he was able to make the show an outstanding success. The Show was virtually divided into two sections; the jumping which he made some of the best in the world;

Col. Sir Michael Ansell, for so long the presiding genius behind the London shows

and the show classes where the emphasis was very much on quality, turn-out and elegance.

The White City, as it became familiarly known (it did not become the Royal International Horse Show until its Jubilee Year in 1957) became very popular, not only with the general public but with the equestrian social public; it was vital for anyone who was anyone to be present at the great Gala performance on the Wednesday evening, invariably attended by the Queen and other members of the Royal Family, when the premier individual show jumping championship of the world was competed for, the King George V Gold Cup. The Members' block, which was comprised mostly of the south side of the stadium, would be absolutely packed; to get a table in the glass-fronted restaurant on that night was a feat indeed. There is no doubt that very quickly the White City established a wonderful atmosphere of its own. From the very beginning when on the stroke of 7.00 p.m. (punctuality being a principal feature of Michael Ansell's organisation) the fanfare sounded and the first horse in the first jumping competition entered the arena, until the very end when bathed in spotlights the band of the Royal Marines played their hauntingly

Famous show winners:

Eagle's Hill, owned by Elspeth Ferguson: In-Hand Champion 1976 and 1978

Enstone Artist, principal stallion in Mrs Dorian Williams' leading Pony Stud

Pendley Maypole, principal mare in Mrs Dorian Williams' leading Pony Stud

Davina Lee-Smith on *Pretty Polly*

Mrs Rosemary Cooke on the Cob *Knobby*

Count Robert Orssich on *Liberty Light*

effective 'Ceremony of Sunset' it was all marvellously exciting and a great and unforgettable experience. Indeed, it could be said that the Royal International at the White City set a standard for shows all over the world: few would deny that the great shows organised by Col. Sir Michael Ansell in England became the envy of the world; something to which all those interested in horses, including many from overseas, hoped to have the opportunity to come to at least once in their lifetime.

Horse of the Year Show arena

Yet within two years another show was launched which in a quite different yet complementary way was to be as successful, if not more successful than the Royal International Horse Show at the White City. This was of course the Horse of the Year Show which was first presented at Harringay Stadium in 1949; again it was master-minded by Col. Ansell who had with him the same outstandingly able team of stewards and officials that he had at the White City.

The Horse of the Year Show was an almost immediate success, although the very first performances were sparsely attended, few people understanding just what the horse show was all about, it being so different to any other horse show. In fact it was based on a show called 'Le Jumping' held in Paris; this was an all go, spectacular show with the audience very close to the ring in a small, intimate indoor stadium, and very much more involved than at an ordinary horse show. At Harringay the same sort of atmosphere was quickly engendered: once people realised just how exciting it all was they flocked to the Horse of the Year Show in enormous numbers. The emphasis was on jumping but there were also show classes, though these were judged in another arena, only the last few minutes of the final judging being held in the main arena. In addition there were various displays, many of which were quickly to become a feature of the show: displays such as the Musical Drive of the Heavy Horses which from the first year it was introduced became enormously popular with the public, and still is. Over the years it has built up into perhaps the most famous indoor show in the world: indeed, other countries have emulated it by having their own Horse of the Year Show.

After ten years the show had to move from Harringay, the new home being the Empire Pool at Wembley. This has in fact proved to be an even more suitable venue for the show. Once established there the show became even more popular; so much so that it soon became impossible to get seats for any performance towards the end of the week, even months in advance. Nowadays all the evening performances are quickly sold out. That this should be so is largely due to the variety of the programme presented. The jumping, which is international, attracting many of the greatest riders in the world is invariably exciting in that small arena. But equally popular are such events and displays as the Pony Club Games mentioned in an earlier chapter; the Parade of Personalities when some 10 or 12 horses, famous in one respect or another, are paraded in the arena; and the dressage displays, usually presented by one of the leading dressage experts in the world. Finally there is the great Cavalcade with which the show ends. After the last prizes and rosettes have been presented, the lights in the arena are lowered, the trumpeters of the Household Cavalry come silently into the arena in the darkness and then suddenly, dramatically, are hit by the spotlights. They play the opening fanfare and into the arena file some 100 or even as many as 130 horses and ponies, each a champion in its own right. They may be humble pit ponies or they may be priceless

The Heavy Horses' display at the Horse of the Year Show

Quality Hunter

Weight-carrying Cob

Above: **David Tatlow on *State Visit***
Left: **David Barker on Lady Zinnia Pollock's *Balmoral***

thoroughbreds, but they are all there, filling the arena until it seems as though there is no space left at all. With the last arrival, the 'star' of the show – the outstanding 'Personality' or an individual or team that has gained international honours – I have the privilege as the official show commentator of reciting the Tribute to the Horse. This was specially written for me in 1957 by Ronald Duncan, the well-known playwright, but also a West Country farmer, in response to my request for some suitable words with which to bring this great Cavalcade to its climax.

This unique climax never fails to be a most moving experience: even though the stadium is crammed with something approaching 10000 people and over 100 horses and ponies are jammed in the ring, there is an almost uncanny silence as each year these words are recited; a silence broken only by the jingle of a bit or a clink of a spur, or perhaps a horse impatiently pawing at the tan.

Below: The Household Cavalry display at the Olympia Christmas International

Where in this wide world can man find nobility without pride, friendship without envy, or beauty without vanity? Here, where grace is laced with muscle and strength by gentleness confined.

He serves without servility, he has fought without enmity. There is nothing so powerful, nothing less violent; there is nothing so quick, nothing more patient.

England's past has been borne on his back. All our history is his industry. We are his heirs, he our inheritance.

Ladies and Gentlemen – The Horse!

In many ways of course it smacks of the theatre; but this is where the Horse of the Year Show is different to any other show in the world. It is in fact a unique spectacular designed round the horse, and as such has an appeal far beyond the ordinary horse loving and horse riding public; it is equally popular with ordinary people, most of whom it seems find the horse exciting to watch; especially, since show jumping has been introduced to television, which seems to add to its glamour. Having seen it on television many want to see the Show itself. Show jumping is one of the few sports that, far from suffering because of television, has actually benefited from it.

The Royal International Horse Show at the White City was itself moved to Wembley in 1962 when it was impossible to hold the show at the White City Stadium because of the new road being built to link the West End with the Western Avenue. For two years the show was held in the outside stadium, but not only did this prove to be impractical in that the vast stadium, holding between 80000 and 100000 people, was far too big for the requirements of the horse show, but the fact that horses were using the hallowed turf on which the Cup Final was played greatly agitated the minds of those whose main interest as far as sport was concerned was football. It was therefore decided to move the show indoors, into the Empire Pool. Ironically, this was by many considered a retrograde step, though the original International Horse Show was of course an indoor show. Equally ironic is the fact that many now resent the anxiety by some people to move the show outside again, forgetting that its great heyday was in fact in the outside stadium at the White City. The difficulty of having both the International

Horse of the Year Show Cavalcade

Brown
HORSE OF THE YEAR

and the Horse of the Year Show in the same stadium is that it is difficult to make the shows sufficiently different. Inevitably one show suffers, and inevitably this is the International because it is not easy in the Empire Pool to produce the kind of elegance that has always been associated with the Show, first at Olympia and later at the White City. The International, therefore, appears to many to be a pale reflection of the Horse of the Year Show, and in effect virtually the same show. In fact the atmosphere at the Horse of the Year Show is totally different to that of the Royal International Horse Show. It could be said that the Royal International at Wembley has lost its own identity and therefore lacks atmosphere. This, however, would not be entirely fair as the Royal International at Wembley is still a superbly presented show, winning the envy and admiration of many responsible for shows overseas. It is just unfortunate that it shares its venue with the Horse of the Year Show. It could be that the Royal International will one day go outside again, but it is not easy to see where it could go, though many people believe that it would be possible once again to hold the show at the White City; whether or not this is so is debatable as since moving to Wembley the show has become not only more sophisticated, but more popular. The White City presents very real problems, both in stabling and in parking, and in the provision of a good second ring which is needed for the judging of the show classes and as a practise jumping arena.

In 1973 a new show was introduced in London. This was the Dunhill Show held at Olympia. It came into being as a result of Dunhill's desire to sponsor a big indoor show round about Christmas. At first the idea seemed not only impractical, but a considerable risk as no one had seriously considered before holding a show so close to Christmas. In any event to launch a new show is always a hazardous occupation. However, after much discussion an organising Committee, of which I had the privilege to be Chairman, was formed with Raymond Brooks-Ward appointed as the Show Director. Held the week before Christmas the show was an immediate success; within five years it was encountering the same sort of experience as the Horse of the Year Show in huge advance bookings from the day the box office was opened. Dunhill withdrew their sponsorship after a year or two, the show subsequently being presented by a series of generous sponsors, each responsible for one day of the show, the length of which has now been extended to six days.

Olympia is totally different from both the Royal International and the Horse of the Year Show. It has sometimes been described as a cross between a horse show and a circus; this is because a feature of the show is the number of displays which are perhaps more associated with the circus or the pantomime than with a horse show. For instance, there has on a number of occasions been very successful camel racing with leading show jumpers taking part; there is the regular Pony Club mounted pantomime which is extremely popular with the younger members of the audience; there is also the Christmas Finale with Father Christmas appearing on his sleigh as snow falls gently from the roof. All this creates a very happy family show and indeed it could be said that the Olympia International, as it is now known, has filled the gap left by the departure of the famous Bertram Mills Circus which was such a feature of Christmas holidays some years ago. Now parents collecting their children from school or paying a last shopping visit to London before Christmas, at the end of the day, or even during the afternoon, go to Olympia for an entertainment which is relaxed and fast moving, ideally suited to a mixed audience. The jumping is still of a very high standard, the show attracting most of the great riders from Europe. Unfortunately many of their entries have to be refused as in such a show it is essential to keep to a carefully pre-arranged timetable which means that the number of jumpers in any one class has to be strictly limited. All in all the show is an

Parade of Young Stock at the Royal Show, Stoneleigh

Judging Hunters at the Royal Windsor

Hickstead arena. *Inset:* Douglas Bunn, maestro of Hickstead

almost ideal mixture of top-class show jumping and entertainment and usually fills a gap in the horse show calendar.

In the few years of its existence the Olympia International has now become very much a feature of the calendar, attracting an audience entirely of its own, thus allowing each of the three London shows to retain its own identity. Those most closely connected with and interested in horses go to the Royal International; those who like spectacles and atmosphere go to the Horse of the Year Show; those who like the more relaxed atmosphere of a Christmas party go to Olympia. The three shows dovetail in an extremely successful manner, each complementing the others.

With well over 2000 shows taking place in Britain between March and October it is obviously not possible to mention more than one or two. Obviously one must mention the great Royal Show, presented by the Royal Agricultural Society of England in July on their show ground at Stoneleigh. This is really more of an exhibition or a fair rather than a horse show *per se*, the greater part of their ground being taken up with stands and displays; the actual horse events playing only a minor part. Then there are the great agricultural shows such as the East of England at Peterborough, the Royal Highland at Ingliston, just outside Edinburgh, the Royal Welsh, the Great Yorkshire and many other county shows, all of which remarkably attract increasing attendances. Even in 1978 most of the major shows were able to boast record attendances, both amongst the entries and the spectators.

The comparatively new Cardiff Show, held each June in the delightful Castle grounds with the splendid ramparts and picturesque peacocks, also deserves mention, if only for the very generous prize money, some £18000, which is donated by the sponsors, Benson & Hedges, for the Professional and Amateur Show Jumping Championships. In four or five years this has grown into a very important international show, attracting leading riders from many nations.

Perhaps unique in the horse show world is Hickstead where Douglas Bunn in the early 1960s opened his All England Jumping Course, as he called it, at Bolney, near Brighton in Sussex. The principal feature of this show, which was originally entirely a jumping show, was the permanent fences in the main jumping arena. These included the famous Irish Bank, the 'Road', a fence where you jumped up on to a platform and jumped off it, a smaller Irish Bank, a Wall, a water jump and the Devil's Dyke. Over the years Douglas Bunn has added a number of new rings and introduced show classes, harness classes, dressage, indeed, almost every equestrian activity that you can think of.

There is little doubt that horse shows in Britain have a greater variety than in any other country. Each year it seems as though more and more classes are crammed into the programme, everything from breeding classes to top-class show jumping with increasingly large prize money. It is sometimes felt that it is illogical that a show jumper can win a first prize of £1000 whereas a champion hunter or pony, each of which today is enormously valuable, can win only £15 or £20, or even less. The fact is, of course, that it is the show jumping that attracts the crowds. The reward in winning a show class is the increase in the value of one's exhibit.

Despite the poor prize money the show classes are invariably filled to bursting, which suggests that the prize money is not the whole purpose of showing. In fact the standard of the exhibits is exceedingly high, particularly with the ponies, the top six or even twelve in any class having exceptional quality. The Hacks, too, many of them coming from the racecourse, are full of quality. The standard of the Hunters is not perhaps quite so high today, largely due to the fact that the best big horses with both quality and substance are snapped up for big prices as show jumpers or eventers. Nevertheless, the overall standard, even of the now well-filled driving, harness and turn-out classes, is remarkably high and a matter of considerable pride to the equestrian world in Britain.

15
Horse Shows Overseas

Britain is of course not the only country to hold major horse shows: indeed, they take place all over the world. Although still associated with the British Isles, one must firstly mention the famous Royal Dublin Society Show held annually at Ballsbridge. This show is unique in its own individual atmosphere, being more of a fair than a horse show in that every horse exhibited is up for sale. No amount of change or trouble has ever allowed this wonderful atmosphere to alter. The Jumping Enclosure, as the main ring is called, is surely the most superb horse show ring or arena in the whole world, with great stands the whole way round the ring which is bound by a variegated hedge of green and yellow box. It, too, has permanent fences such as the Banks and the Walls and the Water Jump, but unlike any other show in the world the main feature at Dublin is the judging of the Hunter Championship rather than the main jumping competitions, with the possible exception of the Aga Khan Trophy, the Team Championship. The parade of the Hunter Champions each afternoon ensures an absolutely packed audience; to win at Dublin must surely be one of the most exciting experiences that a horseman or the owner of a horse can ever enjoy. Many of the horses shown at Dublin come over to Britain and, indeed, go to all parts of the world. Young stock are also judged at Dublin and discerning buyers from many countries come hoping to buy at a moderate price some of the beautiful Irish horses that are shown at the show, but invariably they have to be content with paying very much more than they originally intended.

There are no evening performances at Dublin, yet each performance is sold out throughout the Show week. What other horse show in the world could ensure absolutely packed attendances every afternoon with several thousands of people queuing up to get into the stands? In Ireland, Dublin Show week implies a holiday, official or unofficial: everyone heads in one direction – Ballsbridge.

In the North American continent the three major shows of the autumn circuit are New York, Washington and the famous Toronto Winter Fair. These

Judging Young Stock in the outside rings at Dublin behind the famous jumping enclosure

Above: The Royal Canadian Mounted Police's famous Musical Ride at Ottawa

shows are extremely well organised and very smart occasions, particularly the Toronto Winter Fair where evening dress is *de rigueur* in the evening. As with the major shows in Britain, jumping is probably the most important event at each session, but Hunter classes and Riding Horse classes are always well filled and considered important in themselves. Unlike Britain, except in the Working Hunter classes, the Hunters are all expected to jump and are judged on style. Particularly popular are the classes for the American Saddle Horses, ridden in the American style, where turn-out plays a particularly important part.

Indeed, turn-out also plays a surprisingly important part in the major shows in Australia. The most important show is the Royal Show at Sydney which again is more of a fair and an exhibition than a straightforward horse show. The remarkable parades of prize winners each day, when led by a marshal, create involved patterns and are extremely effective. Melbourne, held in the autumn, is not so large as Sydney but is still a show that is large by ordinary British standards, and attracts very big crowds. At Melbourne the most important class of all is the class for the best turned-out horse and rider. The Gary Owen Trophy for this class is the most coveted award of all, the

Below: The bucking bronco, a feature of even the smallest show in America

Above: **The Piazza di Siena, perhaps the most beautiful show ground in the world**

winner also being bedecked with a huge wreath of flowers, an outsize lei, and a wide blue sash.

As one might expect, in view of the excellence of riders who come to Europe from New Zealand, excellent, well-organised shows are also run at such places as Christchurch, Auckland and Wellington. As with Australia the problem is sufficient international competition.

As far as Europe is concerned most countries have their official CHIOs (Concours Hippique International Officiel): usually they are held in the same place each year. This is not so, however, in France where although there is a big show at Paris the CHIO is now usually held at La Baule, though it was once held at Fontainebleau. In Switzerland, too, the CHIO alternates between Geneva (indoors), and Lucerne with its beautiful lakeside showground. In Italy, however, it is always in Rome that the principal Italian horse show is held, the site being the famous Piazza de Siena, in the famous Borghese Gardens at the top of Via Veneto. This must be one of the most beautiful show grounds in the world, the arena being in a hollow, flanked by terraces and towering cypresses all round. In good weather it is one of the most pleasant experiences that anyone attending a horse

Below: **The leafy show ground at Luxembourg**

show can enjoy. The Italian crowd is very partisan, which is perhaps not surprising remembering the brilliance of their leading riders, the d'Inzeo brothers and the Munich Olympic gold medallist Mancinelli. Spain also has a very beautiful show ground in the famous Club de Campo in Madrid. This is very much a society show, the wealthy Spaniards flocking to Madrid for the occasion. The Spanish CHIO is also sometimes held at Barcelona. In Portugal the CHIO is in Lisbon, another very attractive show though it is not usually considered as one of the major shows of the international circuit.

Rotterdam is in fact a much more important show and is usually attended by teams from the leading show jumping nations all over Europe. This is partly due to its accessibility, with neither mountains nor water to cross for most European teams. It is also because for many years it has had a tradition of being a well organised, and well run show with beautifully built show jumping courses by its presiding genius Herr Jurgens. The major show at Brussels is indoors where there is a vast arena in a huge and very imaginative stadium. The CHIO in Denmark is held in a rather delightful ground near Copenhagen which is not unlike Lucerne. There is a pleasing informality about the show, even when, as in 1970, the Ladies' World Championship was held there, but like most continental shows the timetable is not rigorously adhered to and there can be long periods when very little is happening. It is a pity that the time-keeping at so many continental shows is so unreliable. In the last few years Sweden has made an effort to establish a first-class international show, but although Sweden is increasingly an equestrian nation, returning as far as competition is concerned to what it was between the wars, and although it has an excellent national centre, there is at present comparatively little enthusiasm for show jumping on a large scale. Their show jumping commentator, however, is outstanding and has succeeded in making show jumping extremely popular, on both radio and television, entirely through his own personality.

There are of course almost as many shows in Germany as there are in Britain. The first major show each year is at Hamburg where the Derby is held; this was the first show to stage a jumping Derby, a competition over a very long course with very big fences in which very few clear rounds are anticipated. The CHIO in Germany is at Aachen. This is a huge show ground, even more spacious than Hickstead, with permanent jumps and ornamental lakes. The courses built by Brinkmann are very demanding but very fair: to win at Aachen is therefore always a greatly sought after achievement. At the weekends enormous crowds are attracted to Aachen for the show jumping and the magnificent driving displays which are always such a feature of the show. The German audience is knowledgeable and enthusiastic, it probably being true to say that the overall standard of jumping is higher than at any other show in the world.

There are some good shows in South America notably at Buenos Aires where the World Championships were held in 1966.

Two other major shows have recently become prominent. The first is Palermo in Sicily which has attracted all the leading riders because of the enormous prize money that it offers; the second is Vienna in Austria which staged the European Championships in 1977, though there were some who were not entirely happy with the conditions that were framed for the Championships (each country holding the World or European Championships is allowed to devise its own conditions). There is also, of course, show jumping on the snow at St Moritz.

In Eastern Europe the principal country for holding horse shows is Poland, which in recent times has held a number of Championships. In 1964 the European Junior Championships were held at Budapest. Unfortunately Moscow seldom invites overseas riders to its shows with the result that little is known about the standard at the horse shows held regularly in the USSR. It is hoped that with the Olympic Games in 1980 being held in Moscow, the USSR will be rather more forthcoming in its international involvement.

Shows are now being held regularly in North Africa; indeed, in Iran and Tunisia a great effort is being made to build up the popularity of show jumping. Already in Morocco there are good shows with quite a high standard of jumping but, of course, all these shows in Africa are only international in the sense that others from Africa can compete. Because of the African Horse Sickness regulations no horse can be brought from Africa to Europe; European riders jumping in Africa therefore have to ride horses provided by the hosts. This also goes for South Africa

Traditional entry of a twelve horse team before a packed stadium at a show behind the Iron Curtain

where the great Rand Easter Show is another extremely well organised exhibition, the horses and the equestrian activities playing a comparatively minor role. The Rand show ground is very well laid out with a modern feel about it. The standard of jumping in South Africa is also extremely high as is quickly appreciated if one visits shows at Cape Town, Pietermaritzburg or Port Elizabeth, though the atmosphere of these shows is much more that of a country show. In South Africa they also have a Horse of the Year Show in December. There is no doubt that if South African riders could compete at European shows on their own horses they would take a great deal of beating. Isolated as they are – and the same can be said of Rhodesia – those responsible for horse shows in Southern Africa have applied themselves with great determination and enthusiasm in imitating to the best of their ability the most successful and best run shows in Europe.

As one who has been fortunate enough to visit in one capacity or another, most of these international shows, one cannot fail to be impressed with the individuality that each of these shows retain. Each one has its own atmosphere, its own *ambiance*, partly created by the nation itself, partly by the environment and partly by something that is quite indefinable, but very real: indeed almost tangible. This is the great charm of the show circuit in that each show is different, each has something to contribute, each fits into the overall pattern of the show season and each has its distinctive quality. All this is largely generated by the core of international riders who travel to all these shows and who though basically rivals, and very determined rivals, are all great friends, each enjoying another's success although obviously anxious to win himself. Inevitably it creates a very happy, relaxed atmosphere, unique perhaps in all sport: in all probability helped by the fact that a competitor is not solely involved, but is involved with a horse, who is not wholly predictable. One always has to accept the fact that a horse is also concerned and, just as it can cover up the rider's mistakes, can also counteract all the best and most brilliant efforts of the rider: which is why, in the long run, it is a partnership: each is dependent upon the other, in just about equal proportions.

PART SIX
Organisations

16 National Organisations

The British Horse Society

The British Horse Society (BHS) was formed in 1947 as the result of an amalgamation of the National Horse Association and Institute of the Horse and Pony Club. In its charter it was laid down that the Society existed to promote the interests of horse and pony breeding, further the art of riding and encourage horsemastership, and the welfare of the horse. At the time of its foundation there were some 5000 members: by the time the Society moved from its London headquarters at Bedford Square to the British Equestrian Centre at Stoneleigh in 1967 there were some 15000 members; by 1978 there were more than 25000 members. When all the members of the Pony Club and the Riding Clubs which are affiliated to the BHS are added then there is a membership well in excess of 100000. This sounds a large number, but in relation to the total number of people riding in Britain, perhaps as many as 2000000, it is not as large as it should be.

When the Society was originally formed there was only an Executive Committee and sub-committees representing the different interests in riding at that time, such as combined training and dressage. In the early fifties there were some half-dozen different committees, but by 1978 there were no less than 18. In addition to the General Purposes and Finance Committee these consist of the Dressage Committee, the Combined Training Committee, the Welfare Committee, the Training and Examination Committee, the Development and Liaison Committee, the Riding Clubs Committee, the Combined Driving Committee, the Long-Distance Riding Committee, the Riding Establishments Act Committee, the Horse and Pony Breeds Committee, the English, Scottish, Welsh and Northern Ireland Committees, the International Horse Show Committee, Sponsorship and, of course, the Pony Club which is in fact autonomous. The Chairman of each of the Committees is entitled to sit on the General Purposes and Finance Committee which has in addition four members nominated by the Council of the Society. The Council not only represents the various interests of the Society, but also has representatives of other bodies such as the British Veterinary Association, the British Show Jumping Association, the Hunters' Improvement Society, the Society of Master Saddlers, the National Master Farriers and Blacksmiths Association, the Thoroughbred Breeders Association and the British Driving Society.

It is obvious that both the Council and the General Purposes and Finance Committee have become too large and unwieldy with the expansion of the Society. A move was therefore made in 1978 to redraft the Constitution so that there is a smaller and more streamlined Council and an Executive Committee which consists of two sub-committees, Finance and Policy. The members of the Executive Committee are elected by the Council and represent the Society as a whole rather than specific interests. It was only natural that under the old Constitution, members representing one particular interest of the Society tended in the deliberations of the General Purposes and Finance Committee to be concerned only with that interest. Under the new Constitution representatives of any specialist committee can be invited to take part in discussions concerning that particular interest, but in principle, members of the new executive represent general rather than particular interests. Understandably, it has taken some time and a large number of meetings to produce a new Constitution that is satisfactory to everybody, but there can be little doubt that the work of the Society will be far more effective with the implementation of this new Constitution.

The work of the Society, it could be said, is divided into two sections; there is the competitive side comprising the dressage, combined driving and combined training, and the services side. The latter comprises everything from welfare, examinations, riding schools and so on. Obviously it is the competitive side of the Society that produces the largest income, which therefore subsidises the services; but it would be a mistake to think that the money raised by the competitive functions should be expected wholly to subsidise welfare, inspection of riding schools and so on. In fact, ideally, the income from the membership subscriptions should cover all these activities leaving the income from the competitive side as a bonus, the source for a realistic reserve fund and provision for the expansionist needs of different disciplines.

There is, inevitably and rightly, a certain autonomy in the different sections of the Society, each committee being responsible for running its own affairs. It would, however, be a pity if the Society was not one coordinated whole as the strength of the Society obviously lies in its numbers. It is far more effective in dealing with Government Departments if one can speak with one voice representing 100000 riders, rather than if one can only speak as an independent group representing some 3000 or 4000 riders. That the work of the Society is complex cannot be denied, but in fact if examined carefully it will be seen that each department is directly, or indirectly, dependent upon other departments of the Society. In recent years the Society has organised itself into regions; these coincide with the regions of the British Show Jumping Association and the Pony Club. There are now also County Committees. The purpose of all this is to enable members to feel more in touch with Headquarters and also to feel more independent in their own particular areas and regions. These regions have done tremendous work in interesting local people in the work of the Society and organising various events and social occasions for their benefit; something that could never be done on a national scale. The Society is now in fact assuming more and more the shape of a pyramid with broadly based foundations representing riders in every part of the country, gradually coming up to a peak which is the executive body responsible for the overall administration of the Society. Obviously it is possible that people in regions get more interested in their own region than they do in the Society as a whole. Nevertheless, on balance it must be of the greatest possible advantage to the Society to have these regional and county committees to ensure that all that happens at Headquarters is disseminated amongst the whole membership.

The work of the Society on the welfare side is often overlooked, as indeed is the work that the Society does, not only to inspect schools with the idea of approving them, but also inspecting schools about which complaints have been received. The following statistics give some idea of the comprehensive work of the Society today. In one year some 20000 leaflets were distributed regarding the feeding of ponies kept out at grass in severe weather conditions. A total of 160000 leaflets were distributed on road safety. More than 3000 miles of bridleways were opened due to the efforts of the Bridleways Panel and County Committees. Over 3500 people – mostly young – took the BHS examinations. Over 10000 enquiries were received at Headquarters, the majority of them about the possibility of careers with horses. Over 2000 schools were inspected by the BHS's Inspectors, either schools already approved to ensure that they are still up to standard, or schools where complaints had been received. Some 70 Local Authorities were persuaded to help in the provision of bursaries to young people attending equitation courses. In 1978 the turnover of the Society in financial terms amounts to £1½ million.

To carry out all this work a staff at the Headquarters of the British Equestrian Centre at Stoneleigh of some 70 people is required. Understandably this produces a very large wages bill; at the same time an almost equally large expenses bill is incurred, the senior members of the staff having to travel many thousands of miles each year. Frequently the ordinary rank and file member of the Society does not appreciate the extent of the Society's work. There are now over 400 Riding Clubs and 300 Pony Clubs which have, as it were, to be serviced. There are 66 County Committees and 19 different regions. The membership subscription at the time of writing is £7. As, when the subscription went up in 1975, it was doubled from £3·50, an attempt has been made to keep the subscription to this level, but there is little doubt that it will have to be increased in the near future.

For a Society with a comparatively small membership the figures are not without interest. The total annual expenditure now approaches £200000, of which administration accounts for £128000; the salaries amounting to nearly £80000; postage costs £16000, printing and stationery £14000. Income from subscriptions amounts to £120000, but income from the main events such as the Royal International Horse Show which amounts to £15000, Badminton £25000 or more, Burghley about £20000, all help to increase the income sufficiently to cover what would otherwise be a deficit; sometimes is. Other committees unavoidably run at a loss, such as the English, Scottish, Welsh and Northern Ireland Committees, Welfare, Development, Training and Examinations and the National Equestrian Centre itself, while the Riding Clubs produces a useful profit of anything between £5000 and £10000 each year. From all this it will be seen that the administration of the Society is very costly: not unnaturally members of certain sections of the Society feel that too much money goes on administration at Headquarters. This is probably the case with most Societies, but in fact the charges at Headquarters to each of the different committees are considerably less than the real cost, which means that certain committees are able to provide more healthy figures than is really the case. Other than from a psychological point of view this is more or less irrelevant as each is a part of the whole. Nevertheless, if the Society is to continue to do its essential work, it is obviously necessary for the expenses of each of the different committees to be kept as low as possible, without in any way impairing the efficiency of that committee. Inflation is bound to increase costs but with something so rambling in its ramifications as the BHS people are inevitably going to feel that it is worth only so much to become a member, for the fact of the matter is that even without being a member of the BHS people are still able to enjoy riding at their own level. Obviously to take part in a one-day event or a dressage competition or a driving event one has to be a member of the Society; but many people who benefit indirectly from the inspection of riding schools, welfare, provision of instructors and so on, can still ride quite happily without becoming a member, blissfully unaware in all probability that they are in fact gaining from the work of the Society to which they do not belong.

It could be said that the British Equestrian Centre at Stoneleigh, for which the Society is responsible, is the pivot of the whole of the Society's work. It is essential, therefore, that it should be not only successful but well supported because the value of the work taking place at the Centre can in fact be of value to members all over the country and, indeed, all over the world. Unlike any other national centre, the British Equestrian Centre is not subsidised by the Government, receiving only grants to help with capital improvements and part payment of the instructional staff. It is not easy, therefore, for the Centre to make ends meet; every effort has to be made to increase the income without increasing the fees which might well result in people being unable to afford to avail themselves of the Centre. The British Equestrian Centre has its own very active management committee representing each discipline and the Pony Club. It is determined to keep the costs of the Centre to the Society as low as possible and is indeed hopeful that it may be possible in the near future to make the Centre pay for itself, which would certainly be a remarkable achievement when one remembers that the national centres of other sports cost either the sport itself or the Government anything between £50000 and £100000 a year.

To sum up, the BHS caters as much for the expert as the ordinary horseman. The various committees dealing with the disciplines, such as combined training and dressage, are obviously devoting their efforts towards the expert or the potential expert, but all the other committees devote themselves to the well being, from an equestrian point of view, of the ordinary riding public.

The British Show Jumping Association

The British Show Jumping Association (BSJA) was formed in 1923 when it was first appreciated that there was a need to draw up a set of rules that would be easily understood by riders, judges and spectators. Show jumping up to this time had been virtually without proper organisation, the rules being made up by different organisations for different events. Immediately after the formation of the Association the standard of show jumping in Britain improved and by the early thirties there were a number of first-class show jumpers in Britain, though because the rules were different to those on the continent they were never very successful in international competition. After the war with the almost universal adoption of the International (FEI) rules British riders soon went to the top of the tree.

The stated objectives of the Association today are as follows:

1 to improve the standard of jumping;
2 to provide for the representation of Great Britain in international competitions;
3 to prescribe the general standard of height of obstacles for show jumping;
4 to promote and encourage the holding of shows where jumping competitions are held;
5 to make rules for the judging of jumping competitions;
6 arrange the registration of horses and ponies;
7 to record the results and winnings of horses and ponies in show jumping competitions.

The Association raises its own funds through subscriptions, registration and transfer fees, leases, affiliation fees from shows and the hiring of jumps. It is administered by an executive committee, eight of whose members are elected nationally and ten of whom are regionally elected members. Obviously with only one aspect of equestrianism to be considered, the BSJA is a very much less complex organisation than the BHS. It is also in the strong position of being able to ensure itself an adequate income because only members of the BSJA are allowed to take part in shows which are affiliated to the BSJA. The membership today is around 10000. Recently the subscription has increased to £16, which may sound high but there is good prize money to be won in show jumping, far more than in any of the disciplines of the BHS; it is interesting, however, that as few as 30 riders are fortunate enough to win as much as, say, £2500 in any one season; though the riders at the top frequently earn twenty times that.

The BSJA is extremely strict in the maintenance of its rules, appreciating that their sport is particularly vulnerable to accusations of cruelty. Any rider who is found guilty of cruelty either in training or in performance is liable to a ban of at least a season and possibly a lifetime. In recent years a number of stipendary stewards have been employed whose responsibility is to ensure that there are no malpractices being carried out at shows. They attend most of the major shows and report anything which in their opinion is undesirable to the Stewards of the BSJA who are members, not those necessarily most involved with competitive show jumping, who are carefully selected to deal with any complaints.

Within the BSJA there is a Junior membership, junior show jumping having become particularly popular in the years since the war. As with the Seniors, there is a grading system to ensure that ponies are not asked to jump too large fences before they are ready for it. There is something of a problem today in that with prize money increasing so regularly it is perhaps too easy for a horse to have achieved the amount of prize money required to upgrade it. The result of this is that horses tend to be over-faced, having been upgraded in perhaps a few months by winning one major competition. The BSJA is constantly reviewing this, frequently raising the amount of money that has to be won before a horse becomes, in particular, Grade A. Grade A courses are now of international size and it is all too easy for a horse with great potential to be over-faced and lose its nerve because it is only allowed to jump in Grade A competitions before it is really sufficiently experienced.

Despite the high subscription the BSJA does not find it easy to make a sizeable profit. This is largely due to what one might call the servicing and registration. In their offices at Stoneleigh a large staff is employed to ensure that the winnings of every horse or pony jumping are recorded. The Association is also responsible for providing sets of jumps, maintaining a special department at Aldershot where the jumps are built. This is an expensive operation and although a certain amount of money comes back to the Association through the hiring of these jumps it is nothing like enough to cover the cost, either of timber or labour. Nevertheless, it is probably true to say that Britain is way ahead of most nations as far as the standard of the jumps is concerned. They are not only extremely well made, always to exactly the right dimensions, but they are also made in such a way as to be attractive to the public. Fortunately, what is attractive to the public is usually attractive to the horse, for a well-made fence is inviting; a fence well-built with bold colours will encourage a horse to jump, whereas a flimsy fence will very often receive casual or careless treatment from a horse.

As has been suggested earlier there is much to be said for an amalgamation of the BHS and the BSJA. Understandably, however, the BSJA does not want to become just the nineteenth section of the BHS, carrying only the same importance as, say, Dressage or Horse Trials. The membership of the BSJA, though sympathetic to the ultimate possibility of the two Societies coming together, feels very strongly that it should retain its own identity as, in their opinion – and there are many who will agree with them – show jumping is still the most important equestrian sport in Britain and should therefore be entirely independent. There are in fact other difficulties as far as amalgamation is concerned, but there is no doubt that it is the independence required by the BSJA membership that is most likely to delay any merger of the two Societies.

It is also of interest that the Horse of the Year Show which is generally accepted as the BSJA show has for many years been a major source of income. The BSJA understandably feel that this income should not be shared with the BHS, as it would be if the two Societies were amalgamated. On the other hand, in recent years, since the Royal International Horse Show moved to Wembley the gap between the profits of the two shows has decreased enormously. It could well be that in a few years time the profits of the Royal International will be equal to the profits of the Horse of the Year Show. This would at least remove one objection to the merging of the two Societies.

Perhaps because the majority of the membership is actively involved in a competitive sport it is true to say that the involvement of the membership in their sport is far greater than with the BHS where less than 20 per cent of the membership is actively involved in the various departments of the Society. This leads to the BSJA having a somewhat tough reputation, compared with that of the BHS: in fact the BSJA members are only, quite understandably, dedicated to their sport and therefore take a close interest in any legislation that the BSJA Council introduce. There is little doubt that the BSJA is one of the best organised and, therefore, most effective ruling bodies of show jumping in the world. As a result, it has a very considerable influence on world deliberations concerning the sport of show jumping.

Other Organisations

The Pony Club

The British Horse Society is of course the parent body of the Pony Club, but the Pony Club is itself autonomous. It was founded in 1928 with the following objects:

1 to encourage young people to ride and to enjoy all types of mounted sports;
2 to provide instruction in riding, horsemastership and care of horses;
3 to promote the highest ideals of sportsmanship and citizenship, thereby cultivating character and self-discipline in its members.

With over 300 branches in the British Isles there are some 40 000 members. Overseas there are a further 600 branches. Each Pony Club is run by a Committee which appoints a District Commissioner. One of the unique features of the Pony Club is its annual summer camp.

Originally the Pony Club was based on local Hunts, but nowadays there are many branches in non-hunting countries; the overall interests are therefore far wider. In addition to their own Championships, both for eventing and show jumping, they have dressage competitions and, of course, the Prince Philip Cup for Mounted Games. More recently a Tetrathlon has been introduced with the particular purpose of encouraging more boys to be members of the Pony Club. For the same reason polo has been

The Hunters' Improvement Society's yellow caravan, now replaced with a smaller unit

introduced. There is no doubt that the introduction of these two new sports has achieved that purpose; the number of boys joining each year is now increasing very considerably. Even more important perhaps is the fact that because of the Tetrathlon and polo, boys tend to remain members of the Pony Club longer than they otherwise would. Indeed, one of the problems of the Pony Club is to retain members up to their seventeenth birthday and as Associates.

The Hunters' Improvement and Light Horse Society

This Society, founded over 100 years ago, provides a most useful service by ensuring that good stallions are available to the owners of useful part-bred mares who could never afford the services of a top-class stallion. Through a grant provided by the Levy Board, the Hunters' Improvement and Light Horse Society (HIS) is able to subsidise approved stallions so that only a comparatively small fee is charged for the service to mares. An annual show is held at Newmarket each March, premiums being awarded to those stallions which the judges think worthy of them. These are awarded on a regional basis so that the HIS ensures that in each part of the country there is an HIS stallion available to which mares can be brought for a reasonable fee. In the old days the stallion used to be literally led from stable to stable to cover the different mares, but in recent times the mares are taken in the normal way to the stud. This scheme has done an enormous amount to maintain the high standard of half-bred and three-quarter bred horses which have so long been the pride of Britain. The time is coming, however, when more money will be required if the scheme is to continue. It is hoped therefore that the Levy Board will see its way to increase their grant to the HIS.

The Ponies of Britain Club

This Club was formed by its founder Mrs Glenda Spooner, who is still Chairman, some 30 years ago. Since when it has gone from strength to strength holding two major shows, the Stallion Show in the spring and the Summer Show; a show is also held in Scotland. The breadth of interest covered by the Ponies of Britain is enormous, with everything from stallions and breed classes to leading rein and show pony classes. It not only provides a very useful adjunct to the world of pony breeding and showing ponies, but also engenders a very happy relationship between all those involved.

The National Pony Society

This is the official pony organisation which controls all the pony world activities in the same way as the BHS controls its various disciplines and the BSJA controls show jumping. In the opinion of some there was a need for a special organisation for those most interested in showing and therefore some years ago the British Show Pony Society was formed. It has area branches running their own shows and providing social occasions for the members in the different regions.

There is no doubt that the pony world is very well served as far as organisations are concerned. Indeed, it is fortunate that this is so because, more than in any other department of the equestrian world, there has been an explosion in interest in ponies both from the riding point of view and from the showing and breeding point of view. Unless the whole pony world were properly organised it could be somewhat chaotic.

The British Show Hack and Cob Association

This again is a body that came into being to look after the interests of those who show Hacks and Cobs: it performs a most useful service; as indeed do the other societies that run their own organisations to make sure that their particular interests are not entirely overwhelmed and lost sight of in the very complex composition of the horse world as it is today.

The Association of British Riding Schools

This Association was formed some years ago as the controlling body of the Riding Schools Movement. As with the BHS it has its own inspection scheme to ensure that proper standards are maintained. It is not compulsory for riding schools to belong, but it is obviously in the interests of most to do so.

APPENDIX

BRITISH HORSE SOCIETY
ASSOCIATED ORGANISATIONS

Association of British Riding Schools,
Chesham House,
56 Green End Road,
Sawtry, Huntingdon, Cambs
Tel: Ramsey 830278

British Driving Society,
10 Marley Avenue,
New Milton, Hants
Tel: New Milton 616338
Sec: Mrs P. Candler

British Equine Veterinary Association,
Overton,
Maids Moreton, Buckingham
Sec: P. S. Hastie, MRCVS

British Show Hack and Cob Association,
The National Equestrian Centre,
Kenilworth, Warwickshire
Tel: Coventry 27192
Sec: J. E. Blackmore

British Show Jumping Association,
The National Equestrian Centre,
Kenilworth, Warwickshire
Tel: Coventry 20783/4
Sec: Lt.-Com. W. B. Jefferis, RN (Ret.)

British Show Pony Society,
Smale Farm,
Wisborough Green, Billingshurst, West Sussex
Tel: Wisborough Green 279
Sec: Capt. R. Grellis

British Veterinary Association,
7 Mansfield Street,
Portland Place, London W1
Tel: 01-686 6541

Fédération Équestre Internationale,
F. O. Widmer,
Avenue Hamoir 38,
Brussels 18, Belgium

Hackney Horse Society,
National Equestrian Centre,
Kenilworth, Warwickshire CV8 2LR
Tel: Coventry 27192

Hunters Improvement Society,
National Westminster Bank Chambers,
8 Market Square,
Westerham, Kent
Tel: Westerham 63867
Sec: G. W. Evans

Master of Foxhounds Association,
Parsloes Cottage,
Bagendon,
Cirencester, Glos
Tel: North Cerney 470
Sec: A. H. B. Hart

National Master Farriers' and Blacksmiths' Association,
674 Lofthouse Gate,
Wakefield, West Yorks
Tel: Wakefield 823286

National Pony Society,
Stoke Lodge,
85 Cliddesden Road,
Basingstoke, Hants
Tel: Basingstoke 22906
Sec: Cmdr. B. H. Brown, RN (Ret.)

Ponies of Britain Club,
Brookside Farm,
Ascot, Berks

Riding for the Disabled Association,
Avenue R,
National Agriculture Centre,
Kenilworth, Warwicks
Tel: Coventry 56107
Sec: Miss C. M. L. Haynes

Thoroughbred Breeders' Association,
42 Portman Square,
London W1
Tel: 01-487 4586
Sec: S. G. Sheppard

Worshipful Company of Farriers,
3 Hamilton Road,
Cockfosters,
Barnet, Herts.
Sec: F. E. Birch

17 International Organisations

There is, and always has been, a great deal of individualism amongst horsemen. This is, perhaps, particularly so in Britain, but it is also the case in most countries. It is not true to say, however, that horsemen are so independent that they resist their equestrian activities being properly organised. Equestrianism, like any other sport, is in fact highly organised, both at national and international levels. It is obviously, inevitable that this is so, though naturally it is competitive riding that is far more organised than recreational riding.

Fédération Équestre Internationale

The international organisation is known as the Fédération Équestre Internationale (FEI). It was founded in 1921, the first President being the eminent Frenchman Baron du Teil. The Baron was President until 1927, since when there have been some eight Presidents. Prince Bernhard of the Netherlands was President for ten years until the appointment of Prince Philip, the Duke of Edinburgh, in 1954. He is still President today and has agreed to serve until 1980. His contribution is inestimable.

The purposes of the FEI are set out as follows:

1 To be the sole international authority for the equestrian sports of dressage, jumping, three-day events, driving and any other forms of equestrian sports which the General Assembly may from time to time decide.

2 To promote the organisation of international equestrian competitions throughout the world.

3 To coordinate, standardise and publish the rules and to supervise the organisation of international equestrian events, while allowing the National Federations the widest possible freedom in the arrangement of their programmes.

4 To standardise and approve the rules and programmes for International Championships, Regional and Olympic Games and to control their technical organisation.

5 To provide the means for discussion and understanding between National Federations and to give them support and encouragement, and to strengthen their authority and prestige.

6 To encourage instruction in riding, driving and horsemastership for recreational purposes.

The FEI's principles are as follows:

1 The FEI is based on the principle of equality and mutual respect between all its National Federations without prejudice of race, colour, religion or internal politics. National Federations therefore undertake that their competitors will compete against the competitors of all other member National Federations whenever required and under all circumstances, without exception whatever.

2 The National Federations recognise the FEI as the sole international authority for those equestrian events which are agreed by its members. National Federations agree not to become affiliated to any other equivalent organisation for a similar purpose.

3 The FEI and all National Federations recognise only one Equestrian Federation for each nation.

4 The FEI and all National Federations agree to comply with and be bound by the Statutes, General Regulations, the Rules for the individual disciplines, and any other publications authorised by the General Assembly.

5 The Regulations and Rules governing international equestrian competitions shall apply to all competitors whatever their nationality in all countries whose National Federations are affiliated to the FEI.

6 The National Federations have complete jurisdiction over all competitors (amateur and professional) of their countries.

7 In case of disagreement in the interpretation or application of the Statutes, General Regulations and Rules of the FEI it shall be settled by an arbitration committee consisting of three members of the Bureau appointed by the Bureau for that purpose. The General Assembly of the FEI is the final Court of Appeal.

8 Any sanctions or penalties pronounced by the FEI or by National Federations shall be recognised and enforced by all National Federations.

9 Nothing contained in these Statutes shall authorise the FEI to intervene in matters, equestrian or otherwise, which are essentially within the national jurisdiction of National Federations, nor does it oblige National Federations to submit such matters to the FEI for settlement under these Statutes.

It is of significance that after the 1976 Olympics the following was introduced into the FEI official Statutes:

Competitors of one or several nations cannot come to an event and then refuse to participate in those competitions in which some particular nation is represented for reasons of race, colour, religion or internal politics.

It is perhaps a pity that other sports' federations do not consider a similar statute.

The main body of the FEI is the General Assembly, the composition of which is as follows:

1 All members may be represented at the General Assembly by two delegates, accredited in writing by the President of their National Federation. Only one nominated delegate from each Member has the right to vote.

2 The members of the Bureau, may not represent their own or any other National Federation.

3 National Federations must notify the Secretary General before the date of the meeting of the General Assembly the names of their delegates, nominating the one who will have the right to vote. Delegates may not vote unless the Secretary General has been provided with proper credentials in writing and signed by the President of their National Federation.

4 If an appointed delegate is unable to attend the General Assembly, the National Federation may replace him by another delegate provided the Secretary General is notified 24 hours before the session of the General Assembly. Substitutes must deliver their credentials in writing to the Secretary General before they may attend the meeting.

5 Each Member may undertake to represent one other National Federation which is unable to send delegates to the General Assembly. The delegate or delegates present from any National Federation may exercise not more than two votes, that is to say one vote for their own National Federation and one proxy vote.

The General Assembly only meets once each year, usually in Brussels in December.

The executive body is the Bureau, whose composition and functions are as follows:

1 The Bureau consists of the following 13 members:
  (a) Five officers: the President, the First and Second Vice-President, the Secretary General and the Treasurer.
  (b) Eight, or if the duties of the Treasurer are performed by the Secretary General, nine ordinary members.

2 At least one member of the Bureau must come from either North or Central America, one from South America, one from either Africa, Australia, New Zealand or Asia.

3 In order that the Bureau may be properly advised on matters to do with each discipline, at least two members of the Bureau must be on the FEI list of Official International Jumping Judges, one must be on the FEI list of Official International Dressage Judges, one must be on the FEI list of Official International Three-Day Event Judges, one must be on the list of Official International Driving Judges and one must be a qualified Veterinary Surgeon.

4 Each member shall take office at the close of the session of the General Assembly at which he was elected and he will remain in office over the period of the next four ordinary sessions unless he resigns or relinquishes his membership for any other reason.

5 Membership of the Bureau is entirely honorary and it shall not be remunerated in any way. Members may receive travel and lodging allowances for attendance at meetings of the Bureau, the General Assembly and the FEI Committees, or when officially representing the FEI.

6 A member of the Bureau performing functions of a national character at an event shall temporarily lose his prerogatives as a member of the Bureau.

7 A delegate nominated by the National Federation of the country where the next Olympic Games are to be held shall join the Bureau in a consultative capacity for the meetings at the two annual sessions preceding the Olympic Games and at any other meetings of the Bureau during that period when matters affecting the Games are to be discussed. He shall render a report on the conduct of the equestrian events at the Olympic Games and his recommendations to the Bureau at its meeting at the next annual session of the General Assembly following the Games. His mission will then be completed.

Candidates for the Bureau must be able to speak and read French or English and adequately understand the other language. They must have a proper knowledge of equestrian sport or of one of the disciplines, or of the administration of a National Federation or of the running of an international event.

A retiring member of the Bureau is eligible for re-election.

The voting procedure is somewhat complicated: it is probably enough to say that a candidate must receive an overall majority of the votes entitled to be cast.

The Bureau is responsible for the general direction

FEI BUREAU	
President	Prince Philip, Duke of Edinburgh
1st Vice President	Pedro O. Mayorga (Argentina)
2nd Vice President	John Wylie (Ireland)
Secretary General	Fritz Widmer (Switzerland)
President, Dressage Committee	Col Gustav Nyblaeus (Sweden)
President, Driving Committee	Col Donald Thackeray (USA)
President, Veterinary Committee	Prof Igor Bobylev (USSR)
President, Three-Day Event Committee	Vicomte Jurien de la Gravière (France)
President, Show Jumping Committee	Eryk Brabec (Poland)
President, Juniors Committee	Knud Larsen (Denmark)
Members	Paulino Rivera Torres (Mexico)
	H E Rundle (Australia)
	Graf Landsberg-Velen (West Germany)

and administration of the FEI and for all matters not specifically reserved to the General Assembly by these Statutes or provided for otherwise. The Bureau shall carry out all the duties prescribed for it in these Statutes and in the General Regulations. The Bureau may take decisions on behalf of the General Assembly in cases regarded as urgent by the President, Vice-Presidents and Secretary General. Such decisions must be confirmed at the next session of the General Assembly.

The Bureau, as a rule, meets for several days prior to the General Assembly.

There are eight Standing Committees covering disciplines and eligibility, finance and administration, dressage, show jumping, three-day eventing, driving, veterinary and juniors. There are only four members and a Chairman of each committee.

There are in all some 60 members of the Federation, only France, Sweden, Japan, the USA, Italy, Belgium, Denmark and Germany being founder members from 1921. Great Britain joined in 1925, Australia and New Zealand only in 1951, the USSR in 1952. In recent years a number of African and Asian nations have also joined.

From the above it will be appreciated that the whole international organisation is extremely comprehensive. As with so many similar organisations there is nowadays a risk of politics being involved with nations which play only a minor part in the sport clubbing together to influence decisions which may not always be in the best interests of the sport. It is going to be necessary for the Bureau, under the President, to control the Federation with considerable tact and firmness.

It can be seen how vitally important the existence of the FEI is. Without it, all competitive riding and driving at an international level would be a shambles with different countries following different rules. Before Great Britain joined the FEI – and indeed for many years afterwards – the rules for show jumping in Britain were different to those of the FEI. The price Britain paid was to have to wait until after the war in 1946 for its first victory in an international event.

The names of members of the Bureau are given above.

An appendix at the end of this chapter sets out a comprehensive list of the different Federations with the names and the addresses of their Secretaries.

The British Equestrian Federation

It is obvious from the foregoing that it is each country's own Federation that deals with all international affairs concerning their members. In Britain there is a certain anomaly in that until recently there have been two main equestrian bodies, the British Horse Society (BHS) and the British Show Jumping Association (BSJA). Although it is show jumping that is the sport which is most often represented in international competition, more than dressage, three-day eventing or driving, yet it was the BHS that was the official Federation for so long. All this has now been changed with the formation in 1972 of the British Equestrian Federation. The BHS was not, understandably, anxious to give up its federal role. The BSJA, although so much more involved in international competitive riding, was not, on the other hand, particularly anxious to take on the role. It was in 1971 that with the imminent retirement of Col. Sir Michael Ansell as Chairman of the BHS after nearly 20 years, during much of which time he had also been Chairman of the BSJA, it was suggested that the time was at last ripe for the formation of a Federation. Discussions took place between officers and senior members of both Societies. Col. Ansell with his authority and his persuasive powers persuaded the majority that the formation of a Federation was in the interests of both Societies. The problem was obviously going to be to convince the rank and file members of the respective Societies, each and every one being proud of their own Society's independence.

A draft constitution was produced, discussed at length at each level of the two Societies, a date finally being fixed for the two Societies to ratify the proposal for the formation of a British Equestrian Federation. An unexpected tragedy, however, came near to wrecking all the well prepared plans. Sir Michael Ansell's wife was tragically killed. Shocked and distressed Sir Michael was unable to attend the ratifying meetings. As Vice Chairman of the BHS at that time it fell to me to take the Chair at the BHS meeting at which it was hoped that proposals would be accepted by the Council.

Well aware of strong opposition in certain quarters, it seemed wisest to deal first with the various objections likely to be raised by the BHS members, particularly the fear that the Society would lose its autonomy. I then pointed out the value of a fully representative Federation that would be able to speak with a much more effective voice: especially in dealings with Government Departments and Ministries. A Federation furthermore, I suggested, would obviously be able to deal much more effectively with the FEI and other national Federations. In addition it could be the controlling body of the British Equestrian Centre and in due course, perhaps, act as the licensing authority on behalf of the Government.

There was plenty of comment, a considerable amount of criticism, but I was in the fortunate position of holding a trump card. Shortly before the meeting I had been informed that the BSJA at their meeting that morning had unanimously endorsed the proposal to form a Federation representing both the BSJA and the BHS. There is little doubt that this information silenced the opponents of the scheme who were in any case a minority. The proposal was carried unanimously. Thus, in September 1971, the idea of a British Equestrian Federation was generally accepted by the BSJA and the BHS. It actually came into being in May 1972, and was probably the most important development in the equestrian world in Britain since the amalgamation of the Institute of the Horse and the National Horse Society to form the British Horse Society in 1944 and even perhaps since the formation of the British Show Jumping Association in 1923. To suggest that order was being created out of chaos is an exaggeration, but the creation of the Federation was the logical step that had so long been needed in the horse world in Britain.

The tasks of the Federation were designated as follows:

1 To coordinate the major policy interests of common concern to the British Horse Society and the British Show Jumping Association for the benefit of both bodies, whilst allowing both Societies autonomy according to their constitutions.

2 To be the national authority for equestrian activities and interests, other than for racing, within the United Kingdom; for high-level representation with HM Government; and to act in every way as the national governing body for equestrian sport.

3 To be the sole national authority and be so regarded as the National Federation in all matters concerned with the Fédération Équestre Internationale (FEI) including the authority to nominate representatives to the General Assembly of the Fédération Équestre Internationale. To have the responsibility to negotiate or correspond with the Fédération Équestre Internationale on any subject and the power to establish sub-committees to deal with any particular aspect of its relationship with the Fédération Équestre Internationale.

4 To be responsible for dealing on policy matters with any other National Federation and also with the Organising Committees of the Olympic and Regional Games, Continental Championships and all International Events.

5 To be responsible for confirming the issue of amateur permits and professional licences to competitors.

6 To be the body to which either the British Horse Society or the British Show Jumping Association may appeal or refer for advice and to arbitrate when necessary.

The composition of the British Equestrian Federation consists of a President/Chairman and ten members, and such other persons as may be appointed by the Federation from time to time in consultancy or honorary capacities:

1 Five members to be appointed by the British Horse Society and to include the Chairman of the British Horse Society and the Honorary Treasurer, the remaining members to be nominated by the General Purposes and Finance Committee and ratified by the Council.

2 Five members to be appointed by the British Show Jumping Association and to include the Chairman of the British Show Jumping Association and the Chairman of the British Show Jumping Association Finance Committee. The remaining three members to be appointed by the Executive Committee.

3 The Presidents of the British Horse Society and British Show Jumping Association are *ex officio* members without vote; however, in the event that one of the members from the British Horse Society or British Show Jumping Association be absent the Presidents of the respective Societies may vote in their place.

The President/Chairman holds office for four years commencing on 1 January, following the Olympic Games, but is not eligible for re-election.

Those holding *ex officio* appointments, ie Chairman and Treasurer/Finance Chairman of the British Horse Society and the British Show Jumping Association, hold office for the duration of their tenure in their parent organisations. The remaining members hold office for two years.

The present President/Chairman of the British Equestrian Federation is Col. Sir Harry Llewellyn. The four *ex officio* members are Col. Sir Cecil Blacker (Chairman of the British Show Jumping Association), Dorian Williams (Chairman of the British Horse Society), David Garner (Chairman, Finance Committee of the British Show Jumping Association) and Robert Dean (Treasurer of the British Horse Society). The Director General of the Federation is Maj.-Gen. Jack Reynolds.

APPENDIX

NATIONAL FEDERATIONS AFFILIATED TO THE FEI

Algeria
23, Bd Zirout Youcef
Alger
President: Lt.-Col. A. Aouchiche
Sec Gen: Mr Y. Bouabid

Argentina
Rodriguez Pena, 1934
Buenos Aires
President: Gen. Nr Rodolfo Oscar Reinoso
Sec Gen: Col. Eduardo A. Castaing

Australia
Royal Show Grounds,
Epsom Road,
Ascot Vale 3032, Sydney
President: Mr John Walsh
Sec Gen: Mr J H Clappison

Austria
Theresianumgasse, 33
A-1040 Wien
President: Dr Rudolf Nemetschke
Sec Gen: Mr Seti

Barbados
The Quorum Bagatelle Plantation,
St Thomas Parish, W1
President: Mr Justice Denys Williams
Sec Gen: Miss Sarah B. Hamilton

Belgium
Avenue Hamoir, 38
1180 Bruxelles
President: Chevalier H. de Menten de Horne
Sec Gen: Mr J. Hoffman

Bermuda
'Darrell' Trimingham Hill
Paget 6–19
President: Mr Norman J. Holbrow
Sec Gen: Mr Robert G L Clifford

Bolivia
Casilla 6554
La Paz

Brazil
Rua Sete de Setembro, 81 3° Andar
Salas 301/302
Rio de Janeiro
President: Mr Anisio de Silva Rocha

Bulgaria
Bd Tolboukhin, 18
Sofia 1000
President: Gen. Vladimir Stoytchev
Sec Gen: Mr Luben Naidenov

Canada
River Road, 333
Ottawa, Ontario K1L 889
President: Mr D. Esworthy

Chile
Av Vicuna Mackenna, 44
Santiago de Chile
President: Mr Alberto Montecinos
Sec: Mr Carol Lopicich

Colombia
Apartado Aereo 16987
Bogotá
President: Maj.-Gen. Gustavo Matamoros d'Costa
Sec Gen: Sr Jairo Cardenas Fierro

Costa Rica
PO Box 999
San José
President: Mr R. Ferris MD

Cuba
c/o Comite Olimpico Cubano
Hotel Habana
Habana
President: Mr Armand Tamayo

Czechoslovakia
Na Porici, 12
115 30 Praha 1
President: Mr Frantizek Hoza
Sec Gen: Mr Ivan Sturc

Denmark
Idraettens Hus,
Brondby Stadion 20
DK-2600 Glostrup
President: Mr Knud Larsen
Sec: Mr E K Carlsen

East Germany
Storkower-Strasse 118
1055 Berlin
President: Prof. Dr Habil D. Flade
Sec Gen: Mr M. Breitsprecher

Ecuador
Apartado 123A
Quito
President: Capt. Arturo Suarez Nieto
Sec: Econn Hugo Amores

Egypt
Rue Kasr Elnil, 13
Cairo
Sec Gen: Col. S. Khalifa

Finland
Topeliuksenkatu 41 a
00251 Helsinki 25
President: Mr Viktor Jansson
Sec Gen: Mr T. Olavi Lehti

France
Faubourg St-Honore, 164
F-75008 Paris
President: Mr C. Legrez
Dir Gen: Mr J. Courrege

Great Britain
National Equestrian Centre,
Kenilworth,
Warwickshire CV8 2LR
President: Sir Harry Llewellyn, Bt CBE
Dir Gen: Maj.-Gen. J. R. Reynolds

Greece
Rue G Genadious, 3
Athenes 142
President: Mr Serpieris

Guatemala
Ciudad de Guatemala
Apartado Postal 2674
Guatemala
President: Dr Fernando Beltranena Valladares
Sec Gen: Sr Estuardo Mendez Herbruger

Hungary
Szep Utca 3
Budapest 1053
President: Mr J. Pal
Sec Gen: Mr S. Butor

India
c/o RV Dte, Army HQ West Block 111
1st Floor
R.K. Puram,
New Delhi-22
Sec Gen: Dr Prio Hartono SH

Indonesia
Jalan Kibon Sirih, 37
Jakarta

Iran
Avenue Sepahbod Zahedi, 269
PO Box 11-1642
Teheran
President: Mr Kambiz Atabai
Sec: Mrs Golnar Bakhtiar

Iraq
PO Box n° 441
Baghdad
President: Maj.-Gen. S. A. al-Khalidy
Sec Gen: Lt.-Col. Hamdoun Saeed Ali

Ireland
c/o The Royal Dublin Society,
Ball's Bridge,
PO Box 121
Dublin 4.
President: Mr F. J. O'Reilly
Sec Gen: Mr John E. Wylie

Italy
Viale Tiziano, 70
I-00100 Rome
President: Mr Lino Sordelli
Sec Gen: Mr Gionannie Buffa

Japan
1–2, Kana Surugadai, Chiyoda-Ku
Central PO Box 377
Tokyo 100-91
President: Mr Nobutaka Kiso
Sec: Mr Shozo Hara

Korea
Mukyo-Dong, Chung-Ku, 19
KASA Bidg Room 611
Seoul KWM PO Box 106
President: Mr Joun Sik Kil

Libya
Maidan Abu Sitta
PO Box 4507
Tripoli
President: Lt.-Col. Ali Faitouri
Sec: Col. Giuma Schaban

Luxembourg
Route de Thionville, 90
Luxembourg
President: Mr Georges Wagner
Sec Gen: Mme Molitor

Mexico
Cda de Agustin Ahumada, 31
Lomas de Chapultepec
Mexico City 41 10 D F
President: Sr Agustin F. Legorreta Chauvet
Sec: Sr Ruben C. Rodriguez Monterde

Morocco
Dar-Es-Salam ou BP 742
Rabat – Aguidal
President: Prince Moulay Driss Ouazzani
Sec Gen: Col. Benaissa

Netherlands
Postbus 97 639
NL-2509 GA Den Haag
President: Mr A. Stehouwer
Dir: Mr J. Van Leeuwen

New Zealand
PO Box 1046
Hastings, Hawke's Bay
President: Mrs R. D. Dalley
Dir: Mr N. D. Williams

Norway
Hauqer Skolevei, 1
1351 RUD
President: Consul a.E. Bache
Sec Gen: Mr Kjell Ellingsen

Peru
Estadio Nacional
Puerto 19
Lima
President: Sr Jose Luis Balta Vivanco

Philippines
PO Box 1586
Makati, Rizal 3117

Poland
Sienkiewicza, 12
00-010 Warszawa
President: Dr Pawel-Warchol
Sec Gen: Mr Eryk Brabec

Portugal
Rua do Arco do Cego 90-5
Lisboa 1
President: Col. Jorge Mathias
Sec Gen: Lt.-Col. Minas de Piedade

Puerto Rico
Apartado 5642
San Juan 00 905
President: Mr German Rieckehoff
Sec Treas: Mr Luis Cerra

Rhodesia
PO Box U A 340, Union Avenue
Salisbury
President: Mrs W. Smith
Hon Sec Gen: Mr G. R. J. Hackwill

Romania
Str Vasile Conta, 16
Bucarest 70139
President: Victor Standuescu
Sec Gen: Dr D. Nedelea

Salvador (El)
Edificio Central No 304
San Salvador
President: Mr Rogelio Alfredo Chavez

Senegal
Av William Ponty, 16
Dakar

Singapore
Bukit Timah Racecourse
Singapore 11
President: Mr Tan Choo Keng
Sec: Capt. R. F. Tibbatts

South Africa
PO Box 52365
Saxonwold
Transvaal 2132
President: Mr W. C. Angus
Sec Gen: Mrs L. V. Tothill

Spain
Montesquinza, 8
Madrid – 4
President: Sr José Arango
Sec: Sr Juan Botana

Sweden
Bragevagen, 12
S – 114 24 Stockholm
President: Mr Per Skold
Sec Gen: Mr Hans Ernmark

Switzerland
Blankweg 70
CH-3072 Ostermundigen
President: Col. Hans Britschgi
Sec Gen: Mr R. Pezold

Syria
BP 421
Damascus
President: Salim Jarade
Sec Gen: Maj. Adnan El Abrache

Taiwan
Ke Nan Street, 434
Taiwan, Taipei
President: Lt.-Gen. Tien Shu-Shang
Sec Gen: Mr Chung Yu-Hsiang

Tunisia
Club Hippique de la Soukra
La Soukra
President: Slaheddine Baly

Turkey
Beden Tirbeyesi General Mudurlugu
Ulus, Ankara
President: Ass. Prof. Dr Oktay Kural
Sec Gen: Mr Cenan Sahir Silan

USA
Madison Avenue, 598
New York, NY 10022
President: Mr Richard E. McDevitt
Sec: Mr Frederick Wagner III

Uruguay
Av Agraciada 1546, Piso 10, Sala 17
Montevideo
President: Col. Hugo Medina

USSR
Skaternyi Pereulok 4
Moscow 69
President: Prof. M. P. Kobyzev
Sec Gen: Mrs E. Svischeva

Venezuela
Av Francisco Solano con Los Jabillos
Apartado 3588
Edificio Morichal, Piso 5, Oficina 54
Caracas 101
President: Dr Noel Vanososte
Sec: Mr Ekkehard Krueger

Virgin Islands
PO Box 1542
Charlotte Amalie
St Thomas 00801
US Virgin Islands
President: Mr David A. Bornn

West Germany
Postfach 640
Freiherr-von-Langenstrasse, 13
D-4410 Warendorf/Westfalen
President: Graf D. Landsberg-Velen
Sec Gen: Dr Burandt

Yugoslavia
Rue General Zdanova, 27
Beograd
Sec Gen: Mr Milisaw Milutinovic

PART SEVEN
Personalities and Statistics

18
Brief Biographies

Obviously in a short list of brief biographies it is quite impossible to include many who should by their exploits find a place. I have attempted to produce a list of people who in my mind have contributed most, in one way or another, to the equestrian scene during the post-war years. There are many others who have been immensely successful and have contributed something special in the way of achievement or organisation, but any list has to be limited and many, therefore, are inevitably omitted.

Maj. Derek Allhusen

Maj. Allhusen became interested in three-day eventing soon after it was introduced into Britain in 1949. Previous to that he had been keen on the Modern Pentathlon, representing Britain in the Olympics in 1948. Riding *Lochinvar*, Maj. Allhusen was in the winning British Team for the European Championships in 1967 and 1969. His greatest success, however, was when he captained the team that won the Olympic gold medal in Mexico in 1968; he himself winning the silver medal. From his mare *Laurien*, the first horse on which he came into prominence in three-day eventing, he bred *Laurieston* on which Richard Meade won the Individual Olympic gold medal at Munich in 1972 being also a member of the gold medal winning team. Although Maj. Allhusen's main interest in the equestrian world has been three-day eventing he has been a considerable influence in riding generally, particularly in the Eastern counties. He has done a great deal for the British Horse Society both at regional and national level and could now fairly be described as the elder statesman of combined training.

Col. Sir Michael Ansell

Sir Michael Ansell was in the 5th Royal Inniskilling Dragoon Guards before the war, as a soldier representing the British Army in show jumping events. During the war he received severe injuries, which later resulted in blindness when he was captured and taken prisoner of war at St Valéry in France. During his time in a prisoner of war camp, however, he thought deeply about the future of show jumping and immediately after the war he was elected chairman of the newly formed British Show Jumping Association, and was responsible for making show jumping a major sport. He started by organising the Victory Championships in 1945. In 1947 he was responsible for organising the show jumping events at the new Royal International Horse Show at the White City. He was also responsible for the new show at Harringay, to be known as the Horse of the Year Show. He was chairman of the British Show Jumping Association for 22 years, being also chairman of the British Horse Society and its Director. When the British Equestrian Federation was formed in 1972 he became its first President/Director. He is an honorary member of the Bureau of the FEI, in 1977 being awarded the silver medal of the International Olympic Committee, a rare honour.

Caroline Bradley

Caroline Bradley started her riding in the Pony Club with no special privileges. She first represented Britain at Dublin in 1966 and for the following years was most successful on her horse *Franco*, an ex-racehorse that had been jumped in the Rome Olympics in 1960 by David Barker. She was runner-up for the Ladies' European Championship in Vienna in 1973 on

Caroline Bradley on *Tigre*: World Champion Team gold medal, 1978

True Lass. In 1974 she was 3rd in the Women's World Championships at La Baule, having become a professional in 1973. This undoubtedly prevented her from being selected for the Montreal Olympic Team, but in 1978 she was selected for the winning World Championship Team in Aachen, finishing 5th in the Individual event, having earlier that year won the Queen Elizabeth Cup, the Ladies' Championship at the Royal International Horse Show. Caroline Bradley is probably one of the most consistent riders in the world, her success being particularly meritorious because she has had to achieve it on unmade horses that have become top-class horses due to her own skill.

Hans Brinkmann

Brinkmann was a Cavalry Officer before the war, following in his father's footsteps as a successful international rider. He is now considered to be one of the outstanding course builders in the world, in particular building the famous courses at Aachen, the official international horse show for West Germany. Of the many courses that Mickey Brinkmann, as he is known, has built none did more to establish his reputation than the course he built for the Olympic Games at Munich in 1972. Nor could better courses have been built than those he designed for the World Championship in 1978.

David Broome

David Broome came to the fore when he was only 18 years old on a horse called *Wildfire*, a horse rejected by the King's Troop and bought by his father, Fred Broome, for £75. In a brilliantly successful career David Broome won bronze medals at the Rome Olympics in 1960 on *Sunsalve*, and in the Mexico Olympics in 1968 on *Mister Softee*. He also won the European Championships in 1961 in Aachen on *Sunsalve* and in 1967 and 1969 on *Mister Softee*. In 1970 he won the Men's World Championship at La Baule on Douglas Bunn's *Beethoven*, coming 5th in 1974 and 6th in 1978 when he was in the winning team on *Philco*. He is the only rider to have won the

David Broome (GB) on *Mister Softee*, winning the European Championships in 1969

King George V Gold Cup, the Individual championship at the Royal International Horse Show, on four occasions. In all he has competed in four Olympic Games and for 20 years has been a regular member of the British team and prolific winner. He is Joint-Master of the Curre Fox Hounds in Wales.

Douglas Bunn

Douglas Bunn is best known as the Master of Hickstead, but in fact he was for many years an international rider of considerable reputation himself. His best horse was *Beethoven*, an Irish-bred horse, on which he was narrowly beaten in the King George V Gold Cup in 1961. He was well-known as a boy rider and was 2nd on *Rahin* to Col. Harry Llewellyn and *Foxhunter* in a major competition at the age of 18 when still at Cambridge. It was in 1960 that he opened the famous All England Jumping Course at Hickstead. Since then it has developed into a most successful show jumping arena, having in addition some four or five outside arenas where not only jumping competitions are held but also show classes. In 1975 at the April meeting he introduced the famous cross-country event which has become so popular all over Britain. Hickstead is generously sponsored by W.D. & H.O. Wills. The most famous of all the Hickstead events is the Hickstead Jumping Derby contested over 16 fences, including the famous Bank with its drop of 10 ft 6 in.

Bertalan de Nemethy

Hungarian born Bert de Nemethy, a former Cavalry instructor, is now a naturalised American and has been Coach to the United States Equestrian Team for show jumping since 1955. He was in fact a member of the Hungarian Olympic Team at the 1940 Olympic Games which were of course never held. He has coached no less than five American Olympic Teams, frequently winning medals and on two occasions his team has won the President's Cup. He operates from the team centre at Gladstone, New Jersey where he spends his time not only coaching the team, but training young horses and young riders.

Bertalan de Nemethy

Piero and Raimondo d'Inzeo

Piero was born in 1923, Raimondo two years later. Piero joined the Army as an Officer Cadet, passing out in 1946. In 1956 he helped Italy to win the silver medal at the Stockholm Olympics on *Uruguay*. Meanwhile, Raimondo, after going to Rome University, joined the famous Carabinieri, the Mounted Police. His first Olympic medal was on *Merano* in 1956 when he won the silver, winning the gold on *Posillipo* in 1960. Both Piero and Raimondo have not only been extremely successful and consistent in show jumping all over the world, but they have also been extremely popular. Piero has won the King George V Gold Cup on three occasions, Raimondo has twice won the World Championship on *Merano* in 1956 and on *Gowran Girl* in 1960. In 1975 he won the Grand Prix at Dublin. The d'Inzeos' father was a sergeant in the Italian Cavalry, a pupil of the famous Federico Caprilli.

Raimondo d'Inzeo (Italy), twice World Champion, 1956 and 1960, on *Gone Away*

Graham Fletcher

Graham Fletcher is the son of a Yorkshire farmer at Thirsk. Starting on ponies he graduated to young riders' competitions, first coming to prominence as an 18-year-old on the four-year-old *Buttevant Boy*. In 1970 he won the Cortina car for gaining the most points at the Horse of the Year Show, though he was still under 20. He first jumped for Britain at Rome in 1971, winning the Dublin Grand Prix on *Buttevant Boy* the same year. He was short-listed for the 1972 Olympic Team; in 1975 he won the Aachen Grand Prix and went on to ride *Hideaway* with the Olympic Team in Montreal. Still under 30, he has a great career ahead of him as he is so successful at bringing on young horses and turning them into top international horses.

Graham Fletcher (GB) on *Cool Customer* in 1976

Cynthia Haydon

Cynthia Haydon, the daughter of the late Bob Black, who came from Yorkshire between the wars and set up a very successful Hackney establishment, is generally recognised as the leading and most successful driver in the world. She was taught to drive a team by the late Bertram Mills, driving his team at Olympia before the Second World War. She was the first woman ever to compete in an international driving three-day event, being successful both in the European and in the World Championships. She was also the first person to bring a team of Hackneys into this now highly competitive sport. She is equally well-known in the United States and Canada as she is in Britain, competing regularly with success in New York and at the Winter Fair at Toronto. With her husband, Frank, she is the leading breeder of Hackneys in Britain. In 1978 she decided to curtail her activities, but not to retire completely.

Mrs Cynthia Haydon

Seamus Hayes

Seamus Hayes was the son of Maj.-Gen. Liam Hayes, who bought show jumpers for the Irish Army in the 1930s when their team was most successful. Seamus came to England in 1946 to ride first for Tommy Makin and then for the Masserella family; later he was to ride for Phil Oliver. He was the leading rider in Britain in 1949, 1950 and 1952 when he returned to Dublin to take up an appointment as Instructor to the Irish Army Team; he then set up an establishment of his own on The Curragh. His most successful horse was Lord Harrington's *Goodbye*, a magnificent liver chestnut which cleared 7 ft 2 in. in Puissance events on no less than six occasions. He won the original British Jumping Derby at Hickstead in 1961 and was successful again in 1964. Other famous horses associated with Seamus Hayes are *Snowstorm*, *Sheila* and *Planet*.

Seamus Hayes (Ireland) on *Goodbye*: winner of Hickstead, Derby 1961 and 1964

Bertie Hill

Son of a North Devon farmer, Bertie Hill was a successful point-to-point rider when still in his teens, before taking up event riding as a result of his association with the late Tony Collings who ran the famous Porlock Vale Riding Establishment. In 1952 he rode in the Olympic Games for the first time. In 1956 he was invited to ride *Countryman*, owned by the Queen, and was in the winning gold medal team. Had it not been for an unfortunate experience at the trakener obstacle when he was stuck across the pole, the bank having given way, he would almost certainly have won the individual gold medal. He now runs a training establishment in Devon, which is patronised by many leading three-day event riders.

Debbie Johnsey

Debbie Johnsey was Junior European Champion in 1973. Even before that, riding as an adult, she was successful in many major competitions, being runner-up for the Leading Show Jumper of the Year title at Wembley. She was fortunate in having a brilliant pony, *Champ*, which took her to the top, but she soon established herself successfully in adult events in 1975 on the American-bred *Moxy*, being short-listed for the Olympic Games, in which she was actually a member of the team in 1976. The only girl, and the youngest rider in the field, she finally finished fourth, but many believe that she was cheated of at least a silver medal by the storm postponing the jump-off in the Individual event.

Debbie Johnsey on *Moxy*: fourth in the Olympic Games 1976

Jack Le Goff

Jack Le Goff is the son of a French Cavalry officer. Champion Event rider in France in 1956 and again in 1963, he competed in the 1960 and 1964 Olympic Games leading the French team to the bronze medals in Rome and finishing 6th individually. When he retired from active riding he coached the French team which finished fourth in Mexico in 1968, also producing the individual gold medallist Jean-Jacques Guyon who won the individual gold medal; he also coached the French Junior and Senior Teams from 1965 until 1970 when he took over the responsibility for the training of the USA three-day event team. In 1972 the USA won the Olympic silver medal; in 1974 they won both the team and individual titles in the World Championships held that year at Burghley. In 1976, trained by Le Goff, the USA won the Individual gold and the Team silver medals at the Montreal Olympics.

Col. Sir Harry Llewellyn

As far as equestrian sports were concerned, Col. Harry Llewellyn's first love was racing. He rode *Ego* into both 4th and 2nd places in the Grand National, on the first occasion when still a Cambridge undergraduate. On being demobilised at the end of the war he took up show jumping, establishing his famous partnership between himself and perhaps the most popular show jumper of all time, the legendary *Foxhunter*. He won a bronze medal in the team event in the 1948 Olympics at Wembley and captained the gold medal team at Helsinki four years later. Since retiring from show jumping he has played a major part in the organisation of the sport having been both Chairman and President of the British Show Jumping Association. In 1976 he became the President/Chairman of the British Equestrian Federation, succeeding Col. Sir Michael Ansell. He was knighted in 1977.

Col. Sir Harry Llewellyn, with *Foxhunter*

Eddie Macken (Ireland) on *Kerrygold* in 1974

Eddie Macken

Eddie Macken is still under 30 years old, but he has established himself as one of the greatest horsemen in the world. It is in show jumping that he has particularly succeeded, but he is in fact a brilliant all-round horseman. A pupil of Iris Kellett, he first joined the Irish team with *Oatfield Hills* and *Easter Parade* in the early seventies. In 1974, on the outstanding *Pele* (now *Kerrygold*) he was runner-up for the men's World Championship. In 1975 he became a professional and went to live in Germany in partnership with the Schockemohles. Recently his best horse has been *Boomerang* on which in 1976 he won his first British Jumping Derby at Hickstead. In 1977 he not only repeated the performance, but was 2nd as well. He was also beaten in 1977 by only one tenth of a second in the European Championship, and a quarter time fault in the 1978 World Championships robbed him of an almost certain gold medal. He finished 2nd to Gerd Wiltfang. A week later he won his third Hickstead Derby.

Paddy McMahon

Paddy McMahon, who despite his name is wholly English, has been one of the most popular riders in Britain since he first jumped for the British team in 1973. He was selected to jump in the USA with the veteran show jumper *Tim II*, thus forging a link with the very first Horse of the Year Show at which *Tim II* had been a winner. In 1971 he jumped in Barcelona with *Hideaway*; but his most successful combination was with *Penwood Forge Mill*, foaled in 1964, on which he won the European Championship in 1973. He was on the short list for the 1972 Olympics, but having failed to be selected he immediately won the King George V Gold Cup at the Royal International Horse Show and then won the Victor Ludorum at the Horse of the Year Show a few months later.

Richard Meade

It was at Tokyo in 1964 that Richard Meade first rode in the Olympic Games, reaching the show jumping phase with a winning chance, but in fact his horse *Barberry* had a number of fences down and he finished 8th. In 1966 he was 2nd in the World Championships at Burghley. Since then his has been a success story with Olympic gold medals both in Mexico, on *Cornishman V*, and at Munich on *Laurieston*. He also won at Badminton on *The Poacher* in 1970, being second in

Richard Meade, with *Laurieston*

1973 to Lucinda Prior-Palmer when he rode *Eagle Rock*, who although belonging to Barbara Hammond had in fact been bred by his parents. In the 1976 Olympic Games in Montreal he finished 4th, two years later being included in the Kentucky World Championship team.

Ann Moore

Born in 1950, the eldest of a family of six, Ann Moore won the European Junior Championship on *Psalm* in 1968. She won the Ladies' European Championship on the same horse shortly after her 21st birthday when she was short-listed for the Olympic team, winning the Queen Elizabeth II Cup at the Royal International the same year. Competing in the Olympics she rode brilliantly to pick up the silver medal in the Individual event, still on *Psalm*. The following year she was equal first with Alison Dawes in the Queen Elizabeth II Cup again. When *Psalm* went lame in 1974 Ann Moore decided to retire.

Marion Mould

It was probably the brilliant little pony *Stroller* whom Marion Mould continued to ride in adult classes that really established Marion as an outstanding young rider. She won the Ladies' World Championship at Hickstead in 1965 when she was only 18 years old. She jumped a clear round in the 1964 British Jumping Derby finishing 2nd to Seamus Hayes before going on to win the Queen Elizabeth II Cup for the first time in 1967, winning it again in 1971. In Mexico she achieved a remarkable silver medal in a jump-off for the gold and silver with the American ace Bill Steinkraus. After a year or two out of big jumping she has in the last few years come back with great success and is now one of the leading lady riders again.

Nelson Pessoa

Born in 1935, Pessoa must now be considered one of the veterans of show jumping. He first jumped in London in 1956; in 1960 he decided to live permanently in Switzerland in order to be able to compete frequently in the European shows. He now lives in France. Nelson Pessoa won the Mens European Championships on *Gran Geste*; has won three Hamburg and two British Jumping Derbys in addition to innumerable Grand Prix. He is now professionally riding for Moet and Chandon.

Capt. Mark Phillips

Mark Phillips was an outstanding young rider making his mark in the Beaufort Hunt Pony Club at the Pony Club Championships when he was still in his early teens. He was reserve for the Olympic Games in Mexico in 1968, jumped for Britain in 1970, helped Britain win the World Championship at Punchestown riding *Chicago*. In 1971 he won Badminton for the first time on *Great Ovation*, repeating his success the following year. *Great Ovation* was his mount for the Olympic Games in 1972 where he was a member of the gold medal team. On *Maid Marion* he won the

Capt. Mark Phillips, with *Great Ovation*

Her Royal Highness, Princess Anne on *Goodwill*

three-day event at Burghley in 1973, in 1974 winning Badminton for the third time and on this occasion riding the Queen's *Columbus*. In 1975, the year before the Montreal Olympics, his horses were beset by lameness, but he finished 2nd at Burghley on *Gretna Green* and was eventually reserve for the Olympic team with *Persian Holiday*. In 1976 he turned his attention to show jumping and has already shown considerable ability and achieved a number of successes on Trevor Bank's *Hideaway* in major international events.

His Royal Highness, Prince Philip, Duke of Edinburgh

The contribution that Prince Philip has made to equestrian sports is remarkable. In the first place as President of the FEI he has breathed new life into that organisation responsible for all equestrian sports and much else besides. In drafting new rules and regulations he has made the organisation far more effective and manageable. He has also, by his own enthusiasm, set a magnificent example. There is no doubt that both polo and combined driving owe an enormous amount to his enthusiasm for these sports; his participation firmly putting them on the map. His interest in all sport is well-known: one can only regard his interest in equestrian sports as particularly fortunate.

HRH Prince Philip, Duke of Edinburgh

Her Royal Highness, Princess Anne

Princess Anne showed a great enthusiasm and considerable expertise as far as riding was concerned when she was a member of the Garth Pony Club. She first rode at Badminton in 1971, when she finished 5th. In September that year she rode *Doublet* at Burghley in the European Championship, brilliantly winning the Individual event. As *Doublet* was a notoriously difficult horse this was a great triumph for Princess Anne. The following year she was selected for the British Team for the Munich Olympic Games; unfortunately, however, *Doublet* went lame and so she had to withdraw. In 1973 Princess Anne was selected to defend her European title in Kiev on *Goodwill*, an ex-show jumper, that used to belong to Alison Dawes. This brilliant, but very large horse went well in the early stages of the event, but unfortunately fell at the notorious second fence on the cross-country course. Two years later, however, at Luhmuhlen Princess Anne was again selected and on this occasion finished second to Lucinda Prior-Palmer and *Be Fair*. Her consistency in her chosen sport of eventing has shown that her success is neither a flash in the pan nor due to her Royal parentage. Princess Anne is in fact an outstandingly brilliant horsewoman, possessing the vital qualities of patience and courage.

Lucinda Prior-Palmer

Lucinda Prior-Palmer is indisputably the leading lady three-day event rider in the world. She first joined the British team with her horse *Be Fair* in 1973 when she was selected to represent Britain in the European Championships, having won the Badminton Horse Trials that year. Two years earlier she had been in the winning British Junior Team in West Germany. She won Badminton both in 1976 and 1977, also winning at Burghley in 1977, thus retaining the European title that she had first won two years earlier. After a brilliant clear round across country in the Montreal Olympics, *Be Fair* unfortunately slipped his Achilles tendon and had to be retired. He is, however, now back in work. Despite the loss of *Be Fair* in 1977 Lucinda finished 3rd in the international three-day event in America on *Killaire* and was 2nd in the Netherlands on *Village Gossip*.

Malcolm Pyrah

Malcolm Pyrah was 23 years old before he decided on a career with horses, after a brief period as a civil servant, and was fortunate in that he was associated with the Massarella family who were responsible for launching him as an international rider. His greatest successes have been with *Law Court*, *Trevarrion* and *Lucky Strike*. He became a professional in the early 1970s, but in 1975 he reverted to amateur status, though unfortunately this was never ratified by the Olympic Committee which debarred him from taking part in the Montreal Olympics. One of the most brilliant and attractive riders Malcolm Pyrah is also one of the most likeable, being very popular with his colleagues, both at home and overseas. He was in the British winning World Championship team at Aachen in 1978.

Peter Robeson

Peter Robeson's father jumped for Britain immediately after the war. In 1947 on his home-bred mare, *Craven A*, Peter Robeson made an immediate impression, being selected for the 1952 Olympic team for which eventually he was reserve. In 1956 he won a bronze medal at the Stockholm Olympics on *Scorchin'*. In 1964 he won an Individual bronze medal on *Firecrest*, winning the King George V Gold Cup in 1967. He was short-listed for the Olympic team in 1972 and rode *Law Court* in the Olympics in Montreal in 1976. His Olympic involvement thus spans no less than 20 years; a remarkable achievement. He is considered both by the experts and by his rivals in the field of show jumping as the most classic rider in show jumping today.

Peter Robeson on *Craven A* in 1955. He was Olympic reserve in 1952 and Olympic bronze medallist on *Firecrest* in 1964

Alwin Schockemohle

Alwin Schockemohle was born in 1937, starting to ride soon after the war, and at 17 years old becoming a pupil of Hans Winkler at Warendorf. He was reserve in the Stockholm Olympics in 1956, both in show jumping and in the three-day event. He won his first major international competition at Aachen in 1957, becoming a member of the gold medal team at Rome in 1960. In 1965 having been German champion on three occasions he set up the German high jump record on *Exakt*, clearing 7 ft 4 in. In four consecutive European Championships he was placed 2nd; to Mancinelli in Rome in 1963, to David Broome in Rotterdam and Hickstead in 1967 and 1969, and to Paddy McMahon at Hickstead in 1973. He was also fourth to David Broome in the Men's World Championship in 1970. In 1976, however, he finally succeeded in achieving his greatest success when winning the Individual gold medal at the Montreal Olympics on *Warwick Rex*. Plagued with back trouble he then, regretfully, decided to retire.

Hugo Simon

Hugo Simon was in fact bred in Germany, but had a duel nationality through an Austrian grandmother and therefore decided to ride as an Austrian when he realised that his chances of getting a place in the German Olympic team for the Munich Olympics in 1972 were only slight. Riding as an individual he did in fact finish 4th. He is certainly one of the most popular and effervescent riders on the show jumping circuit and in *Lavendel* and *Flipper* he has had two brilliant horses. He created a considerable sensation (and was fined 100 dollars) in 1975 when he refused to have a dope test after one of his horses had won at Rotterdam. His own horse is now *Gladstone*.

Harvey Smith

Harvey Smith literally jumped to fame when he produced *Farmer's Boy* in 1954 having bought it at the York Sales for £40. Three years later he represented Britain with this horse at Dublin. His next successful horse was *War Paint*, which he bought for £200 at

Harvey Smith

Lucinda Prior Palmer on *Be Fair*

Hugo Simon (Austria) on *Lavendel* at the Horse of the Year Show

Leicester, winning the Puissance at the Horse of the Year Show with it at Wembley some five months later when he cleared over 7 ft. He also, on that occasion, tied with Mr Robert Hanson's Canadian-bred, *O'Malley*, which he also rode with great success for a number of years. But his first really outstanding horse was *Harvester*, on which he won the John Player trophy for the first time; an event he has won on no less than seven occasions, including in 1978. He won the King George V Gold Cup in 1970 on *Mattie Brown*, on which he also won the British Jumping Derby at Hickstead in 1970 and 1971. Harvey Smith rode in the Olympic Games in Mexico in 1968, but he has never been entirely successful either in the Olympics or the World or European Championships. He does, however, each year probably win more prize money from show jumping than any other competitor, perhaps in the world. His two sons, Robert and Stephen, are now successfully following in their father's footsteps. There is no doubt that although he is a controversial character Harvey Smith has made a great contribution to the sport of show jumping.

Pat Smythe (Koechlin-Smythe)

Pat Smythe was only 17 years old when she first produced *Finality* to win a major event at the Royal International Horse Show, but it was *Tosca* and *Prince Hal* that firmly established her, not only as a leading lady rider in Britain, but a leading lady rider in the world. She won the European Championship four times, starting in 1957 on *Flanagan*, on which she also won it in Madrid and Hickstead. She was the first lady rider to ride in the Olympic Games at Stockholm in 1956 when on *Flanagan* she won a bronze medal. She also rode in the 1960 Olympics in Rome having in 1958 won the Queen Elizabeth II Gold Cup at the Royal International Horse Show, an event which had eluded her for many years. Her example and her success has perhaps been the greatest inspiration to young riders and is largely responsible for the popularity of show jumping today.

Hartwig Steenken

Steenken first became internationally famous when he won the Men's European Championship at Aachen in 1971 on his brilliant mare *Simona*. He was in the gold medal German team at Munich in 1972, and in 1974 won the World Championship, again on *Simona*, at Hickstead. In 1975 he was runner-up for the European Championship in Munich, but in 1977 he was involved in a serious car accident which resulted in his death in January 1978. His loss to the Germans at the same time as the retirement of Alwin Schockemohle and Hans Winkler is irreparable.

Hartwig Steenken (Germany) on *Simona*: World Champion, 1974

William Steinkraus

Bill Steinkraus is undoubtedly the outstanding American show jumper since the Second World War. He first rode for the American team in 1951, winning a bronze medal in Helsinki in the 1952 Olympics, be-

William Steinkraus (USA) on *Snowbound*: Olympic gold medallist, 1968

coming Captain of the Olympic team in 1955. In 1956 he was both 1st and 2nd in the King George V Gold Cup, winning it again in 1964. He rode in the Rome Olympics in 1960 to win a silver medal, but unfortunately missed the 1964 Olympics in Tokyo because his brilliant horse, *Snowbound*, went lame at the critical moment. In 1968 he won the Individual gold medal on *Snowbound* in Mexico, four years later leading the Americans to another silver medal in the Munich Olympic Games. He then retired as a show jumper, wishing to devote more time to family life and to music, but he was immediately elected President of the USA team and is a regular CBS commentator.

Christine Stuckelberger

Christine Stuckelberger, a Swiss by birth, won the 1976 Olympic Games on her magnificent Holstein, *Granat*, winning the European Championship the following year and in 1978 winning the World Championships at Goodwood. *Granat* is an extremely impressive horse but sometimes appears to be almost too strong for Christine who is very petite. She has, however, achieved consistent successes on this magnificent horse and few would dare to suggest that there is any other combination capable of beating them, though there is no doubt, due to the mistakes by *Granat*, they had an anxious moment at the World Championships at Goodwood, from the German riders Harry Boldt and Dr Schulten-Baumer.

Paul Weier

Most people would regard Paul Weier as Switzerland's most distinguished show jumping rider. On his brilliant horse *Wildfeuer* and later the German-bred *Wulf*, he has had victories all over Europe, coming 3rd in the 1971 European Championships. He is married to Switzerland's leading lady rider, Monica Bachmann.

Maj. Paul Weier

Col. Frank Weldon

Though an outstandingly successful three-day event rider, especially with *Kilbarry* on which he won the Team gold at Stockholm in 1956 and four consecutive European titles between 1953 and 1957, winning Windsor, the 1955 replacement for Badminton, and Badminton itself in 1956, yet today he is best known as the architect of Badminton, the leading three-day event in the world. His courses which are highly imaginative, demanding but always safe, have set an example for three-day event course building the world over. Frank Weldon came to eventing from the racecourse, being a keen point-to-point rider and later very successful under rules, winning the RA Gold Cup at Sandown in 1956 and 1957. He is the equestrian correspondent for the *Sunday Telegraph*. His contribution to the three-day event world is immense.

Col. Frank Weldon, with *Kilbarry*

Sheila Willcox

Sheila Willcox first came to the notice of those responsible for organising three-day events when at Windsor in 1955 she produced a small but active little horse called *High and Mighty* which put up a very creditable performance. In 1957 she initiated a Badminton hat-trick with *High and Mighty*, winning the third year on *Airs and Graces*. *High and Mighty* was by a thoroughbred, *Little Cloud*, out of a Highland cross Arab mare. After competing at Windsor the partnership was only narrowly beaten by Frank Weldon and *Kilbarry* at Badminton the following year before embarking upon their hat-trick. Unfortunately Sheila Willcox was very seriously injured in a fall at Tidworth breaking her spine. However, she recovered sufficiently not only to take up riding again, but to train successfully three-day event horses, being invited to train the Canadian team for the Montreal Olympics. Sheila is a perfectionist and there is little doubt that she owes her success to her extraordinary patience and determination.

Sheila Willcox, with *High and Mighty*

Col. V. D. S. Williams

Col. 'Pudding' Williams was in the 5th Royal Inniskilling Dragoon Guards, but retired after the First World War to start a stud at his home in Northamptonshire and to show hunters and hacks. Becoming both Secretary and Joint-Master of the Grafton Hounds he quickly built up a great reputation for himself as a judge of a horse and an organiser of equestrian affairs. He was one of the founders of the British Show Jumping Association, and was partly responsible for the amalgamation of the Institute of the Horse and the National Horse Society which became the British Horse Society, becoming its first Chairman and later its President. He was also one of the founders of the Pony Club in 1928. However, it is perhaps his introduction into this country of dressage in the mid-thirties that most firmly established his reputation in the field of equitation. Despite considerable resistance, which was still in evidence after the war, he persevered and aroused sufficient interest in dressage to ensure that people whose opinion was respected took it seriously. He was greatly helped by his second wife, Brenda, who became the first lady to ride in the Grand Prix de Dressage in the Olympic Games at Stockholm in 1956, riding again in the Rome Olympics when she was over 60 years old. Col. Williams was the first British person to be invited to judge in the Olympic Games in dressage. His home at East Burnham Park was open house to any enthusiast for equitation with the result that he was responsible for introducing to top-class riding such people as Bertie Hill, Richard Meade and Maj. James Templer. Indeed, many of the leading riders today admit that they owe much of their success to him. He was trainer for the three-day event team that won the gold medal at Stockholm in 1956, and was a regular judge at the leading three-day events of the world until he was over 80 years old.

Hans Winkler

As winner of the gold medal for show jumping in Stockholm in 1956 on his brilliant Hanoverian mare, *Halla*, Hans Winkler established himself as one of the great post-war show jumpers. He was the winner of the World Championship in Madrid and again in Aachen. He also won the European Championship in 1957. *Halla*'s last appearance in the Olympics was in 1960 in Rome, being retired to stud the following year, but with such horses as *Fortune* and *Enigk* and *Torphy*, Hans Winkler remained not only at the top of the German tree, but as a leading rider worldwide. He helped to win four Team gold medals for Germany and indeed was still with the German team in Montreal where he won a silver medal. He has great influence at

Gerd Wiltfang (Germany) on *Duell* at Hickstead

Hans Winkler, with *Halla*

Warendorf where he is always prepared to help young German riders. He is, moreover, extremely popular in international circles.

Gerd Wiltfang

Gerd Wiltfang took up show jumping in 1944 when he was 18 years old. Two years later he became German champion. In 1972 Gerd Wiltfang was a member of the winning German Olympic team on *Askan*, then believed to be the most valuable show jumper in the world. Possessed of a quite exceptional eye for a stride, in 1978 he won the Individual World Championship on *Roman*.

Gerd Wiltfang

19 Statistics

OLYMPIC RECORDS

SHOW JUMPING

		Gold	Silver	Bronze
1896	Event not held			
1900	Paris	Aimé Haegeman (Belgium) *Benton II*	Georges van de Poele (Belgium) *Windsor Squire*	de Champsavin (France) *Terpisichore*
	Teams:	No team event held		
1904–1908	Event not held			
1912	Stockholm	Jean Cariou (France) *Mignon*	Rabod W. von Kröcher (Germany) *Dohna*	Emanuel de Blommaert de Soye (Belgium) *Clonmore*
	Teams:	**Sweden** C. Gustaf Lewenhaupt Gustaf Kilman Hans von Rosen	**France** Michel d'Astafort Jean Cariou Bernard Meyer	**Germany** Sigismund Freyer Wilhelm Graf von Hohenau Ernst-Hubertus Deloch
1920	Antwerp	Tommaso Lequio (Italy) *Trebecco*	Alessandro Valerio (Italy) *Cento*	C. Gustaf Lewenhaupt (Sweden) *Mon Coeur*
	Teams:	**Sweden** Hans von Rosen Claes König Daniel Norling	**Belgium** Herman d'Oultremont André Coumans Herman de Gaiffer d'Hestroy	**Italy** Ettore Caffaratti Giulio Cacciandra Alessandro Alvisi
1924	Paris	Alphonse Gemuseus (Switzerland) *Lucette*	Tommaso Lequio (Italy) *Trebecco*	Adam Królikiewicz (Poland) *Picador*
	Teams:	**Sweden** Åke Thelning Axel Ståhle Åge Lundström	**Switzerland** Alphonse Gemuseus Werner Stuber Hans Bühler	**Portugal** Antonio Borges de Almeida Helder de Souza Martins José Mousinho de Albuquerque
1928	Amsterdam	František Ventura (Czechoslovakia) *Eliot*	Pierre Bertran de Balanda (France) *Papillon*	Charles Kuhn (Switzerland) *Pepita*
	Teams:	**Spain** José Navarro Morenés José Alvarez de los Trujillos Julio Garcia Fernández	**Poland** Kazimierz Gzowski Kazimierz Szosland Michal Antoniewicz	**Sweden** Karl Hansen Carl Björnstjerna Ernst Hallberg
1932	Los Angeles	Takeichi Nishi (Japan) *Uranus*	Harry Chamberlin (USA) *Show Girl*	Clarence von Rosen Jr (Sweden) *Empire*
	Teams:	No nation completed the course with three riders		
1936	Berlin	Kurt Hasse (Germany) *Tora*	Henri Rang (Romania) *Delfis*	József von Platthy (Hungary) *Sellö*
	Teams:	**Germany** Kurt Hasse Marten von Barnekow Heinz Brandt	**Holland** Johan Jacob Greter Jan Adrianus de Bruine Henri Louis M. van Schaik	**Portugal** José Beltrão Luiz Marquês do Funchal Luiz Mena e Silva

SHOW JUMPING *(Continued)*

		Gold	Silver	Bronze
1948	London	Humberto Mariles Cortés (Mexico) *Arete*	Rubén Uriza (Mexico) *Harvey*	Jean Françoise d'Orgeix (France) *Sucre de Pomme*
	Teams:	**Mexico** Humberto Mariles Cortés Rubén Uriza Alberto Valdés	**Spain** Jaime Garcia Cruz José Navarro Morenés Marcelino Gavilán y Ponce de Léon	**Great Britain** Harry Morton Llewellyn Henry Morison V. Nicoll Arthur Carr
1952	Helsinki	Pierre Jonquères d'Oriola (France) *Ali Baba*	Oscar Cristi (Chile) *Bambi*	Fritz Thiedemann (Germany) *Meteor*
	Teams:	**Great Britain** Wilfred Harry White Douglas Stewart Harry Morton Llewellyn	**Chile** Oscar Cristi Cesar Mendoza Ricardo Echeverria	**USA** William Steinkraus Arthur John McCashin John Russell
1956	Stockholm*	Hans Winkler (Germany) *Halla*	Raimondo d'Inzeo (Italy) *Merano*	Piero d'Inzeo (Italy) *Uruguay*
	Teams:	**Germany** Hans Winkler Fritz Thiedemann Alfons Lütke-Westhues	**Italy** Raimondo d'Inzeo Piero d'Inzeo Salvatore Oppes	**Great Britain** Wilfred Harry White Patricia Smythe Peter Robeson
1960	Rome	Raimondo d'Inzeo (Italy) *Possillipo*	Piero d'Inzeo (Italy) *The Rock*	David Broome (GB) *Sunsalve*
	Teams:	**Germany** Hans Winkler Fritz Thiedemann Alwin Schockemöhle	**USA** Frank Chapot William Steinkraus George Morris	**Italy** Raimondo d'Inzeo Piero d'Inzeo Antonio Oppes
1964	Tokyo	Pierre Jonquères d'Oriola (France) *Lutteur*	Hermann Schridde (Germany) *Dozent*	Peter Robeson (GB) *Firecrest*
	Teams:	**Germany** Hermann Schridde Kurt Jarasinski Hans Winkler	**France** Pierre Jonquères d'Oriola Janou Lefebvre Guy Lefrant	**Italy** Piero d'Inzeo Raimondo d'Inzeo Graziano Mancinelli
1968	Mexico	William Steinkraus (USA) *Snowbound*	Marian Coakes (GB) *Stroller*	David Broome (GB) *Mister Softee*
	Teams:	**Canada** Jim Elder Jim Day Tom Gayford	**France** Janou Lefebvre Marcel Rozier Pierre Jonquères d'Oriola	**Germany** Alwin Schockemöhle Hans Winkler Hermann Schridde
1972	Munich	Graziano Mancinelli (Italy) *Ambassador*	Ann Moore (GB) *Psalm*	Neal Shapiro (US) *Sloopy*
	Teams:	**W Germany** Fritz Ligges Gerhard Wiltfang Hartwig Steenken Hans Winkler	**USA** William Steinkraus Neal Shapiro Kathryn Kusner Frank Chapot	**Italy** Vittorio Orlandi Raimondo d'Inzeo Graziano Mancinelli Piero d'Inzeo
1976	Montreal	Alwin Schockemöhle (W Germany) *Warwick Rex*	Michael Vaillancourt (Canada) *Branch County*	François Mathy (Belgium) *Gai Luron*
	Teams:	**France** Hubert Parot Marcel Rozier Michel Roche Marc Roguet	**W Germany** Hans Winkler Paul Schockemöhle Alwin Schockemöhle Soenke Soenksen	**Belgium** Eric Wauters François Mathy Edgar Guepper Stanny van Paeschen

* Due to Australian quarantine regulations the equestrian events were not held in Melbourne with the other sports.

THREE-DAY EVENT

Year	Venue		Gold	Silver	Bronze
1896–1908	Event not held				
1912	Stockholm		Axel Nordlander (Sweden) *Lady Artist*	Friedrich von Rochow (Germany) *Idealist*	Jean Cariou (France) *Cocotte*
		Teams:	**Sweden** Nils Adlercreutz Axel Nordlander Ernst G. Casparsson	**Germany** Friedrich von Rochow Eduard von Lütcken Richard G. von Schaesberg-Thannheim	**USA** Benjamin Lear John C. Montgomery Guy Henry
1920	Antwerp		Helmer Mörner (Sweden) *Germania*	Åge Lundström (Sweden) *Yrsa*	Ettore Caffaratti (Italy) *Traditore*
		Teams:	**Sweden** Helmer Mörner Åge Lundström George von Braun	**Italy** Ettore Caffaratti Garibaldi Spighi Guilio Cacciandra	**Belgium** Roger Moeremans d'Emaus Oswald Lints Jules Bonvalet
1924	Paris		Adolph D. C. van der Voort van Zijp (Netherlands) *Silver Piece*	Fröde Kirkebjerg (Denmark) *Meteor*	Sloan Doak (USA) *Pathfinder*
		Teams:	**Netherlands** Adolph D. C. van der Voort van Zijp Charles F. Pahud de Mortanges Gerard P. C. de Kruijff	**Sweden** Claes König Torsten Sylvan Gustaf Hagelin	**Italy** Alberto Lombardi Alessandro Alvisi Emanuele di Pralormo
1928	Amsterdam		Charles F. Pahud de Mortanges (Netherlands) *Marcroix*	Gerard P. C. de Kruijff (Netherlands) *Va-t-en*	Bruno Neumann (Germany) *Ilja*
		Teams:	**Netherlands** Charles F. Pahud de Mortanges Gerard P. C. de Kruijff Adolph D. C. van der Voort van Zijp	**Norway** Arthur Quist Bjart Ording Eugen Johansen	**Poland** Josef Trenkwald Michal Antoniewicz Karol de Rommel
1932	Los Angeles		Charles F. Pahud de Mortanges (Netherlands) *Marcroix*	Earl Thomson (USA) *Jenny Camp*	Clarence von Rosen Jr (Sweden) *Sunnyside Maid*
		Teams:	**USA** Earl Thomson Harry Chamberlin Edwin Argo	**Netherlands** Charles F. Pahud de Mortanges Karel J. Schummelketel Aernout van Lennep	(There was no third team medal)
1936	Berlin		Ludwig Stubbendorf (Germany) *Nurmi*	Earl Thomson (USA) *Jenny Camp*	Hans Mathiesen-Lunding (Denmark) *Jason*
		Teams:	**Germany** Ludwig Stubbendorf Rudolf Lippert Konrad von Wangenheim	**Poland** Severyn Kulesza Henryk Rojcewicz Zdislaw Kawecki	**Great Britain** Edward Howard-Vyse Alec Scott Richard Fanshawe
1948	London		Bernard Chevallier (France) *Aiglonne*	Frank Henry (USA) *Swing Low*	J. Robert Selfelt (Sweden) *Claque*
		Teams:	**USA** Frank Henry Charles Anderson Earl Thomson	**Sweden** J. Robert Selfelt Nils Olof Stahre Sigurd Svensson	**Mexico** Humberto Mariles Cortes Raul Campero Joaquin Solano Chagoya
1952	Helsinki		Hans von Blixen-Finecke (Sweden) *Jubal*	Guy Lefrant (France) *Verdun*	Wilhelm Büsing (Germany) *Hubertus*
		Teams:	**Sweden** Hans von Blixen-Finecke Nils Olof Stahre Karl F. Frölen	**Germany** Wilhelm Büsing Klaus Wagner Otto Rothe	**USA** Charles Hough Walter Staley Jr John Wofford
1956	Stockholm		Petrus Kastenman (Sweden) *Iluster*	August Lütke-Westhues (Germany) *Trux von Kamax*	Francis Weldon (GB) *Kilbarry*
		Teams:	**Great Britain** Albert E. Hill Francis Weldon A. Lawrence Rook	**Germany** August Lütke-Westues Klaus Wagner Otto Rothe	**Canada** James Elder Brian Herbinson John Rumble
1960	Rome		Lawrence Morgan (Australia) *Salad Days*	Neale Lavis (Australia) *Mirrabooka*	Anton Bühler (Switzerland) *Gay Spark*
		Teams:	**Australia** Lawrence Morgan Neale Lavis William Roycroft	**Switzerland** Anton Bühler Hans Schwarzenbach Rudolph Günthardt	**France** Jack L. Le Goff Jean R. Le Roy Guy Lefrant

THREE-DAY EVENT *(Continued)*

		Gold	Silver	Bronze
1964	Tokyo	Mauro Checcoli (Italy) *Surbean*	Carlos Moratorio (Argentina) *Chalan*	Fritz Ligges (Germany) *Donkosak*
	Teams:	**Italy** Mauro Checcoli Paolo Angioni Giuseppe Ravano	**USA** Michael Page Kevin Freeman J. Michael Plumb	**Germany** Fritz Ligges Horst Karsten Gerhard Schultz
1968	Mexico	Jean-Jacques Guyon (France) *Pitou*	Derek Allhusen (GB) *Lochinvar*	Michael Page (USA) *Foster*
	Teams:	**Great Britain** Derek Allhusen Richard H. Meade Reuben Jones	**USA** Michael Page James Wofford J. Michael Plumb	**Australia** Wayne Roycroft Brian Cobcroft William Roycroft
1972	Munich	Richard H. Meade (GB) *Laurieston*	Alessa Argenton (Italy) *Woodland*	Jan Jonsson (Sweden) *Sarajevo*
	Teams:	**Great Britain** Mary D. Gordon-Watson Bridget Parker Richard H. Meade Mark Phillips (non-scorer)	**USA** Kevin Freeman Bruce Davidson J. Michael Plumb	**West Germany** Harry Klugmann Karl Schultz Ludwig Goessing
1976	Montreal	Edmund Coffin (USA) *Bally-cor*	John Plumb (USA) *Better & Better*	Karl Schultz (W Germany) *Madrigal*
	Teams:	**USA** Edmund Coffin John Plumb Bruce Davidson Mary Tauskey	**West Germany** Karl Schultz Herbert Bloecker Helmut Rethemeier Otto Ammermann	**Australia** Wayne Roycroft Mervyn Bennett William Roycroft Denis Pigott

GRAND PRIX (DRESSAGE)

		Gold	Silver	Bronze
1896–1908	Event not held			
1912	Stockholm	Carle Bonde (Sweden) *Emperor*	Gustaf-Adolf Boltenstern Sr (Sweden) *Neptun*	Hans von Blixen-Finecke (Sweden) *Maggie*
1920	Antwerp	Janne Lundblad (Sweden) *Uno*	Bertil Sandström (Sweden) *Sabel*	Hans von Rosen (Sweden) *Running Sister*
1924	Paris	Ernst Linder (Sweden) *Piccolomini*	Bertil Sandström (Sweden) *Sabel*	Xavier Lesage (France) *Plumard*
1928	Amsterdam	Carl F. F. von Langen (Germany) *Draufgänger*	Charles Marion (France) *Linon*	Ragnar Olson (Sweden) *Günstling*
1932	Los Angeles	Xavier Lesage (France) *Taine*	Charles Marion (France) *Linon*	Hiram Tuttle (USA) *Olympic*
1936	Berlin	Heinz Pollay (Germany) *Kronos*	Friedrich Gerhard (Germany) *Absinth*	Alois Podhajsky (Austria) *Nero*
1948	London	Hans Moser (Switzerland) *Hummer*	André Jousseaume (France) *Harpagon*	Gustaf-Adolf Boltenstern Jr (Sweden) *Trumf*
1952	Helsinki	Henri St Cyr (Sweden) *Master Rufus*	Lis Hartel (Denmark) *Jubilee*	André Jousseaume (France) *Harpagon*
1956	Stockholm	Henri St Cyr (Sweden) *Juli*	Lis Hartel (Denmark) *Jubilee*	Liselott Linsenhoff (Germany) *Adular*
1960	Rome	Sergey Filatov (USSR) *Absent*	Gustav Fischer (Switzerland) *Wald*	Josef Neckermann (Germany) *Asbach*
1964	Tokyo	Henri Chammartin (Switzerland) *Woermann*	Harry Boldt (Germany) *Remus*	Sergey Filatov (USSR) *Absent*
1968	Mexico	Ivan Kizimov (USSR) *Ikhor*	Josef Neckermann (W Germany) *Mariano*	Reiner Klimke (W Germany) *Dux*
1972	Munich	Liselott Linsenhoff (W Germany) *Piaff*	Elena Petuchkova (USSR) *Pepel*	Josef Neckermann (W Germany) *Venetia*
1976	Montreal	Christine Stückelberger (Switzerland) *Granat*	Harry Boldt (W Germany) *Woycek*	Reiner Klimke (W Germany) *Mehmed*

WORLD CHAMPIONSHIPS

SHOW JUMPING

Men's World Championships

Year	Venue	Place	Rider / Horse
1953	Paris	1	Francisco Goyoago (Spain) *Quorum*
		2	Fritz Thiedemann (Germany) *Diamant*
		3	Pierre d'Oriola (France) *Ali Baba*
1954	Madrid	1	Hans Winkler (Germany) *Halla*
		2	Pierre d'Oriola (France) *Arlequin*
		3	Francisco Goyoago (Spain)
1955	Aachen	1	Hans Winkler (Germany) *Halla*
		2	Raimondo d'Inzeo (Italy) *Nadir*
		3	Ronnie Dallas (GB) *Bones*
1956	Aachen	1	Raimondo d'Inzeo (Italy) *Merano*
		2	Francisco Goyoago (Spain) *Fahnenkonig*
		3	Fritz Thiedemann (Germany) *Meteor*
1960	Venice	1	Raimondo d'Inzeo (Italy) *Gowran Girl*
		2	Carlos Delia (Argentina) *Huipil*
		3	David Broome (GB) *Sunsalve*
1966	Buenos Aires	1	Pierre d'Oriola (France) *Pomone*
		2	José Alvarez de Bohorques (Spain) *Quizas*
		3	Raimondo d'Inzeo (Italy) *Bowjak*
1970	La Baule	1	David Broome (GB) *Beethoven*
		2	Graziano Mancinelli (Italy) *Fidux*
		3	Harvey Smith (GB) *Mattie Brown*
1974	Hickstead	1	Hartwig Steenken (W Germany) *Simona*
		2	Eddie Macken (Ireland) *Pele*
		3	Hugo Simon (Austria) *Lavendel*
1978	Aachen	1	Gerd Wiltfang (W Germany) *Roman*
		2	Eddie Macken (Ireland) *Boomerang*
		3	Michael Matz (USA) *Jet Run*
	Team Event (first time)	1	Great Britain
		2	Holland
		3	USA

Women's World Championships

Year	Venue	Place	Rider / Horse
1965	Hickstead	1	Marion Coakes (GB) *Stroller*
		2	Kathy Kusner (USA) *Untouchable*
		3	Alison Westwood (GB) *The Maverick*
1970	Copenhagen	1	Janou Lefebvre (France) *Rocket*
		2	Marion Mould (née Coakes) (GB) *Stroller*
		3	Anneli Drummond-Hay (GB) *Merely-a-Monarch*
1974	La Baule	1	Janou Tissot (née Lefebvre) (France) *Rocket*
		2	Michele McEvoy (USA) *Mr Muskie*
		3	Barbara Kerr (Canada) *Magnor*

Since 1978 joint Championship for men and women

THREE-DAY EVENT

		Team	Individual
1966	Burghley	1 Ireland 2 Argentina (only two teams finished)	1 Carlos Moratorio (Argentina) *Chalon* 2 Richard Meade (GB) *Barberry* 3 Virginia Freeman-Jackson (Ireland) *Sam Weller*
1970	Punchestown	1 Great Britain 2 France (only two teams finished)	1 Mary Gordon-Watson (GB) *Cornishman V* 2 Richard Meade (GB) *The Poacher* 3 James Wofford (USA) *Kilkenny*
1974	Burghley	1 USA 2 Great Britain 3 W Germany	1 Bruce Davidson (USA) *Irish Cap* 2 Michael Plumb (USA) *Good Mixture* 3 Hugh Thomas (GB) *Playamar*
1978	Kentucky	1 Canada 2 W Germany 3 USA	1 Bruce Davidson (USA) *Might Tango* 2 John Watson (Ireland) *Cambridge Blue* 3 Helmut Rethemeier (W Germany) *Ladalco*

DRESSAGE

		Team	Individual
1966	Berne	1 W Germany 2 Switzerland 3 USSR	1 Josef Neckermann (W Germany) *Mariano* 2 Reiner Klimke (W Germany) *Dux* 3 Harry Boldt (W Germany) *Remus*
1970	Aachen	1 USSR 2 W Germany 3 E Germany	1 Elena Petouchkova (USSR) *Pepel* 2 Liselott Linsenhoff (W Germany) *Piaff* 3 Ivan Kisimov (USSR) *Ikor*
1974	Copenhagen	1 W Germany 2 USSR 3 Switzerland	1 Reiner Klimke (W Germany) *Mehmed* 2 Liselott Linsenhoff (W Germany) *Piaff* 3 Elena Petouchkova (USSR) *Pepel*
1978	Goodwood	1 W Germany 2 Switzerland 3 USSR	1 Christine Stückelberger (Switzerland) *Granat* 2 Uwe Schulten-Baumer (W Germany) *Slibovitz* 3 Jennie Loriston-Clarke (GB) *Dutch Courage*

PRESIDENT'S CUP

The award for the world team championship, based on each country's best six Nations Cup results in a season. The figure in brackets represents the number of points.

1965	Great Britain (35)
1966	USA (27)
1967	Great Britain (37)
1968	USA (34)
1969	W Germany (39)
1970	Great Britain (27·5)
1971	W Germany (37)
1972	Great Britain (33)
1973	Great Britain (34)
1974	Great Britain (37)
1975	W Germany (39)
1976	W Germany (32)
1977	Great Britain (35·5)
1978	Great Britain (36)

EUROPEAN CHAMPIONSHIPS

SHOW JUMPING

Men's European Championships

Year	Venue	Place	Rider, horse
1957	Rotterdam	1	Hans Winkler (Germany) *Sonnenglanz*
		2	Bernard de Fombelle (France) *Bucephale*
		3	Salvatore Oppes (Italy) *Pagoro*
1958	Aachen	1	Fritz Thiedemann (Germany) *Meteor*
		2	Piero d'Inzeo (Italy) *The Rock*
		3	Hans Winkler (Germany) *Halla*
1959	Paris	1	Piero d'Inzeo (Italy) *Uruguay*
		2	Pierre d'Oriola (France) *Virtuoso*
		3	Fritz Thiedemann (Germany) *Godewind*
1961	Aachen	1	David Broome (GB) *Sunsalve*
		2	Piero d'Inzeo (Italy) *Pioneer*
		3	Hans Winkler (Germany) *Romanus*
1962	London	1	David Barker (GB) *Mister Softee*
		2	Hans Winkler (Germany) *Romanus*
			and Piero d'Inzeo (Italy) *The Rock*
1963	Rome	1	Graziano Mancinelli (Italy) *Rockette*
		2	Alwin Schockemöhle (Germany) *Freiherr*
		3	Harvey Smith (GB) *O'Malley*
1965	Aachen	1	Hermann Schridde (Germany) *Dozent*
		2	Alfonso Queipo le Llano (Spain) *Infernal*
		3	Alwin Schockemöhle (Germany) *Exakt*
1966	Lucerne	1	Nelson Pessoa (Brazil) *Gran Geste*
		2	Frank Chapot (USA) *San Lucas*
		3	Hugo Arrambide (Argentina) *Chimbote*
1967	Rotterdam	1	David Broome (GB) *Mister Softee*
		2	Harvey Smith (GB) *Harvester*
		3	Alwin Schockemöhle (Germany) *Donald Rex*
1969	Hickstead	1	David Broome (GB) *Mister Softee*
		2	Alwin Schockemöhle (W Germany) *Donald Rex*
		3	Hans Winkler (W Germany) *Enigk*
1971	Aachen	1	Hartwig Steenken (W Germany) *Simona*
		2	Harvey Smith (GB) *Evan Jones*
		3	Paul Weier (Switzerland) *Wulf*
1973	Hickstead	1	Paddy McMahon (GB) *Penwood Forge Mill*
		2	Alwin Schockemöhle (W Germany) *The Robber*
		3	Hubert Parot (France) *Tic*
1975	Munich (Amateurs only)	1	Alwin Schockemöhle (W Germany) *Warwick*
		2	Hartwig Steenken (W Germany) *Erle*
		3	Sonke Sonksen (W Germany) *Kwept*
1977	Vienna	1	Johan Heins (Holland) *Seven Valleys*
		2	Eddie Macken (Ireland) *Kerrygold*
		3	Anton Ebben (Holland) *Jumbo Design*

Deborah West and *Baccarat* at Badminton in 1970

5
50
45
15
40
20
35
30
25

SHOW JUMPING *(Continued)*

Women's European Championships

Year	Venue	Place	Rider and horse
1957	Spa	1	Patricia Smythe (GB) *Flanagan*
		2	Giulia Serventi (Italy) *Doly*
		3	Michelle d'Orgeix (France) *Ocean*
1958	Palmermo	1	Giulia Serventi (Italy) *Doly*
		2	Anna Clement (Germany) *Nico*
		3	Irene Jansen (Netherlands) *Adelbloom*
1959	Rotterdam	1	Ann Townsend (GB) *Bandit*
		2	Patricia Smythe (GB) *Flanagan*
		3	Anna Clement (Germany) *Nico* and Giulia Serventi (Italy) *Doly*
1960	Copenhagen	1	S. Cohen (GB) *Clare Castle*
		2	Dawn Wofford (GB) *Hollandia*
		3	Anna Clement (Germany) *Nico*
1961	Deauville	1	Patricia Smythe (GB) *Flanagan*
		2	Irene Jansen (Netherlands) *Icare*
		3	Michelle Cancre (France) *Ocean*
1962	Madrid	1	Patricia Smythe (GB) *Flanagan*
		2	Helga Kohler (Germany) *Cremona*
		3	Paola de Goyoaga (Spain) *Kif Kif*
1963	Hickstead	1	Patricia Smythe (GB) *Flanagan*
		2	Arline Givaudan (Brazil) *Huipil*
		3	Anneli Drummond-Hay (GB) *Merely-a-Monarch*
1966	Gijon	1	Janou Lefebvre (France) *Kenavo*
		2	Monica Bachmann (Switzerland) *Sandro*
		3	Llala Novo (Italy) *Oxo Bob*
1967	Fontainebleau	1	Kathy Kusner (USA) *Untouchable*
		2	Llala Novo (Italy) *Predestine*
		3	Monica Bachmann (Switzerland) *Erbach*
1968	Rome	1	Anneli Drummond-Hay (GB) *Merely-a-Monarch*
		2	Giulia Serventi (Italy) *Gay Monarch*
		3	Marion Coakes (GB) *Stroller* and Janou Lefebvre (France) *Rocket*
1969	Dublin	1	Iris Kellett (Ireland) *Morning Light*
		2	Anneli Drummond-Hay (GB) *Xanthos*
		3	Alison Westwood (GB) *The Maverick*
1971	St Gallen	1	Ann Moore (GB) *Psalm*
		2	Alison Dawes (née Westwood) (GB) *The Maverick*
		3	Monika Leitenberger (Austria) *Limbarra de Porto Conte*
1973	Vienna	1	Ann Moore (GB) *Psalm*
		2	Caroline Bradley (GB) *True Lass*
		3	Monica Weier (Switzerland) *Erbach*

Since 1975 joint Championship for men and women.

THREE-DAY EVENT

Year	Venue	Team	Individual
1953	Badminton	1 Great Britain (no other team finished)	1 Lawrence Rook (GB) *Starlight* 2 Francis Weldon (GB) *Kilbarry* 3 Hans Schwarzenbach (Switzerland) *Vae Victis*
1954	Basle	1 Great Britain 2 Germany (only two teams finished)	1 Albert Hill (GB) *Crispin* 2 Francis Weldon (GB) *Kilbarry* 3 Lawrence Rook (GB) *Starlight*
1955	Windsor	1 Great Britain 2 Switzerland (only two teams finished)	1 Francis Weldon (GB) *Kilbarry* 2 John Oram (GB) *Radar* 3 Albert Hill (GB) *Countryman*
1957	Copenhagen	1 Great Britain 2 Germany 3 Sweden	1 Sheila Willcox (GB) *High and Mighty* 2 August Lütke-Westhues (Germany) *Franko* 3 Jonas Lindgren (Sweden) *Eldorado*
1959	Harewood	1 Germany 2 Great Britain 3 France	1 Hans Schwarzenbach (Switzerland) *Burn Trout* 2 Francis Weldon (GB) *Samuel Johnson* 3 Derek Allhusen (GB) *Laurien*
1962	Burghley	1 USSR 2 Ireland 3 Great Britain	1 James Templar (GB) *M'Lord Connelly* 2 German Gazyumov (USSR) *Granj* 3 Jane Wykeham-Musgrave (GB) *Uyebrooks*
1965	Moscow	1 USSR 2 Ireland 3 Great Britain	1 Marian Babirecki (Poland) *Volt* 2 Lev Baklyshkin (USSR) *Ruon* 3 Horst Karsten (Germany) *Condora*
1967	Punchestown	1 Great Britain 2 Ireland 3 France	1 Eddie Boylan (Ireland) *Durlas Eile* 2 Martin Whiteley (GB) *The Poacher* 3 Derek Allhusen (GB) *Lochinvar*
1969	Haras du Pin	1 Great Britain 2 USSR 3 W Germany	1 Mary Gordon-Watson (GB) *Cornishman V* 2 Richard Walker (GB) *Pasha* 3 Bernd Messman (W Germany) *Wiendspeil*
1971	Burghley	1 Great Britain 2 USSR 3 Ireland	1 HRH Princess Anne (GB) *Doublet* 2 Debra West (GB) *Baccarat* 3 Stewart Stevens (GB) *Classic Chips*
1973	Kiev	1 W Germany 2 USSR 3 Great Britain	1 Alexander Evdokimov (USSR) *Jeger* 2 Herbert Blocker (W Germany) *Albrant* 3 Horst Karsten (W Germany) *Sioux*
1975	Luhmuhlen	1 USSR 2 Great Britain 3 W Germany	1 Lucinda Prior-Palmer (GB) *Be Fair* 2 HRH Princess Anne (GB) *Goodwill* 3 Peter Gornuschko (USSR) *Gvsar*
1977	Burghley	1 Great Britain 2 W Germany 3 Ireland	1 Lucinda Prior-Palmer (GB) *George* 2 Karl Schultz (W Germany) *Madrigal* 3 Horst Karsten (W Germany) *Sioux*

DRESSAGE

Year	Venue	Team	Individual
1963	Copenhagen	1 Great Britain 2 Romania	1 Henri Chammartin (Switzerland) *Wolfdietrich* 2 Harry Boldt (Germany) *Remus* 3 Henri Chammartin (Switzerland) *Woermann*
1965	Copenhagen	1 W Germany 2 Switzerland 3 USSR	1 Henri Chammartin (Switzerland) *Wolfdietrich* 2 Harry Boldt (Germany) *Remus* 3 Reiner Klimke (Germany) *Arcadius*
1967	Aachen	1 W Germany 2 USSR 3 Switzerland	1 Reiner Klimke (Germany) *Dux* 2 Ivan Kisimov (USSR) *Ikor* 3 Harry Boldt (Germany) *Remus*
1969	Wolfsburg	1 W Germany 2 E Germany 3 USSR	1 Liselott Linsenhoff (W Germany) *Piaff* 2 Ivan Kisimov (USSR) *Ikor* 3 Josef Neckermann (W Germany) *Mariano*
1971	Wolfsburg	1 W Germany 2 USSR 3 Sweden	1 Liselott Linsenhoff (W Germany) *Piaff* 2 Josef Neckermann (W Germany) *Van Eick* 3 Ivan Kisimov (USSR) *Ikor*
1973	Aachen	1 W Germany 2 USSR 3 Switzerland	1 Reiner Klimke (W Germany) *Mehned* 2 Elena Petouchkova (USSR) *Pepel* 3 Ivan Kalita (USSR) *Tarif*
1975	Kiev	1 W Germany 2 USSR 3 Switzerland	1 Christine Stuckelberger (Switzerland) *Granat* 2 Harry Boldt (W Germany) *Woycek* 3 Karin Schluter (W Germany) *Liostro*
1977	St Gallen	1 W Germany 2 Switzerland 3 USSR	1 Christine Stuckelberger (Switzerland) *Granat* 2 Harry Boldt (W Germany) *Woycek* 3 Uwe Schulten-Baumer (USSR) *Slibovitz*

INDEX

Page numbers in italics denote illustrations

ACKNOWLEDGEMENTS

The Publishers wish to thank the following for supplying illustrations for use in this publication:

All-Sport: 78, 79, 211. **Ian Ball**: 58, 59, 62, 63, 66, 67, 71, 75, 93, 129, 140, 174–5, 215, 219. **R. & H. Chapman**: 165 (*top right*). **Gerry Cranham**: 136, 203. **Findlay Davidson**: 49 (*bottom left*), 50 (*bottom*), 51, 52 (*top left and bottom right*), 53 (*bottom*), 73, 74 (*right and centre left*), 76 (*top*), 77 (*top*), 82, 87, 138, 157, 164, 165 (*centre left*), 166–7, 177 (*top*), 183, 204, 206 (*left*), 208 (*left*), 213 (*right*), 216 (*top*), 217 (*left*), 220 (*bottom*). **David Ellis**: 123. **Fotomas Index**: 115, 141. **John Grant**: 120. **Haig-McAlister Limited**: 35, 38. **John Hedgloe**: 149, 151, 154, 156. **Clive Hiles**: 22, 65 (*bottom*), 172–3 (*bottom*). **Horse and Hound**: 48 (*bottom* left), 165 (*bottom right*), 207 (*bottom right*), 213 (*left*). **E. D. Lacey**: 23, 36, 40, 41, 48 (*top left and bottom right*), 52 (*centre*), 54–5, 56, 57, 60, 61, 64, 68, 70, 72 (*bottom*), 75, 76 (*bottom left and right*), 77 (*bottom left and right*), 88, 89, 94–5, 102–3, 137, 168–9, 205, 207 (*left*), 209, 214, 228–9. **Leslie Lane**: 24–5, 29, 47, 49 (*bottom right*), 50 (*top*), 65 (*top*), 74 (*top left*), 83, 84, 85, 92, 98, 99, 101, 126, 139, 165 (*top left*), 172 (*top left and right*), 176–7 (*bottom*), 178–9, 192, 210 (*right*). **The Mansell Collection**: 15, 91, 187. **Frank Meads**: 111 (*top left*), 112, 116 (*centre*), 122, 125. **Monty**: 46, 49 (*top*), 52 (*top right and bottom left*), 53 (*top*), 74 (*bottom left*), 96, 206 (*right*), 207 (*top right*). **Pony and Light Horse**: 26–7, 32, 109, 113, 130, 131, 132 (*bottom*), 163, 170, 171.

OTHER GUINNESS SUPERLATIVES TITLES

Facts and Feats Series:

Air Facts and Feats, *3rd ed.*
John W. R. Taylor, Michael J. H. Taylor and David Mondey

Rail Facts and Feats, *3rd ed.*
John Marshall

Tank Facts and Feats, *2nd ed.*
Kenneth Macksey

Car Facts and Feats, *2nd ed.*
edited by Anthony Harding

Yachting Facts and Feats
Peter Johnson

Motorcycling Facts and Feats
L. J. K. Setright

Business World
Henry Button and Andrew Lampert

Music Facts and Feats
Robert and Celia Dearling with Brian Rust

Art Facts and Feats
John FitzMaurice Mills

Soccer Facts and Feats
Jack Rollin

Motorboating Facts and Feats
Kevin Desmond

Animal Facts and Feats
Gerald L. Wood FZS

Plant Facts and Feats
William G. Duncalf

Structures – Bridges, Towers, Tunnels, Dams . . .
John H. Stephens

Weather Facts and Feats
Ingrid Holford

Astronomy Facts and Feats
Patrick Moore

Guide Series:

Guide to French Country Cooking
Christian Roland Délu

Guide to Freshwater Angling
Brian Harris and Paul Boyer

Guide to Saltwater Angling
Brian Harris

Guide to Field Sports
Wilson Stephens

Guide to Mountain Animals
R. P. Bille

Guide to Underwater Life
C. Petron and J. B. Lozet

Guide to Motorcycling, *2nd ed.*
Christian Lacombe

Guide to Bicycling
J. Durry and J. B. Wadley

Guide to Waterways of Western Europe
Hugh McKnight

Guide to Water Skiing
David Nations OBE and Kevin Desmond

Guide to Steeplechasing
Richard Pitman and Gerry Cranham

Other Titles:

The Guinness Book of Answers, *2nd ed.*
edited by Norris D. McWhirter

The Guinness Book of Records
edited by Norris D. McWhirter

The Guinness Book of 1952
Kenneth Macksey

The Guinness Book of 1953
Kenneth Macksey

The Guinness Book of 1954
Kenneth Macksey

Kings, Rulers and Statesmen
Clive Carpenter

The Guinness Book of Antiques
John Mills

The Guinness Book of Winners and Champions
Chris Cook

History of Land Warfare
Kenneth Macksey

History of Sea Warfare
Lt-Cmdr Gervis Frere-Cook and Kenneth Macksey

History of Air Warfare
David Brown, Christopher Shores and Kenneth Macksey

English Pottery and Porcelain
Geoffrey Wills

Antique Firearms
Frederick Wilkinson

The Guinness Guide to Feminine Achievements
Joan and Kenneth Macksey

The Guinness Book of Names
Leslie Dunkling

100 Years of Wimbledon
Lance Tingay

The Guinness Book of British Hit Singles
edited by Tim and Jo Rice, Paul Gambaccini and Mike Read

The Guinness Book of World Autographs
Ray Rawlins

Derby 200
Michael Seth-Smith and Roger Mortimer

The Official Centenary History of the AAA
Peter Lovesey